OF MOOSE AND MEN

A Wildlife Vet's Pursuit of the World's Largest Deer

DR. JERRY HAIGH

ECW Press

Published by ECW Press
2120 Queen Street East, Suite 200, Toronto, Ontario, Canada M4E 1E2
416-694-3348 / info@ecwpress.com

LIBRARY AND ARCHIVES CANADA CATALOGUING IN PUBLICATION

Haigh, J. C. (Jerry C.)
Of moose and men : a wildlife vet's pursuit of the world's largest
deer / Jerry Haigh.

ISBN 978-1-77041-091-6
ALSO ISSUED AS: 978-1-77090-211-4 (PDF); 978-1-77090-212-1 (EPUB)

1. Haigh, J. C. (Jerry C.). 2. Moose. 3. Wildlife veterinarians—
Canada—Biography. I. Title.

QL737.U55H35 2012   599.65'7   C2011-906977-6

Editor for the press: Jennifer Knoch
Cover and text design: Tania Craan
Front and back cover photos: Jerry Haigh
Printing: Trigraphik   1   2   3   4   5

The publication of *Of Moose and Men* has been generously supported by the Canada Council for the Arts which last year invested $20.1 million in writing and publishing throughout Canada, and by the Ontario Arts Council, an agency of the Government of Ontario. We also acknowledge the financial support of the Government of Canada through the Canada Book Fund for our publishing activities, and the contribution of the Government of Ontario through the Ontario Book Publishing Tax Credit. The marketing of this book was made possible with the support of the Ontario Media Development Corporation.

PRINTED AND BOUND IN CANADA

"It is not real work unless
you would rather be doing something else."

— *Sir James Barrie, Convocation Address,*
St. Andrews University, 1922

For Jo.

• CONTENTS •

• ACKNOWLEDGEMENTS •

I offer a special vote of thanks to Vince Crichton, who is the senior moose biologist working in Canada today. He received the Distinguished Moose Biologist Award in 1988 and was elected president of the North American Moose Foundation in 2005. He not only wrote the foreword to this work but also commented on some important issues and generously allowed the use of some of his photographs.

Elder Barry Ahenakew generously shared both history and words about moose from the Cree perspective, and Darryl Chamekese of the Saskatchewan Indian Cultural Centre was an invaluable resource and shared personal stories about moose.

Special thanks also to those who read and commented on whole chapters, set me right on important facts, and allowed me to use some of their wonderful photos and artwork: George Bubenik, Ken Child, Kris Hundertmark, Tom Knight, Andrzej Krzywinski, Susan Kutz, Mats Lindquist, Adrian Lister, Richard McCabe, Alexander Minaev, Jane Mingay, Nigel Monaghan, Milla Niemi, Jessica Paterson, Bill Samuel, Julia Sigwart, Bob Stewart,

Gerhard Stuewe, Jimmy Suttie, Ken Tustin, Nicholas Tyler, Victor van Ballenberghe, and Murray Woodbury.

In order to do as thorough job as possible, one of my self-imposed tasks was to try and gain an understanding of the status of moose in the early twenty-first century, and to that end I contacted biologists from just about every range country, U.S. state, and Canadian province where moose exist. I read as many volumes as I could of the *Proceedings of the North American Moose Workshop*, not just the publications from the workshops I was lucky enough to attend. These workshop proceedings morphed into the journal *Alces*, whose front-cover mandate reads: "A Journal Devoted to The Biology and Management of Moose." I owe the contributors and editors sincere thanks for their hard work. I also consulted several books that contained useful information. When those attempts failed, I went, with some care, to the Internet. In the end I was able to obtain information on fifty-five regions—including five separate ones in Russia, which I think is excusable because there are nine time zones involved.

I made several calls to colleagues whom I had met at various moose conferences over the years and had help from numerous biologists whom I have never met. Apart from those named above, others who replied to my queries and sent me valuable information that I could not have obtained from books and journals were: Gundega Aizupiete, James Allen, Anis Aoude, Jon Arnemo, Jim Baker, Linas Balciauskas, Kimberlee Beckmen, Roger Bergström, Dean Beyer, John Blake, Erika Butler, Nigel Caulkett, Terry Chapin, Kjell Danell, Pjotr Danilov, Mark Drew, John Fletcher, Brett Elkin, Sunne Häggmark, Doug Heard, Yeen Ten Hwang, Bill Jensen, Jon Jorgensen, Doug Jury, Lee Kantar, Kalin Kellie, Steve Kilpatrick, Sébastian Lefort, Anders Lie, Ray Longmuir, Christopher Lyons, Peter Macdonald, Colin Mackintosh, Rick Marshall, Don McInnes, Tuire Nygrén, Danila Panchenko, Bob Patenaude, Brent Patterson, Rolf Peterson, Memoree Philipp, Margot Pybus, Mike Ramsay, Jim Rettie, Bengt Roken, Christine Ruggere, Dwayne Sabine, Steve Schmitt, Helen Schwantje, Karen Simonson, Christopher Smith, Norman D. Smith, Sharon Snowshoe, Erling

Solberg, Sarah Spencer, Rob Tether, Raisa Tillikainen, Dale Toweill, and Randy Wright.

Past and present members of my writers' group gave me much valuable feedback. They are Wilfred Bird, George Bitz, Eve Kotyk, Kurt van Kuren, Rebecca Lloyd, Judy McCrosky, Bobbi Mumm, Gayle Smith, and Jon Watts.

This work would not have been possible without the dedication and patience of my wife, Joanne, who read and re-read every word and made many useful suggestions.

Finally, my editors. Mcaghan Craven kept an eagle eye on everything and made invaluable contributions to the entire enterprise. Jen Knoch of ECW Press tidied up the loose ends, organized the layout and photos and made important suggestions.

Credit goes to all of these generous people, but errors and omissions are entirely my own responsibility.

Storytelling comes alive in this book by Jerry Haigh, the Glasgow veterinarian who documents his travels from Scotland via Africa to Saskatchewan.

Linking education and the future of moose presents a formidable challenge to wildlife managers and biologists. This retired Glasgow vet does a service toward this end by touching on many fascinating aspects of this boreal forest icon by giving the reader a glance into many aspects of moose biology and management — a vital task, since an informed public is essential for its future.

Of Moose and Men is the story a young vet from the balmy climate south of the equator ending up in moose country with temperatures of −40°C, a relocation that inevitably made his tweed pants a tad stiff! Haigh's compulsion for writing and storytelling gives the reader an insight into his fascinating life as a Canadian veterinarian with an interest in wildlife.

The book deals with the serious side of a vet's life but also the humorous (such as Mrs. Bullwinkle putting the run on the Glasgow vet), calling on a cast of characters that many of us in the wildlife field have experienced, and who in their own way give character to the book. He has made a concerted effort to contact informed individuals in various parts of the world to bring some semblance of order to his knowledge of moose and credibility to the stories.

From a wildlife management perspective, *Of Moose and Men* gives the reader a superficial glimpse into the moose world, touching on many of the complex issues pertaining to moose biology and management, and offering an accessible entry point into some of the tasks of wildlife biologists and veterinarians. The book might also be called "moose biology made simple," because the author's writing style will capture the imagination and interest of readers, whether this is their first encounter with this formidable animal or whether, like Haigh, they've spent decades in its pursuit.

Dr. Vince Crichton

CHAPTER ONE

A BREATHTAKING START

A big move from Africa to Canada; weather as I did not know it;
a disastrous start with a fortunate ending.

UNDERSTAND JOB OFFER SASKATOON STOP
ON SAFARI IN RWANDA TRANSLOCATING
ELEPHANTS STOP WILL MAKE CONTACT ASAP
ON RETURN TO KENYA STOP HAIGH.

Working in the half-dark of a crowded post office jam-packed with Rwandans and three other "Europeans" (as any white person was called), I struggled to compose the telegram. For reasons of economy, it had to contain the fewest possible words and still be intelligible after winging its way through the wires and across the aether to Canada. I arrived at the post office without a writing implement of any kind, but luckily a charming and well-dressed matron loaned me a pencil. After crossing out redundancies like pronouns and other surplus words, I tore the fawn-coloured sheet off the pad. Next, I had to negotiate the throng occupying the room, making my way from the heavily scarred wooden shelf I had been working at toward the metal wicket, where I discovered I was about fifth in line (or maybe tenth, as the line was somewhat disorganized) for attention.

As I waited I looked around at the stained walls that had probably once been cream-coloured but were now a spiderweb-covered dark brown. The brown paint that had once coated the concrete floor showed through in a few places where it was not caked with rust-red mud that had been tracked in on the shoes or bare feet of customers. The streets were mud-puddled from the downpour of the previous night.

Eventually I got to the front of the queue, where I found that I could hardly see the clerk behind the grime-covered glass sheet. I bent down and spoke through the grate.

"I'd like to send this cable to Canada," I said to him, only to receive a blank stare. I had forgotten that I was in a francophone country. I switched to French, which was also a mistake, as I ran out of vocabulary after the initial *"Je veux."* I changed gears again to Swahili, which allowed us to understand one another.

I was in Kigali, Rwanda's capital, in mid-April 1975 and had not long come off the phone with my wife, Jo, who was at our home in Kenya. After the normal greetings she said, "A man named Nielsen called from Canada. They have offered you the job at the vet college."

"Did you say they've offered it to me?" I asked in a mixture of elation and hope that I had not misunderstood her.

"Yes, he wants you to call. It's wonderful news, isn't it?"

"Have you got the number?"

She read out the long number, which I tried to memorize, and then I realized that with the nine-hour time difference it would be 4 a.m. in Saskatoon. Not a good time to call. Conversely, by the time Nielsen would be in his office it would be 1 a.m. in Kigali, and I would not be able to use a phone, as the post office would be closed. The times were simply not going to mesh. In those pre-Internet, pre-fax days, a telegram was the only solution to my problem. And I was intent on getting my response to him as quickly as I could.

Dr. Nielsen was offering me a post as a zoo and wildlife veterinarian at the University of Saskatchewan's Western College of Veterinary Medicine. I had applied several months earlier and been waiting to hear for some time. Of course, Nielsen called when I happened to be away from home for several weeks.

I was in Kigali on a brief break during a prolonged exercise of culling and translocating the last of Rwanda's wild elephants. What follows is the story of what happened six months later, and then the thirty-odd subsequent years after my family and I left Kenya to take up life in Canada.

When I finished up the first leg of the Rwanda project I went back home to Lunatic Lane at the foot of Mount Kenya for a brief visit to see Jo and our four-year-old daughter, Karen. I desperately wanted to chat with Jo about our possible future and tell bedtime stories to Karen. As soon as I could arrange the tickets I flew to Canada, not so much to be interviewed for the position as to find out more about the country, the work, and the working environment. I needed to see what this job, which had called for a veterinarian with clinical wildlife experience, was all about. The position advert had also mentioned that zoo work would be part of the mix, and I needed to see what that meant.

I knew almost nothing of Canada, but the job offer was too attractive to turn down without a good look. For several reasons Jo and I knew that we had to move on from Kenya. Not least of these was that we had not only Karen but also another child on the way, and we wanted to ensure they had a good education and future. While Jo's medical practice at the Nanyuki Cottage Hospital was thriving, my own private practice had shifted to depend to a large extent on intermittent wildlife work. The large animal side of my work—the horse, sheep, and cattle part—had recently taken a serious hit when the farms of several of my clients—those upon whom I relied for monthly, bread-and-butter, herd-health work—had been sold to the Kenyan government in "Africanization" programs. The new owners had been given small plots between five and twenty acres in size, and they had barely enough resources to buy seed, let alone cattle. There had been a rural landscape shift: from a small number of relatively wealthy families owning dozens or hundreds of head of livestock, to a large number of families with practically nothing for a vet to do.

My arrival in Saskatoon on the first of May, late at night, carrying a piece of cardboard on which I had printed my name, sticks in my mind for two reasons. The first is that I was at once approached by a tall, distinguished-looking man with slightly greying hair, who identified himself as Ole Nielsen, Jo's caller, and dean of the college. That he would take the trouble to meet me personally spoke volumes about him. (Volumes that would be confirmed when he left Saskatoon after a distinguished career that included two terms as dean. He moved on to assume the leadership of another Canadian veterinary school at Guelph, Ontario.) The other reason that evening in May still remains fresh has to do with the weather. I was used to the cold of Glasgow but not madly impressed with the just below zero temperature and the snowstorm that greeted us as we left the airport and headed to Dr. Nielsen's Volvo station wagon. Luckily Nielsen had had the foresight to borrow a full-scale goose-down parka for me. I hardly took it off for the next week, despite the fact that many Saskatonians were in light jackets or even shirt-sleeves after coming through the bitter cold of the prairie winter, something I had yet to learn about.

"You can generate your own job description on the wildlife side of things. We don't really have a precedent or example to work with" was how Dr. Nielsen put it when we met next day in his office. "As for the rest, it will be 50 per cent zoo medicine and some teaching. We have fixed up a visit to the zoo later today, and then tomorrow you can meet some of the rest of our faculty."

What a golden opportunity—to be told to write your own job description!

One highlight of those six days was a trip I took with Dr. Gary Wobeser, a quiet athletic man about 1.78 metres in height, who would go on to win the Canadian Senior Men's Biathlon championship. Gary had joined the faculty the year before I arrived, after completing his Ph.D. in wildlife pathology. We drove for five hours in his monster bottle-green station wagon to the Cabri Sandhills of southern Saskatchewan, where Gary had been conducting a study of die-offs in one of the province's most charismatic species, the white-tailed deer. His reputation in the world of wildlife diseases was already in the ascendancy.

Back home in Kenya it did not take Jo and me long to make the decision to move. Our son, Charles, arrived on time in July, but with the somewhat unusual record of my being drafted as second surgeon for Jo's Caesarean delivery when the resident on duty did not respond to repeated calls over the Nairobi Hospital public address system.

Six weeks later we left Kenya and had a short stint in Scotland and Holland to introduce our new son to his proud grandmothers and other family members. I left for Canada in mid-September to start on the next chapter of our adventure, and Jo and the kids stayed with her parents in Holland for some extra rest time. When she did arrive we stayed with the Neal family, whom we had met in Meru National Park, Kenya, when Dick Neal was conducting research on the breeding biology of kangaroo rats.

I was a total North American greenhorn. The first mistake I made was to buy a Ford Pinto, not knowing about *Unsafe at Any Speed*, the book consumer advocate and environmental crusader Ralph Nader had written, which focused on the exploding gas tank of the infamous vehicle. Comparing it to the cars in Kenya and Europe, Jo thought it was enormous until she saw a few of the others on the road, most of which dwarfed it.

While with the Neals, we searched for a house, heeding a piece of advice we had never heard before. It was the aphorism that only three things mattered in house purchasing: location, location, and location. In this regard we were lucky because, even though there was a housing shortage at the time, we found a nice bungalow that backed right onto a park. Karen could leave through the back gate and walk across the grass (or snow) right to school. The basement was unfinished so I could put my woodworking hobby to good use. Over time, the African hardwood crate that had carried our goods and chattels across the ocean became a coffee table and matching set of armchairs, with upholstery by Jo, who has great skill with many forms of craft.

The ramp at the front entrance of the Western
College of Veterinary Medicine in 1975.

UNIVERSITY OF SASKATCHEWAN ARCHIVES, PHOTOGRAPH COLLECTION, A-4888

In the meantime, I dove into my work at the university. Even before the family arrived, and only three days after I arrived to start my new job, I found myself dealing with an animal crisis that was partly of my own making. It was what would technically be called an iatrogenic emergency: a symptom or illness brought on unintentionally by something that a doctor does or says.

In this case it was the "does" rather than the "says."

The patient was an emaciated white-tailed deer doe, who stood with drooping ears about five metres from me. She was on the other side of the page-wire fence that surrounded the enclosure she shared with a group of shaggy bison. Bison are about the same size as the Cape buffalo, with which I was more familiar from my years in Africa.

I guessed that hers was not typical behaviour for a deer, but I needed no guesswork to know that she was dreadfully thin and that something needed to be done. Of course this is exactly why Brent Pendleton, the animal foreman at the zoo, had asked me to take a look at her. I had met Brent briefly three months previously when I first visited Saskatoon. In the interval he had grown a red beard, and it took me a moment to recognize him.

It was obvious that the only way I was going to be able to examine the animal was to immobilize her with a drug cocktail. But doing that proved to be a problem. I had little choice in the manner of approach because of the utterly useless design of all the large animal enclosures at the zoo. In every case the open-ended shelters for the animals had been placed exactly in the middle of the pens. With no doors on the shelters, and absolutely no other way of trapping an animal for any kind of examination, I was in a quandary. I mused that such a layout nicely matched the paradigm of "the ideal family home" in Saskatoon, with the single family dwelling in the middle of a garden. The architect who had laid out the plans for the zoo, which was quite new, obviously had no concept of animal behaviour or needs. Indeed, the fences around every pen were set in straight lines, with sharp angles, just like suburban fences in a city. Humans may be the only species on Earth that have created home territories with straight boundaries. The home ranges of animals are never set so rigidly, and of course they often overlap.

The pens at the zoo were a huge step up, however, from those at the previous site of the animal collection. Those enclosures resembled what can charitably be described as a roadside menagerie at the Golden Gate Park in the city's west end. By all accounts, and from looking at some of the old photos, the park was an eyesore. In 1964 Saskatoon's city council decided to purchase the animals and equipment from the Golden Gate and held them there until they could be moved across the city to Forestry Farm, which had been one of the very important silviculture sites for the province since 1913. The new animal park opened in 1972, three years before my arrival, and any veterinary work had been carried out on an ad hoc basis by whomever could find the time or had some of the necessary skills.

After looking at the sick deer, Brent and I walked back to the office, and I prepared an immobilizing dart. I had not yet had the time to order the supplies I needed for such a job, but luckily there was a small supply of the right drugs at the college, and I had brought some with me. My choice was limited: either a super-potent morphine-like substance called M99 or a cattle sedative called Rompun. I had used both, separately and in combination, on a wide range of African species from elephants to tiny antelopes half the size of the deer, so I had some idea of where to start in terms of dosage. Moreover, Dr. Ron Presnell, a small-animal surgeon at the college, had recently published an article on the use of this very combination of drugs on white-tailed deer. The big surprise, when I read his paper, was that the dose Presnell suggested was almost exactly what I would have used two months earlier on a white rhino that weighed about ten times as much as the deer.

Armed with a darting pistol, a dart, plenty of experience with similar-sized animals from Africa, and the knowledge from Presnell's paper, I walked with Brent back to the two-acre bison pen. There we met up with Jureen, one of the older keepers, close to retirement age, who had come over from Golden Gate Park and was on large-animal duty. The deer had hardly moved in the intervening half hour and was still standing looking more or less straight at me.

I tried to manoeuvre to a good spot for a shot at the heavier muscles of her hindquarters, but there was no way to manage it. She was not going to cooperate. After about ten minutes, however, during which time Brent became concerned that she would move out of range, she turned her front end slightly sideways. I now had a chance at a shot into her shoulder or neck. Of the two, the shoulder looked like the poorer option. The ridge on her shoulder blade was clearly visible and the other bones also stood out. A heavy dart there would surely hit the bones and could break something. I took one more look at the neck, realizing that it, too, did not have much muscle mass, and pulled the trigger on the gas-powered pistol.

The dart flew true—it was only about four metres to the target— and the effect was instantaneous and dramatic. The animal fell onto her side as if pole-axed. Jureen had probably never seen a deer immobilization before, as all animal captures at Golden Gate had been done with a lariat. Brent had only seen one or two such procedures and none on a deer. To see this new vet, hot off the press from Africa and hired because of his extensive experience with wildlife capture, achieve such an amazing result was probably quite something.

Something it was, but not something good. I knew at once that we had a problem, but I did not yet know how serious that problem was. Immobilized animals, even under the very best of circumstances, usually take a few minutes to go down. Only in the last three or four years have we come close to achieving immobilizations in under two minutes, and this one was under two seconds. The closest thing I had ever seen to such a speedy take down was the result of a hunting rifle and a lead bullet.

I was over the fence in a trice and placed my stethoscope on the deer's chest. She was alive, but her breathing was irregular to say the least. One moment she was not breathing at all, the next it was going nineteen to the dozen. Then her breathing stopped again for about twenty seconds before going immediately back to a rapid pattern. I had read of this pattern, but I had never seen it before. It is known as Cheyne-Stokes respiration and is caused by damage to the respiratory centres in the central nervous system. The situation was serious, and I suggested to Brent that he call on the two-way radio to have someone bring the zoo van to the site so that we could take her to the veterinary teaching hospital, about four kilometres from the zoo.

The van, driven by another keeper, soon arrived and entered the bison pen at the back gate. We loaded the deer and headed out. I got into my own vehicle near the office and followed what was essentially now an ambulance. Of course I had fallen behind the van and was doing my level best to catch up, exceeding the speed limit, when I saw a flashing red light in my rear-view mirror. I knew that this was probably bad news for me, but I chose to ignore it, hoping I would be able to explain my way out of the situation in due course. When I arrived at the hospital parking lot, the deer was being unloaded onto a gurney and wheeled in through the big overhead doors.

I turned quickly to speak to the gentlemen in blue who were in the car with the flashing light. "I'm sorry I didn't stop before, but that deer is in a crisis, and she is my patient. Excuse me while I run in to see how she is doing. I'll be back as soon as I can."

With that I spun round and followed the gurney. By the time I got to the anesthesia suite, Dr. Peter Cribb, the anesthesiologist at the college, was hovering over the deer with his stethoscope.

It was soon over. The deer's breathing became even more irregular, and about eight minutes after we got to the college it stopped altogether. She was on oxygen but there had been no time to administer any emergency drugs, even if there had been any that would have done the trick.

"I'll just go and sort things out with the police, and then I'll go down to the post-mortem room and see if they can give us any ideas of what happened," I said to Peter.

I turned to head back to the loading gate, only to see one of the policemen peering through the glass aperture in the door right at the anesthesia suite. I opened it up and apologized to him, but the only response I got was, "Can I see your driving license, sir? You know that you were exceeding the speed limit, don't you?"

The upshot was that I had to pay a substantial fine.

As for the deer, wildlife pathologist Gary Wobeser was on duty and showed me what had happened. The dart needle had managed to find its way into the centre of the vertebral column by an almost impossible route. At the junction between each of the seven bones of the neck, there are minute holes through which nerves enter the spinal cord from various parts of the neck and thorax. In a white-tailed deer these holes, which go by the proper name of dorsal root canals and carry the nerve of that name, are almost exactly the same diameter as the needle I had used for the immobilization: smaller than a meat skewer. I would wager that I could fire a thousand, or maybe many thousands, of shots at a skeleton of a deer-sized animal and never manage to achieve what I did by driving that needle through that tiny hole. The dart, which would have emptied in a flash, compounded the injury by instantaneously dumping three millilitres of fluid into a virtually non-existent space and the sensitive nerve tissues of the spinal cord itself. No wonder her breathing was disrupted. No wonder the deer did not survive. The dart was almost as deadly as a rifle bullet.

It turned out that there would have been little I could have done about the deer's emaciated condition. She had a cancer of the kidney, which had already spread to neighbouring tissues. I reasoned that the accidental "bullet" saved her any further suffering, and I was able to put this event behind me and get on with my new job, which included setting up a herd health program for all the animals in the zoo. Assisted by a home-grown darting system that caused almost no injection-site damage, in the next sixteen years I handled and immobilized dozens of white-tailed deer, as well as other similar-sized deer and I'm happy to say I did not lose one of them.

CHAPTER TWO

WHAT'S IN A NAME?

That which they call a moose (or is it an elk?);
origins; DNA; the moose in Cree culture

I arrived at the zoo fresh from Africa, carrying with me a fascination with how things are named in the scientific world and how they got to where they are today. Who is related to whom? How closely? From day one I was faced with a puzzle that I needed to solve.

Right next to the pen in which my deer patient had lived was an attractive, one hectare–sized enclosure with some fence-protected spruce trees and a pond. Six large deer—an antlered male and three females with two of their calves—lived in this area. The identifier sign attached to their fence confused me a bit because the residents looked to me like overgrown versions of the Scottish Red Deer, with which I was quite familiar. In fact, the sign revealed that they were elk.

On my way from Kenya to Canada to begin my new job, I had stopped off in Munich to attend a wildlife conference. One afternoon all the delegates went to the zoo. Lying contentedly in one of the pens was a large, dark-brown, almost-black creature. The German sign on the wall of the enclosure read *Elch* (luckily subtitled in English as Elk), *Alces alces*. But this animal bore virtually no resemblance to the creature I was now looking at in Saskatoon. Apart from anything else, the Latin name on this sign, shown as it should be in italics, was *Cervus elaphus*, which is indeed the taxonomic name of the deer I was familiar with from my days in Scotland and my trips to the Highlands, trout rod in hand. Those Latin names matter because they define all living things, no matter what language you speak. I knew that any article I might write about a wild animal would have to include its taxonomic name.

An alternative name for elk on the sign in Saskatoon was also listed: wapiti.

I knew immediately that this needed sorting out, and with the vet college library's copy of *The Mammals of Canada* in hand, it did not take me long to solve at least part of the puzzle.

I learned that wapiti is the name used by Cree and Shawnee, and no doubt other members of the Algonquian language group, to describe the creature's white rump. When Europeans colonized North America, the wapiti, a very close relative of the European red deer, acquired the handle "North American elk" and is known as such in major texts. Elk is used as the common abbreviation, which of course takes us back to the European scene.

In several European languages, the large dark-haired creature I had seen in Munich, whose males carry antlers for part of the year, are called elk or Eurasian elk in English, or something similar such as *alg* (Swedish), *elg* (Norwegian), *elch* (German), *eland* (Dutch), and *alce* (Italian). In North America, they are moose.

Why moose? I puzzled.

It is impossible to guess why European immigrants decided that what we now call a moose was what they knew as an elk (or *elg*, if they were Vikings). Perhaps this naming debacle happened later than Vinland, though, and some short-sighted immigrant explorer saw a large animal through some bushes and wanted it to be something familiar. Perhaps, if he or she came from England, where moose had long since vanished, he had never actually seen a Eurasian moose but had heard of them. He called the big beast an elk, but of course he had seen what was already known by several of the peoples who had lived on the continent for thousands of years as a wapiti. This perhaps solves the problem of the North American elk's name, but what about that of the North American moose?

I am lucky enough to live in the very city where the Cree people of Saskatchewan have their headquarters. Many years after encountering the naming puzzle at Forestry Farm Park, I got in touch with Darryl Chamakese, who is the Cree Language Developer at the Saskatchewan Indian Cultural Centre. He gave me a warm welcome when I visited his office and was soon delving into a couple of dictionaries to see what he could find, as he was as intrigued as I about the elk/elch/ moose puzzle.

He explained that the name in Cree is *môshwa* or *môswa* (pronounced *mooshwuh*) and that the *môs* root occurs repeatedly in moose-related words. One word that has crossed almost unaltered in English is *Môsomin*, which are moose berries. This has become the name of a small town in southern Saskatchewan, Moosomin.

A larger Saskatchewan community also takes its name from the moose. The city of Moose Jaw has at least two claims to fame. It is linked, at least by the city tourism boosters, to the infamous Chicago gangster Al Capone, but for me, its wonderful Festival of Words is the major attraction because it brings authors and readers together in what may well be the friendliest and most delightful three-day jamboree of literature anywhere. Since my first visit as a reader I have puzzled over the origins of the city's name. There are conflicting accounts.

Two Moose-Javians, as they are called, repeated an oft-told tale that an early traveller in the area repaired his Red River cart with a moose's jaw bone. This story seems to fit nicely into the urban myth or April Fool's class of etymologies. One half-reasonable theory about Moose Jaw's name is that on a map, or viewed from the hills above, the river that runs through the community looks like a moose's jaw. Of course a moose's jaw, to all but the most carefully observing anatomists, looks pretty much like a wapiti's jaw. Maybe the city has been misnamed all along. What seems most likely is that the name derives from Cree sources, either from *mōscâstani-sîpiy*, which means "a warm place by the river," or phonetically the even closer *mōsegaw*, meaning "warm breezes."

Of course, if you have spent many years of your life living within a few hundred metres of the equator, as I did, the concept of warm breezes at –30°C requires some imagination.

The English "moose" is probably derived from *moosu*, meaning "he strips off," a Narragansett word, or maybe from the Abenaki *mus*, both languages being part of the Algonquian group. The word moose appears to have first entered English through repeated use by one or two Englishmen, either Thomas Hanham, who was named in the first Charter of Virginia issued by King James VI of Scotland (a.k.a. King James I of England; it depends upon your view) in 1606, or Admiral John Smith, explorer and author, who wrote about Pocahontas to King James's wife, Queen Anne, in 1616. Pocahontas was a member of an Aboriginal tribe who lived in the Tidewater region of what is now the state of Virginia, and she and her people also spoke a language of the Algonquian family. It is fun to speculate that she may have had a role in the adoption of a word from her native tongue into the English of her husband, John Rolfe.

As I waded deeper and deeper into the Native and English etymology of elk/wapiti, and then moose, I became more and more curious about the moose's taxonomic name, *Alces*, and how it became the accepted name in the scientific world. It does match the Italian term, and perhaps that became the Latin chosen by the famous eighteenth-century Swedish scientist Carl Linnaeus, the father of taxonomy. He called the moose *Alces alces* in 1758.

Almost a hundred years later there appeared a curious anomaly when, in 1854, the word *muswa* appeared as a scientific description of moose in North America. A professor Edward Forbes, writing about creatures seen during a North American expedition, called the creature *Alces muswa: The Moose-deer.* He then added "Muswa of the Cree

Indians." Of course he was ninety-six years too late, as Linnaeus had preempted him, but beautiful illustrations of the antlers and some of the bones accompany the very detailed descriptions of the skeleton.

When I started working on moose in 1975, it was pretty straight-forward. Each living thing had two names, a genus and a species. All moose around the globe were *Alces alces*. From there the system went to subspecies names and a third handle was added to delineate the region where the animals were found. At that time seven subspecies were described. In the 1990s an eighth, from the extreme eastern part of Eurasia, was added.

The accompanying map shows how various moose subspecies are geographically separated, although on neither the Eurasian nor the North American land mass are the boundaries absolute; the types tend to merge into one another. A good example lies in Canada's British Columbia, which has the distinction of having three races within its boundaries: *gigas* in the extreme north, *andersoni* in the central regions, and *shirasi* in the south, where it borders with Idaho and Washington.

One thing that caught my eye right away as I tried to satisfy my curiosity was that the Eurasian races were said to have sixty-eight chromosomes, while those of North America had seventy. I learned that, rather than the Americans gaining two chromosomes along the way somehow, what had most likely happened was that a pair of chromosomes among the seventy had tagged on to another pair and so reduced the total in the Eurasian subspecies.

With this information added to my mental library I wondered if moose really could all be dubbed under the heading of a single species. If obviously similar creatures had the same number of chromosomes then they were usually considered to be the same species. In dogs, think Great Danes and dachshunds. If they can get it on (maybe the dax stands on a chair?), they will produce pups. Of course, in the case of these breeds, it was human intervention or fashion choice that led to the bizarre differences we see today.

In the 1970s nobody seemed to know if the moose of North

America could interbreed with those of Eurasia, and the chances of anyone trying to find out were slim to nil (and still are). It would be fun to find out, but the cost of such a trial would be prohibitive, never mind the paperwork! Other similar-looking creatures with differing chromosome numbers can breed successfully, of course, but they usually have sterile offspring. And this outcome, sterility, has long been used to help us categorize animals as separate species.

The best-known example of two animals breeding with a sterile product is the cross between the horse and the donkey. The chromosome numbers of these two distinct species also differ by only two—sixty-four and sixty-two respectively—and we know that the foals are robust, make great pack animals, and have a reputation for stubbornness, but are nevertheless sterile. The name for these animals, mules, has even stretched beyond the animal and become part of the lexicon to describe any sort of hybrid, especially if it has a tendency to bloody-mindedness.

We have no idea if the model of the horse and donkey cross will apply in moose, but there are species, including the house mouse, in which differing chromosomes numbers do not prevent successful creation of fertile young.

And then came DNA. That is not strictly true, of course, as any high-school student of biology will quickly tell you. When James Watson and Francis Crick published their landmark study in 1953, they changed science in the way that many others before them had done. Today they rank with Archimedes, Copernicus, Galileo, Newton, and Darwin as big thinkers. However, DNA technology had not yet been turned to moose biology in 1975. When in 1983 California scientist Kary Mullis developed the ability to, as he stated, "pick the piece of DNA you're interested in and have as much of it as you want," his work led to the ability to look at tiny portions of the DNA chain and so differentiate groups of animals to a remarkable degree. By using a technique called polymerase chain reaction (PCR), which is really just a chemical Xerox machine, Mullis could create enormous numbers of those tiny portions in a very short time to allow a close look at them. This revolution allowed scientists to determine to a remarkable degree where an animal came from.

In the late 1980s and early 1990s DNA techniques were in use for moose and beginning to answer some of my questions, but even in 1997, when the landmark book *Ecology and Management of the North American Moose* was published, the really refined use of DNA had not become mainstream.

Since that 1997 book, approximately half of all the scientific papers ever published on moose genetics have appeared. The main consensus now is that there are probably eight subspecies: four in Eurasia, four in North America. However, it is not that simple. There are dissenting opinions that claim two main species *A. a. alces* in Europe and western Asia and *A. a. americana* in eastern Asia and North America. A main argument for this proposal was the finding of seventy chromosomes (the North American number) in four animals from Sakha in the Yakutia region, which lies roughly in the middle of the moose range on the Eurasian continent. This is too small a sample to be a reliable representation of all of them, however, and takes no account of the extreme eastern race shown in the map.

Kris Hundertmark, who is a professor at the University of Alaska, Fairbanks, and was awarded the Distinguished Moose Biologist award in 2007, has worked on moose taxonomy for many years. His award citation states, "No other person has published as many papers on the genetics of moose as Kris." He told me that moose are his favourite animals and that outside his work he is a keen photographer and, like me, enjoys fly-fishing.

When I wrote to him and asked about the current situation, he opened his reply with "Moose taxonomy is certainly confusing at the moment." He and his colleagues have spent as much time as anyone trying to sort out the puzzle and have concluded that there are three groups of moose—European, Asian, and North American—but that the amount of variation among those groups is very small. At most, the North American–Asian split is only 10,000 years and the Eurasian one somewhere around the 30,000- to 50,000-year mark. Both ranges

Map of approximate global distribution of eight subspecies of moose.

A. a. a. = A. a. alces	A. a. g. = A. a. gigas
A. a. p. = A. a. pfizenmayeri	A. a. an. = A. a. andersoni
A. a. c. = A. a. cameloides	A. a. s. = A. a. shirasi
A. a. b. = A. a. burturlini	A. a. am. = A. a. americana

* introduced in Newfoundland
§ introduced from Alberta to the Cape Breton highlands in 1948–1949

COURTESY KRIS HUNDERTMARK WITH CAPE BRETON ADDITION BY THE AUTHOR

of years are a mere blip in the history of the planet, no more that the diameter of the period at the end of this sentence relative to the entire book.

Kris explained to me that the differing chromosome numbers are of minor importance and that all moose are quite closely related. On the question of differing chromosome numbers and the possibility that offspring of crosses might be sterile, he was less certain.

Paleontologists generally agree that the first creatures that can be dubbed *Alces* appeared in the fossil record about two million years ago. With one exception—the broad-fronted moose, which appeared in both Eurasia and North America—moose ancestors arose in Eurasia. Those that can be called by the double genus and species name *Alces alces* are much more recent, arising about 100,000 years ago in the Yakutia region of what is now Russia.

I am intrigued by another thing about moose. How did modern moose get into North America? Although they are fantastic swimmers and are known to have moved tens of kilometres to colonize islands in Europe, there is no doubt that moose came to what is now Alaska by land.

At least two versions apply.

The scientific one is that they came across the Bering land bridge during a glacial period some 14,000 years ago at the end of the last ice age. What is enticing, and a worthy challenge for a modern Sherlock Holmes, is that according to Hundertmark the moose of the Americas are not as closely related to those living on the shores of the Bering Strait as they are to those of the Yakutia, which is centred some 3,000 kilometres to the west.

The Aboriginal version of moose origins differs significantly. Apart from helping me with Cree names and moose-related words, Darryl Chamakese went the extra mile when he arranged for me to meet an interesting Cree Elder who, he said, knew much more about moose than he did. After I picked him up at his office, Darryl took me to meet Barry Ahenakew, a solidly built, serious-looking man in his fifties, who was a bit cautious about speaking to me but opened up when I told him what I had on my mind and gifted him a copy of one of my books to show him the kind of work I was doing.

Over the course of three sessions and several cups of coffee (tea in my case), Barry shared several stories about Cree history and told me even more Cree words related to antlers and moose. He was adamant that the stories were not folklore or legends, but the history of his people. As I grew to know him a bit I realized that he was a hugely respected Elder, and he confirmed this for me when he told me that a group of Australian Aborigines had travelled all the way to Saskatoon to consult with him about a land claim issue.

On our second trip to meet Barry, Darryl told me that Barry is indeed special, and then used Cree words that I could not grasp and which he later explained in an email. He wrote, "Barry is *kihté-aya*, a term derived from two words. *Kihté* means great. . . . Great because this being has reached a certain pinnacle of life steeped in sacred and life-giving knowledge. *Aya* means a being; this could mean a human being or a spiritual being. *Kihté-aya* describes a person respected, wise, and called upon in times of need, but in its translation into English it loses much of its deeper and more beautiful meaning."

Darryl went on to say that "an 'Elder' does not think of himself as better than anyone else. It is through him that the words of Elders pass and he or she does not claim ownership of this knowledge. He or she is merely a conduit."

Over the course of our meetings, Barry took me deeper into the Cree moose culture and language about it. He confirmed some research I had done about Cree nations across Canada. In Saskatchewan there are three main groups, the Plains Cree, the Swampy Cree, and the Woodland or Bush Cree. A little farther east there are the Rocky Cree and farther east yet, around James Bay, are the Moose Cree. As a group, among themselves, they are simply known as *Iyiniwak*: The People.

The wide geographic range of the Cree people also accounts for the many differences in the name of the central figure in the mythology and history of these people. In Saskatchewan, he is known as Wesakechak, but there are many variations across the continent, and even an Anglicized one in the name of a common bird of the boreal forests, the whisky jack or grey jay. These days, stories about him often depict him as a trickster, but Barry explained that he is much more than that.

This is the moose origin history that Barry shared with me:

At one time we were the most technologically advanced people on Earth, with airplanes and heavy weapons. We lived on an island in the ocean to the east of where we are now. The Creator saw how we were damaging everything and he caused the island to start sinking. Because Wesakechak had the technology, he built a raft and put all the creatures on it, as well as the people. He paddled west and eventually found land. The moose were among the first to leave, and those first moose, which are sacred spiritual beings, are known as *Mōswa Atayōkan*. They migrated to the west, as did the humans and all the other animals that you see today.

With the naming and origin conundrums out of the way, it was time to get back to work at the zoo.

CHAPTER THREE

A TRIP TO BANFF

A wild elk chase; a new system for injecting animals;
a pivotal meeting that would resonate for thirty-five years.

While it was interesting to partially solve the elk and moose naming puzzle, it did not get me any further with the general zoo work and my increasing need to improve the welfare of darted animals. My experience with the white-tailed deer was probably the last straw. I had seen deep bruising, and even bleeding, from the entry site after darting soft-skinned antelopes like impala and had been wondering for some time if there was any way of changing the darting process, or perhaps the instruments used. I was faced with several animals of more or less the same size here in Saskatoon and did not want any more wrecks like that first white-tailed doe. The list of animals in my care included the remaining whitetails in the collection and three other species of small deer, as well as carnivores like wolves and even two African lions, George and Queenie—the undoubted star attractions of the entire menagerie.

Within a month of my arrival (while I puzzled over the darting challenge and doodled ideas on scrap paper), I began to learn my way around the world of zoo medicine and the politics of the veterinary college (much the more difficult challenge), and I received an unexpected call.

"Good morning. Is that Doctor Jerry Haigh?" came the carefully modulated voice over my office phone.

"Yes, this is Jerry. What can I do for you?"

"This is Bim Hopf, from the Calgary Zoo. I'm the veterinarian here, and I hear that you have lots of experience with wild animal capture. We have an unusual problem. Somebody has killed our bull elk with a crossbow, and the director has managed to negotiate the donation of a replacement from Banff National Park."

"With a crossbow!" I replied. "That's pretty crazy."

"I agree with you. I wonder if you could get here and join me with the capture, as I've no experience with that sort of thing."

"I'd be delighted," I replied almost without thinking. "How do I get to Calgary?"

Three days later I was on an Air Canada flight to Calgary, which I knew very little about (I had only heard that it hosted some sort of rodeo thing), and three hours later Bim and I were sitting in his truck watching a young bull elk subside gently in the snow as the dart in his left hip took effect.

Warden Perry Jacobson, a squat round-faced man in his forties, had fired the metal dart that Bim had made up after we talked about doses. The elk did not run far, and then he lay still with his head up until the truck and trailer approached him through a fifteen-centimetre-deep blanket of snow. We all grunted the animal up the ramp into the trailer and took deep breaths as Perry lifted and latched it securely. After Bim gave the animal an antidote and quickly left by the side door, we watched through the ventilation panels until he stood up. Two hours later we were back in Calgary, and soon after we dropped the tailgate of the trailer, the big bull walked quietly out into what would be his new home.

It was too late to get back to Saskatoon, and Bim invited me into his home to meet his family and spend the night. Over a delicious meal of lasagna we chatted about Bim's work at the zoo and soon discovered that we were both concerned about darting animals and the need to find some way of doing it that would be less traumatic than the thump of a heavy metal dart. A big creature like the elk we had just ferried from Banff could no doubt handle the impact, but smaller creatures might have a problem, and the smaller they got, the greater was the risk to them. I had read of an unfortunate small dog that had been killed outright when a dart had gone right through his chest wall.

"I've been fiddling with the idea of using a blowpipe and plastic syringe," I told Bim. "There was an article in the *Veterinary Record* a while back where a couple of guys adapted a syringe and used it to capture wild monkeys in Malaysia. They employed local tribesmen, the Orang Asli, to fire their long pipes—about four metres long—up into the canopy. These people have lived in the forests as long as anyone knows and are deadly accurate. Of course, they use poisons, but the researchers used tiny doses of PCP."

The long name for PCP is a twenty-six-letter alphabet soup—phenylcyclohexylpiperidine—but it is more commonly known as phencyclidine (mercifully further shortened to PCP). Even a few drops will produce hallucinations in people, so the dose for the monkeys had been truly minute.

"I thought you couldn't get that stuff anymore," replied Bim.

"You can't get it here, I know that. It's too dangerous. They must have had a source, and of course they may have done the work a few years back and only recently reported it."

PCP was (and sadly remains) a street drug. The term "recreational" hardly seems to fit the accounts that I read about the drug and its use at the time. These were more like horror stories. I read about one young man who tore his own eyes out under the influence. In another report, a man threw himself down an elevator shaft because he thought he could fly. The stuff had over twenty street names, including Angel Dust and Hairy Jerry (it could not have applied to me, given my inherited bald state). One researcher found that PCP induces symptoms in humans that are virtually indistinguishable from schizophrenia.

There is no way of knowing what sort of hallucinations were

A fallow deer buck with a blowdart in its shoulder.
The immobilizing drug cocktail is beginning to work.
JERRY HAIGH

suffered by the animals subjected to capture with this drug while it was
in use, but it had disappeared from the legal market by the late 1970s.

"I've been thinking about the same dart thing," said Bim. "Let's
head to the basement after dinner and see what we can come up with."

I showed Bim what I had been fiddling with, as it was easy to do
on a simple workbench. It involved cutting up plastic syringes and
sticking needles through them to see if I could create a propulsion

system for a dart to empty when it hit the target, but not before. I seemed to have this more or less licked, but I could not get the thing to fly straight when I tried to propel it through a piece of plastic pipe.

"I've got a propulsion system worked out," I said. "If we use two plungers at the back we can insert some butane between them straight from a cylinder with a fine needle. I don't have one here, but you can get butane at any drug store, the same stuff you use to refill cigarette lighters. All we have to do is block the needle at the business end of the syringe so that no drugs will emerge from it until we want them to. I have that part solved by blocking the needle tip and drilling a hole in its side. Then you cover that hole with a collar that will be pushed back on impact with skin. What I have not figured out is how to get the thing to fly properly."

The solution was simple and elegant, and it was Bim who spotted it. Walking over to the dartboard on the wall, he picked up a dart and pointed to the plastic flights. "Why don't we try putting something like this—maybe a bunch of wool—into the rear face? That should stabilize it."

We tried a couple of the newly improved prototypes, which seemed to work pretty well. We both hit the target without trouble from the standard eight-foot (2.4-metre) distance from the dartboard, but made no effort to go for double top.

Back at home I worked out the minor bugs in the system and was soon making up darts and needles on the workbench at the zoo, which had a well-equipped workshop with a drill press and myriad other tools.

One of the most pressing reasons for all this fiddling about with plastic darts was that I had to get going on the main challenge at the zoo. As far as I could make out, no vaccines of any sort had ever been given to the animals. There were several carnivores in the collection, and they were all susceptible to one or more nasty, usually lethal, viral infections. In addition, there were wolves, coyotes, foxes, badgers, and raccoons, all susceptible to canine distemper, which is a common disease of dogs. A vaccination program for this group of animals was a high priority.

An unusual pair of dog-like animals was also part of the collection. The sign on their cage stated that they were dingoes from Australia. The cage was almost certainly a carry-over from Golden Gate Park. It was totally inadequate and consisted of a wooden-framed wire contraption with a footprint about four by four metres and just over two metres in height. A much-chewed wooden box just big enough for both animals sat in one corner. If the surely miserable occupants really were dingoes, how they got from Down Under to the Canadian prairies was a complete mystery to me and everyone else.

The lions George and Queenie also needed to be vaccinated, but how was I going to get at them? Teaming up with the keepers would allow me to catch the smaller animals with heavy-duty butterfly nets designed specifically for the task, but the only time I had ever heard of nets being used to deal with lions dated back to the times of the Roman circuses and the gladiators. Gladiators were considered dispensable, and I'm sure the event organizers never had to deal with the office of Occupational Health and Safety.

The first dose of the vaccine was easy to give. The lions would do almost anything for some meat scraps, and as a keeper fed them through the page wire I was able to slip a needle under their skin and give the injection. But only just. Before the syringe plunger had gone fully home the lions were on the move, and after that they would never let me anywhere near them. Even at fifty paces away they knew precisely who I was and would growl while they moved away from my approach. It wasn't just my outline. One Sunday the next year I visited with my family and carried one-year-old Charles on my shoulders. The lions recognized me at once, again at fifty paces.

One dose of vaccine was not going to provide the pair with the protection they needed. I had to get a second one in, and do it within thirty days. This is what led to my efforts with the blowpipe. The visit to Calgary and the brainstorm with Bim had come at just the right time.

Getting the vaccine booster injections into the lions was easy with the new darting system. After a little practice, I found I could shoot the dart to its target pretty accurately. With a pipe about 1.5 metres long I could blow the dart and hit a fist-sized target reliably from about ten metres, and that was as far as the lions could go in their too-small pen. They did not like it much, of course, and became even more distrustful of me for many months afterwards. Many zoo vets face the same distrust and have animals react negatively when they approach with any sort of pipe- or rod-like object.

Naturally, I talked about the blowpipe and dart development with colleagues, in particular Dr. Peter Cribb, a graduate of the Royal Dick Veterinary College in Edinburgh who had come to Canada with his family and started out as a private practitioner in Fort St. John near British Columbia's border with Alberta. Peter asked one question whose implications I had not considered.

"Are you sure this thing is going to be legal and not classed as a restricted weapon?"

"I'm not planning to use it on anything other than animals," I replied.

"You might be wise to check," he said.

I started my round of checks with a call to the local detachment of the Royal Canadian Mounted Police, whose secretary directed me to the province's office of the Attorney General. In due course I received a carefully worded reply above the signature of Roy Romanow, who would later become the premier of Saskatchewan, to the effect that the blowpipe would not be restricted as long as it was not used on humans but remained a tool for animal work.

For the next thirty-odd years I never used anything but a blow-pipe system on captive animals that needed to be drugged and could not be hand-injected. The system was also widely adopted in the zoo world, and several excellent improvements were made when commercial versions came on the market. The blowpipe and its descendants have become standard equipment all over the world for the capture of animals, both in zoos and in the wild, for species ranging from fish to elephants.

A week after those second injections into the lions, I was feeling as though I had overcome a major hurdle in my new career in Canada. In retrospect, it was therefore surprising when another career-changing (and -augmenting) event happened so close on the heels of the first one. It was a connection that took me to four continents and work with deer species ranging from moose to red deer in Europe and New Zealand, axis deer in Australia, reindeer in Mongolia, and a deer of questionable origin on Rota, a tiny island in the Mariana chain in the Pacific Ocean. I received a message from the receptionist in the Large Animal Clinic at the college. She called me on the internal phone.

"Dr. Haigh, there is a man down here in the waiting room who wants to talk to someone about drugs for moose capture." I was quickly on my way, as this sounded interesting.

The only person in the waiting area was a stocky man with a dark well-trimmed beard, about 1.72 metres tall, who introduced himself as Bob Stewart when I said, "Were you looking for some moose drugs? I'm Jerry Haigh."

CHAPTER FOUR

OF MOOSE AND MEN

First efforts at moose capture and the effects of winter;
language and accent differences cause a brief hiccup.

"If I hit the pilot with the dart we are all done for," I said to myself as I rehearsed my safety speech.

It was six weeks after my first meeting with Bob in the clinic reception area, and I was sitting in my room at Bainbridge Lodge in northeastern Saskatchewan before going in to breakfast and joining the rest of the moose capture team.

Once we had finished eating I opened up my drug box and started my spiel, although I decided to tone down the opening line, as I really did not know how they might react.

"We are working with a super-potent opioid—a morphine-like drug," I said, "and we need to be very careful how we handle it. Of course, I'm the one most at risk because I might accidentally inject myself, so please take a look at these vials. This one has red ink on it, and that spells danger. It contains the immobilizing drug Fentanyl. Don't touch it. This one is marked with green, meaning safety, or go. It contains Naloxone, a specific antidote to any opioid. If I inject myself with the Fentanyl and need help, this is the one you need to use—give me a couple of ccs and then keep an eye on me to make sure

31

I'm breathing. Top me up with another cc if I get drowsy and my breathing slows down."

Then I added the line about the possible accidental darting of the pilot. "But don't worry, I've had lots of firearms safety training, and the business end of the barrel will never be inside the helicopter when there's a dart in the gun."

When I sat with Bob Stewart in the reception area of the Large Animal Clinic six week earlier he had said, "I'm with the Department of Natural Resources. We are getting prepared for a long-term moose study in the Cumberland Delta, and Gary Wobeser told me that you would be the guy to contact. I'm here to see if you can let me have some succinylcholine—Anectine or Sux—for the program. We plan to capture a substantial number of them over the next couple of years, and we need to dart them from a helicopter."

There were so many layers to Bob's proposal that I hardly knew where to start. First of all, I had only been in Canada for six weeks, and here was my first opportunity to get into the work I loved: in the field, studying free-ranging wild animals. I knew that whatever the zoo work might have to offer, it was not going to satisfy me professionally.

"What's the study about?" I asked.

"We want to find out a lot about habitat use, population size, home range, and so on. No detailed study of moose biology has been done in Saskatchewan, and there aren't many anywhere else, either. The Alaskans have one on the go, and there is some work being done in Alberta. We want to see what's what here."

"What are the plans?"

"We intend to capture some moose, put visual collars on them that can be easily seen from the air, and see how they fare. We will be doing survey flights from a fixed-wing aircraft twice a year, and if the collars are big and bright enough we should be able to find the animals. To do that we need to capture them by darting them from a helicopter. Later, if we can get the funds, we hope to go to radio collars," said Bob.

"I've done lots of darting in Africa: rhino, elephant and several kinds of antelope, so that should be no problem," I replied. "However, there is a bit of an issue about your choice of drug. I'm not sure that Anectine is the best drug these days, and I think I can offer you a better alternative. I can get some modern drugs that have an antidote. Moreover, I can get them for free and can come and help you with the work, as it fits my job description exactly."

"I've looked at the literature and have discovered that not many people are using Sux anymore. But we can't legally get our hands on M99. I know some biologists are using it, but it's a narcotic and they're not licensed for it. Anyway, I thought we'd try something that is at least legal," Bob replied, leaning forward. "But I know Anectine isn't ideal, either. If you have something better, and free, I'm interested."

Bob was skeptical about Anectine because he had read what little literature there was at the time on moose capture, and most of the articles from the 1960s mentioned Anectine: merely a paralyzing agent that has no effect at all on an animal's ability to sense what is happening to it, which is a major animal-welfare issue. By that time, Anectine was no longer in use in Africa because modern morphine-like drugs called opioids—like M99 and the Fentanyl that I had been using for six years—were much safer and also ensured the patient was unaware of anything that happened after the drugs took effect. As well, when using an opioid for animal capture the duration of immobilization could be readily controlled, as opioids have effective antidotes that can be administered when the researcher or clinician is ready to usher the patient back to consciousness. Moreover, these drugs can be topped up if the animal shows signs of waking up at an inopportune moment, which certainly cannot be safely done with Anectine. Animals dosed with Anectine are also likely to go from paralyzed to fully awake in seconds, which would create an interesting situation for a researcher dealing with a beast the size of a moose, not to mention a grizzly bear (a species on which Anectine had been used for a while at that time).

"Why don't we head upstairs for a coffee and chat some more?" I suggested.

"Don't have time right now," Bob said, standing and stretching his right leg, "but if you can dig into things a bit and get back to me, I'd like to pursue this."

We exchanged telephone numbers and he headed out the door to his truck.

I was electrified. I had been burning a lot of hours studying for the board exams that I needed to pass in order be licensed to practice veterinary medicine in Saskatchewan, doing little else than covering my zoo duties every day and hitting the books. Although there were only three weeks to go before the tests, I decided that a diversion was a must: my brain seemed to be frying with facts.

My first stop was the well-stocked college library to get myself up to speed and search for scientific articles about moose capture. There were a couple from the '60s that described the use of paralyzing agents, and one from 1970 that seemed to document the first time M99—which Bob had referred to and was the drug I had used in my first white-tailed deer case—had been employed. There was not much else, but I did find one important thing. I confirmed my suspicions that Anectine had a very narrow safety margin in moose and further-more, its effective dose at some times of year was more than its lethal dose at others. Quite why this was so was not clear, but it probably had something to do with the seasonal changes in body condition that occur in many animals living in northern climes. Adding this new piece of information to the animal welfare concerns I already had about the drug ruled Anectine out completely in my book.

My next step was to try and find out if any Canadian wildlife vets were working on a similar kind of field project and call them. I already knew that we had a very strong team working in pathology, parasitology, and epidemiology at the college, as we had started to meet once a week in a sort of informal "Wildlife Group." However, there did not seem to be any vets in Canada who had experience with moose capture.

Early next morning, I called Dr. Richard Maarsboom of Janssen Pharmaceuticals in Belgium. He had already helped me so much with the opioid Fentanyl that I had used for six years in Kenya, on everything from rhinos to the tiny dik-dik and on those elephants in Rwanda. I figured that it was something I could try on some Canadian animals, and here was the opportunity. He was keen to help by supplying the drugs gratis, and he pointed me to the regulatory authorities in Canada with whom I would have to deal for import permits.

After the call to Belgium, I dialled Ottawa to speak to a Dr. Campbell of the national drug authority. His thick west of Scotland brogue put me at ease.

"Good morning, Dr. Campbell. My name is Jerry Haigh, but you don't know me from a bar of soap. I'm calling from the Western College in Saskatoon, but I'm a Glasgow grad. It sounds like you're a Glasgow man, yourself. Did you graduate there?"

"Aye, 1945, but I've been in Canada a long while," he said.

"I've recently arrived from Kenya, and I'm hoping to get hold of some Fentanyl for moose research."

He was at once helpful, asked me how much I needed, and told me which forms to fill out. I had already calculated doses for twenty animals, with a fudge factor to spare in case of dart misses or some other unforeseen thing. The doses were based upon African beasts familiar to me and similar in size to moose, such as eland or buffalo.

"Two grams should be enough," I said.

"That shouldnae be a problem. Just send me the paperwork. We should have no trouble getting it in from Belgium."

At this point, satisfied that I'd done the proper groundwork, I called Bob, and we began to plan for the trip.

"I've booked a helicopter for the second week of December. Can you get up to Bainbridge Lodge on the 6th or 7th?" he asked.

"How do I get there?"

"Head to Prince Albert, cross the North Saskatchewan River, turn right to Nipawin and keep going on Highway 55 on the gravel to the T junction with Highway 9. The lodge is right there. I'll book a room for you. It'll take you about five hours."

So, six weeks later, on a crisp December morning, with a poached eggs and bacon breakfast inside me, I listened to the CBC Radio weather reporter tell me that it was −18°C as I backed carefully out of our slippery driveway and headed out of town, north toward the Saskatchewan River Delta and my first wildlife research experience in Canada.

I passed snow-covered fields and drove through a series of small towns, each with at least one tall wooden granary towering above the landscape. I crossed the bridge over the partly frozen North Saskatchewan River, a wide sheet of ice disappearing to my right round a long bend, and turned east. More towns, more snowfields, and then, four hours after my departure, I found myself entering unfamiliar territory. I was driving the clinic's big, old, mustard-coloured Chevrolet Impala through a boreal forest mix of tall, straight, silver-trunked aspen devoid of any greenery and spruce trees, whose dark green branches were festooned with snow. The Porcupine Hills rose to my right, and I caught occasional glimpses through the gaps in the trees on my left of a wide flat area that looked like prairie. The road was obviously heavily used, the snow packed hard into the gravel and deep in the ditches where ploughs had thrown it. Several big trucks stacked with logs came at me, barely giving me enough room to pass without ending up in the ditch.

The "prairie" I was seeing snippets of was anything but. From the maps I had obtained I realized that I was passing along the southern edge of the Saskatchewan River Delta that straddles the Saskatchewan–Manitoba border. At 10,000 square kilometres, it is the largest of only five inland river deltas in North America. When we flew over large parts of it in the next week, I saw that it was a network of frozen waterways and small lakes, interposed with mile after mile of bush and trees.

At the time, we called the delta the Cumberland Delta, and so do most people to this day. However, it is more correctly named for the Saskatchewan River. Indeed all river deltas are everywhere named for the river that supplies them, as in Okavango, Mackenzie, and so on. I suppose "Cumberland" comes from the community of Cumberland House, which lies at the northern edge of the Saskatchewan River Delta.

This community was an important trading post in the early days of the Hudson's Bay Company and was founded in 1774 by Samuel Hearne.

At Bainbridge lodge I met with the rest of the crew: Wayne Runge, a tough-looking, blond, solidly built biologist with the department, who was based in Prince Albert, and Terry Roc, a colleague and friend of Bob's, slimmer than Wayne, dark-haired, and about my height at 1.82 metres. I also met the vital link to our entire operation, Cliff Thompson, the slightly stooped helicopter pilot, whose green and white Bell Jet Ranger was parked about fifty metres from the buildings.

I climbed up the five steps that led to a short deck attached to a trailer, and in there I met the hosts and owners of the lodge, Janet and Cliff Carter. It was Janet who asked what I'd like for dinner, saying, in the same breath, "I've just come from making a big load of pasta. I've got a tomato and meat sauce to go with. How does that sound?"

Taking the hint, I said, "I'll look forward to it, but I'd love a cup of tea. Where can I put my stuff while the water is boiling?"

I have a thing about tea. The water must be boiling when added to the leaves or bag, and I prefer that the mug or pot be pre-warmed. The hot water that comes out of coffee machines just doesn't cut it. My family have heard this mantra so many times—especially in the U.S. where the hot brown water that passes for tea usually tastes as if it has come out of a roadside ditch—that they simply roll up their eyes or look embarrassed when I start on my little rant.

Cliff showed me to another trailer, and I dumped my bags, drug box, and dart gun. Then it was back to the dining room and what turned out to be a really excellent meal, the first of many over the next several trips to Bainbridge in the ensuing years.

The first thing we did in the morning was exchange safety protocols. After my little speech and demonstration, Cliff spent a few minutes telling us where not to walk around helicopters, with special reference to the spinning tail.

I turned to Cliff and said, "I need some help with the darting—our success is going to be 80 per cent or more based on your skill. Have you done this kind of work before?"

Cow moose and calf running beneath the helicopter.
JERRY HAIGH

"No, but I've flown plenty of surveys. What have you got in mind?"

"I'm sure it's straightforward, but I've found that if you, as pilot, can get me slightly behind and above the animal, about thirty or forty feet away from him, I can get a shot away into his rump. The key is that for a few seconds we need to be moving at exactly the same speed as him. That thing," I pointed to the gun that was leaning in the corner, "is not very accurate and has a pretty low muzzle velocity, so even at close range I can easily miss if we are overtaking or falling back."

"Shouldn't be a problem, but we'll do a couple of dry runs if you like."

"Let's see how things work out," I said.

We all packed into the helicopter and donned our headsets. Bob was in front next to Cliff, and Terry, Wayne, and I—not to mention all the drugs—were on the back seat.

It took me some time to work out whether I should wear the headset over my toque, or vice-versa. Wool headgear had not been required in Kenya, but here the temperature was well below freezing,

The white vulval patch on this female moose is clearly visible.
GERHARD STUEWE

and I knew that when it came to darting my head would be halfway out of the window, with the wind from both our forward motion and the downdraft of the helicopter blades exaggerating everything many fold. I figured it would be like doing a hundred on an open motorcycle through an Arctic blizzard. Eventually, the wool stayed close to my bald head and the headphone clip rode on top of it.

It took us little time to find our first moose; the delta had the highest concentration of them anywhere in the province—something over two animals per square kilometre at the time.

"It's a bull," said Bob.

"But it hasn't got any antlers," I said, puzzled. "Surely they would be still attached, at least until March or so."

"No, mature bulls usually shed in early December, not like other deer. The key thing to look for is the white vulval patch under the tail. Only females have that," he replied.

"We're too heavy to do a dart run with this many people on board, so I'll just drop Terry and Wayne off by that beaver lodge," said Cliff over the intercom. "That'll give Jerry more room to move back there. Then, we'll go and see how things are."

As it turned out we did not need a dry run. The bull had not gone far and was standing in tall willows not two hundred metres away from where he had been when we first spotted him. In less than ninety seconds, including the time that it took Cliff to herd the bull into a clear spot, he had a dart in his left hip. Without any prompting from me, Cliff took the machine up high, and we circled gently for a few minutes. All the while I kept a close eye on the stopwatch that I used for this kind of work. After six minutes the animal began to show signs of drug effects. His gait changed to a sort of goose step, and he began to circle rather aimlessly. At first this was encouraging, but when after a further five minutes he was still at it, I became a bit worried.

"I'm beginning to think we may not have enough of a dose in him," I said. "If he hasn't gone down on his own pretty soon, we may have to intervene. If we can be ready to land near him in three or four minutes, we may be able to get close enough to handle him. Either that or I could top him up with another dart."

I was basing this scenario on my experiences with African animals and was pleased that I had brought some rope along. As luck would have it, the bull moved over quite close to where Terry and Wayne were standing. They had had a grandstand view of the whole thing from the top of the beaver lodge. We put down on the same pond where we had left them, and at this point the exercise took on the look of a cross between a rodeo and a circus as we all tried to grab the animal. Of course, trying to grab a moving bull moose—even one that is drugged and has shed its antlers—when standing in thirty centimetres of snow and trying to avoid bushes that are taller than you are, is bound to look pretty circus-like. Luckily no one had a movie camera, and we were all too busy trying to work to laugh at ourselves.

Finally, an opportune moment arose. As the moose came past me I reached up and slipped the noose I had made from the rope over his head. It did not reach all the way around, and I could not reach up over two metres, but it did catch and hold on his long nose. I called to the

OF MOOSE AND MEN

First moose capture, December 1975. The animal has been fitted a collar. The project later gained the funds to use radio collars. Bob Stewart (left), Wayne Runge (behind), Terry Roc (right).

JERRY HAIGH

other team members, and pretty soon we had him hobbled and down. If the moose had not been close to the beaver lodge I doubt we could have caught him, as it took all four of us to get him under control.

Then the work began. Terry and Wayne began measuring his body—length, chest circumference, leg length, and so on—and collecting hair samples. Bob, after a couple of anxious moments waiting to hear how his first live moose up close and personal was faring, went back to the helicopter and pulled out a fifteen-centimetre-wide, brightly coloured collar, pale blue with yellow patches. He returned, opened up his tool kit, and got out a hole punch and a box of stout rivets and riveting gun.

I pulled my stethoscope from the outside pocket of my parka and slipped the plastic earpieces into place. They were like icicles. Ever since that moment I have had the good sense to keep my stethoscope in an inner insulated pocket. With the business end of the instrument on the moose's chest, I listened for a while and monitored his heart and breathing, which seemed fine, although a bit faster than I might have wished.

"How's he doing?" asked Bob.

"Seems fine. Heart rate about eighty per minute, breathing already slowing down to twenty per minute. I'd expect a slower heart rate in an animal of this size, but I think that the rate is probably due to the fact that we had to chase him. I'll keep an eye on it. I'll check it every few minutes," I said.

After I had collected a blood sample from the jugular vein and put it inside my parka pocket, where it would not freeze in the −22°C conditions, I stepped back to take a look at our first success (so far: he had not yet woken).

Besides the very obvious collar, the bull had one strange thing about him. Parts of his shoulders and neck were almost completely bald. We looked more closely at him and discovered a mass of ticks hidden right up against the skin adjacent to the bald patches. I did not know then that the so-called "moose tick" or "winter tick" was a problem every year for these big animals. In time, biologist Bill Samuel from the University of Alberta would work out, with his graduate students, the life cycle of this pest and show that it has the potential to kill moose late in the winter, particularly if the temperatures get really cold. Moose can die when, in response to the irritation caused by hundreds, sometimes thousands, sometimes many many thousands of ticks, an animal rubs off the ten-centimetre hollow hairs that protect it from the cold. When that happens the moose simply cannot retain enough body heat to survive and enters a negative energy balance, eventually dying of what amounts to starvation. Bill has made a movie of the so-called "ghost" moose that suffer from this condition. They are white and ghostly because the only hairs left over large parts of their bodies are the white remnant stubs of the original, long black and dark-brown coat. Samuel has also published an informative book called *White as a Ghost: Winter Ticks and Moose*. Most recently he linked up with *National Geographic* and produced a short film that is available on You Tube (search *Can Ticks*

Kill Moose?), which shows both the life cycle and the effects of the ticks on a moose.

I have since learned from various sources that 100,000 of these uninvited guests have been counted on a single moose and that they were known as a major problem for moose over a hundred years ago when Ernest Thompson Seton, the noted author, wildlife artist, and co-founder of the Boy Scouts of America, viewed "winter ticks as a greater 'enemy' of moose than were wolves, bears, and cougars."

The most mind-boggling report of infestation by winter tick (the species' Sunday name is *Dermacentor albipictus*) came from Dwight Welch, who was the senior author on a paper about the death of a zoo reindeer from a heavy tick infestation. Dwight was one of Bill Samuel's graduate students, and when I went to track this report down for more detail I got more than I bargained for.

In the article that appeared in the prestigious *Journal of Wildlife Diseases*, Dwight and his co-authors state, "A total of 411,661 winter ticks (25 ticks per square centimetre) were collected." That is more or less the same area as the fingernail on my pinkie! Of course most of the ticks collected were the tiny nymphs, which, within two weeks of arrival on the reindeer, would have changed from the pinhead-sized larvae to nymphs after they have sucked some blood. After another blood meal, they develop into adults. It is the adult females that swell to a bluish raisin-sized bag of blood, which most people cringe upon seeing.

It makes me almost begin to itch just thinking about them.

I asked Dwight for more details as I tried to envision someone actually counting that many ticks and staying awake. Dwight put me on to Chris Wilke, who was working as technician for Bill Samuel at the time and is the man who actually did the count.

This is part of what Chris wrote to me: "Yes, I do remember this animal well. It's hard to forget something so extraordinary. . . . For good or bad (I'm not sure which), I did a complete count on this animal. While sectioning the hide I remember seeing a lot of adult ticks on the PM [postmortem] room floor, which I thought was unusual until I started to look closer at the hide and the floor around

OF MOOSE AND MEN

Moose with extensive hair loss due to winter tick.
The animal is severely debilitated.

BILL SAMUEL

me. There were literally thousands of ticks (of all life stages) still on the PM room floor after sectioning. These ticks did not get counted."

Not surprisingly, the reindeer had died, almost certainly from of being bled out by voracious ticks. But it turns out that no full necropsy was conducted, so the actual cause of death is unknown. I think I would just about keel over if I had twenty-five ticks on every square centimetre of my body. Every square centimetre.

Chris wrote further about my speculation on the ability to stay awake while counting ticks: "As for the staying awake comment, I really didn't have a problem with that as the numbers were so mind-boggling, I found it hard to sleep and I was quite anxious to get a final tally. . . . There were lots of all-nighters doing that project. For that I relied on everybody's standard—strong coffee."

But back to 1975. While the bald areas on the moose were interesting, we had a job to do. Bob and the others finished up the measuring, and I checked the vital signs again. All seemed well.

"If we're all done, I'll give him the antidote," I said. I was hoping that its effects on the moose would be as spectacular and immediate as they were on African animals, but I did not let the others know because I wanted to surprise them.

After I had injected the antidote into the vein on his foreleg we stood back a few metres while the moose lay upright. After about twenty seconds his ears twitched, his near eye opened as if a light switch had been flicked, and five seconds later he jumped to his feet and disappeared at a fast trot into the tall thicket of alder bush. In retrospect, we were probably not standing far enough away from him. If he had come toward us, we would not have had time to get out of the way. Indeed, two years later, when I was using my Super 8 camera to catch some memories for posterity, a cow moose got up and came straight for me. I was just able to dive away, but she ran right over the tripod and completely wrecked it. The camera survived.

"Wow! That was pretty smooth," said Wayne. "It's a good thing you've done this sort of thing before. I don't think we would have caught him without that rope."

"You're right," I replied. "I think we need to up the dose a tad, maybe by 20 per cent or so. That recovery is impressive, isn't it?"

Bob had booked us into the lodge for ten days, but with the dense population of moose, and the success of the drug combination (especially after upping the dose), we used up all twelve of the collars, each one marked with a different pattern, by the fifth day. There was no point in sticking around, although we did use two hours of the last morning to fly out, *sans* darts, and check for collared animals. The seven that we found all seemed fine. As we were not using radio collars at this stage we had not expected to find all of them, but Bob was pleased to see that the pale blue and yellow of the bands around their necks showed up clearly against the dark hair, the white snow, and the leafless brush.

"We are planning to do some more in February," said Bob. "I hope to have some radio collars by then. Can you get some more drugs?"

"I've still got to do some Christmas shopping at home," I replied. "I'll put that on my list."

I hoped to call Ottawa on the Monday after my return, but I had to deal with something of a crisis that day, so it was on the Tuesday after that first successful moose collaring exercise that I called.

"David Campbell here" was the greeting when I finally got past the switchboard operator.

"Dr. Campbell, Jerry Haigh again. I'd like to get hold of some more Fentanyl."

"What? You've only just had some, a month ago. How can you have used that much? I thought you had at least a year's supply."

"It was only two grams, and each animal needs about one hundred milligrams, so that's only twenty animals at best. We got twelve, and we have another capture session coming up in February."

"How can you use one hundred milligrams per animal? That's a huge dose. I thought they only needed a couple, at the most," he said.

"Well, they do weigh upwards of four hundred kilos."

"Remind me what beast this is."

"We are studying moose in northeastern Saskatchewan, putting collars on and looking at diseases and so on."

I could almost sense a light going on at the other end of the line. He chuckled.

"I misunderstood. When you said moose I was thinking of the daft cliché about the Scots accent, you know the one: 'There's a moose loose aboot this hoose.' I suppose it goes back to the famous Robbie Burns poem, you know, 'To a Mouse.' As in 'Wee, sleekit, cow'rin, tim'rous beastie.'"

His Glasgow background, his knowing that I came from the same place (although I lack the accent), and the unusual request had led him astray.

CHAPTER FIVE

PETRUSKA

A moose with a problem; an adventurous couple;
blowguns for beginners.

The thing I extracted from the black garbage bag on the bench looked like a deflated soccer ball from the days when all soccer balls were a uniform dark brown colour. As I looked at its surface, I could see tiny pencil-thin bones under the opaque brown membrane and some other hard structures, one of which might have been a tiny skull. One perfectly circular depression that must have been an eye socket lay uppermost under the frozen covering.

I was standing in the garage-cum-storage area of Miles and Beryl Smeeton's home in Alberta the day after getting a call for help.

"Hello, Dr. Haigh, this is Miles Smeeton." The friendly, cultured voice on the line indicated the caller came from a British background. "I'm calling from Cochrane. I got your name from one of your students, chap named Roger Bate. We are worried about our moose, Petruska, who has given birth to a calf and a very strange-looking, shrivelled-up thing, and we'd like someone to see her. She's not eating, and the live calf is looking pretty groggy."

It was the last day of May in 1976, and little did I know that this call would propel me toward getting to know one of the most interesting couples I have ever met. As I would find out much later, Miles and his wife, Beryl, may have been the most extraordinary, not to say unconventional, couple of the twentieth century.

"Can you get to Calgary tomorrow? If you can catch the mid-morning flight I'll meet you at the airport. We'll cover your costs, of course."

"I'll see what I can do," I replied, "but can you tell me if we can get close enough to her for me to examine her?"

"We groom her regularly. She is completely bonded to my wife, Beryl, who raised her from a day-old. I'm not sure how close she will let strangers come when she has a calf, but I think you will be all right."

He was not quite correct, and had it not been for my rugby and tennis history I might not be telling this tale.

The next morning, as I left the plane and headed down the hall toward the luggage carousel, where we had agreed to meet, I found myself wondering what this man would look like. He had told me he was tall, and his voice was not that of a young man. I need not have worried. Standing a full head above the other people near the luggage carousel, was a pencil-thin, white-haired man with piercing blue eyes and a huge beak-like nose.

I guessed him to be 1.95 metres tall, but later found out that he was just over 2 metres, something he would never admit to because in Malton, the lovely market town in England's Yorkshire Dales where he was raised (and where my first girlfriend came from), he would have been considered a freak.

I walked straight up to him, and before I could say a word he spoke. "Dr. Haigh?" I nodded and he went on, "Delighted to meet you. It was good of you to come at such short notice. Have you got any luggage to collect?"

What luggage I had was a small fibreglass case that contained a variety of drugs, most of them in case I needed to immobilize the patient, the rest antibiotics to treat the moose. The case also held also a variety of syringes ranging from my homemade darts to large ones that I would need to administer penicillin. I also had the 1.5-metre blowpipe that I had carried on board, along with the letter from Saskatchewan's Attorney General permitting me to use it. I figured that without that letter I would never have been able to get past the security staff in Saskatoon, and trying to explain would almost certainly have led to complications and delays.

"Good to meet you Mr. Smeeton. I don't have any luggage. I have booked a return flight late this evening, as I have a class to teach tomorrow morning at 7:30."

"What a pity. We are going out to dinner with friends, and they are keen to meet you. It will be a bit rushed, but we can go on from their place to the airport. And by the way, please call me Miles," he replied.

"I'm Jerry," I countered. Then we made our way to the car park, where we got into a somewhat battered old quarter-ton Datsun truck.

As we rattled along the fifty or so kilometres west out of the city, we soon struck up a friendly conversation and found that we had very similar backgrounds. The thread started with British military links. My father had been in the Highland Light Infantry (the Glasgow Regiment) and had done his war service in the King's African Rifles in East Africa and later Burma. Miles, born in 1906, eight years before my father, had done most of his military service in India and had ended up as brigadier with Probyn's Horse during the last days of World War II in Burma. Miles had been to school at England's famous Wellington College, which has always been best known for the number of graduates who have gone on to serve in the army. This is hardly surprising, given that the school was named for the hero of Waterloo. I had been at school in Sherborne, and Wellington had been one of our major sports rivals at cricket and rugby. I had played tennis against Wellington, both at home and away.

While I had never been in India, Miles had been in Kenya, and we had some mutual acquaintances there. As for India, my wife, Jo, was born and brought up there and had lived in Ootacamund (Ooty) for many years, a place the Smeetons had visited but before Jo moved there. Eventually our conversation came around to the situation at hand.

"What's the problem with the moose?" I asked.

"She delivered a normal calf and then a tiny shrivelled-up thing that looks for all the world like a mummy. Beryl will tell you more," he replied.

As we drove west and then north the road changed to a gravel surface, and then we turned west again toward a long line of hills foregrounding the snow-covered peaks of the Rockies. We travelled along a high mesh fence behind which patches of trembling aspen and stands of dark green spruce were interspersed with open ground.

"This is our place," said Miles. "We've got a quarter-section fenced and you'd think that this would give us some sense of security, but a couple of years ago someone took it upon themselves to shoot one of our tame bulls from out here on the road. We found him dead—his name was Peterkin—just lying over there in that clearing near the fence. The culprit never collected anything. Sheer bloody vandalism. We had two other bulls, Castor and Pollux. They were Petruska's twin sons by Peterkin."

"Named for stars in the Gemini constellation?" I asked.

"Yes, originally the sons of Leda, brothers of Helen of Troy. We don't have them both anymore, Castor jumped out a couple of years ago," he replied.

We stopped at a high gate, and I hopped out to open it. The drive had a tall fence on both sides leading down to the house. Miles explained that it was for security and to keep the moose away from the house and the front gate. A couple of hundred metres down the drive we came to a pine-clad house built somewhat in the hip-roofed style of a Dutch barn.

"Wow! This is beautiful," I said. "How long have you been here?"

"We've only lived here for seven years. We bought the place in '67 when our daughter Clio was working at the Calgary Zoo, but we didn't come to live here until '69, after the last of our sailing adventures. It took quite a time to build our house, and for a while we lived in a shack as it was being done."

"Sailing adventures?"

"We left India after the war. I resigned from the army and after a few years in British Columbia on Saltspring Island we bought a yacht called *Tzu Hang*. We set off on our adventures and ended up here."

During the ten years in Kenya, and then the move to the prairies, I had lost touch with my own sailing days as a teenager and student and had no idea that "sailing adventures" for Miles meant twenty years at sea in a forty-six-foot yacht, an eight-year circumnavigation, and their last journey, at age sixty-three, going westward around, and *doubling* (sailing from 50° South on one side to 50° South on the other) Cape Horn instead of taking the easy route through the Panama Canal or even flying. Doubling Cape Horn is considered the Everest of the sailing world and had only been accomplished in a small yacht by three other sailors at the time. My messing about in boats was child's play in comparison to what Miles and Beryl had accomplished.

Only later did I find out (not from Miles) that he had written five books about those trips. That first one, *Once Is Enough* (1959), has become a sailing classic, translated into many languages. In it he describes their journey from Tasmania to Chile with friend, solo-ocean sailor, and master carpenter John Guzzwell. They twice tried to round Cape Horn (the second time without John) but were foiled by two dismastings after being turned over in full somersaults. The first resulted after a pitchpoling: they were turned end-over-end by a massive rogue wave. As if those two events were not enough, the book also provides an account of how Beryl was swept off the deck into mountainous seas by that first wave that was so powerful her one-ton breaking strain lifeline snapped. Astonishingly she managed to get back on board. Karma? Who knows?

If she had not been able to swim back and be helped on board by Miles and John, I would not have been enjoying the scene or travelling to Alberta to look at a sick moose.

We entered through the side of the house and then I had another surprise. The garage was really a large storage area containing freezers, shelves, a variety of boxes, and a lavatory bowl next to a hand-washing sink. From there we moved into a sitting room on the northern side of which was a staircase with three right-angled turns around a metal pole rubbed shiny with frequent use.

Miles explained. "My knees are done for. I can climb up, but I come down on the pole, like a fireman. Come on up and meet Beryl."

Beryl had heard us coming and greeted me as I emerged, gopher-like, from the well of the staircase. She was a strikingly beautiful seventy-year-old with fine bones and a slim figure topped by long hair done up in a bun.

"Good afternoon, Jerry. It was good of you to come at such short notice."

The second-floor, cedar-panelled room was dominated by a huge daybed, suspended from the ceiling by chains. On one side were a table made from a cable drum and chairs made from varnished wooden barrels. There were at least half a dozen Persian-type rugs on the floor. All around the sides of the room in cupboards and on shelves were items collected from all over the world. The most striking of these were two ancient Chinese egg jars and an original painting of a yacht under jury rig.

"Is that your boat? I asked.

"Yes," replied Miles. "That was *Tzu Hang* after we were overturned and had fixed something up to get back to land. That painting was used as the front cover for my book about our first trip in her."

The view to the west must have been carefully chosen when the house was being planned. Through the big picture window the mountains captivated in much the same way Mount Kenya had the power to always drag my eye. The difference between this Rockies vista and the Kenyan one lay in the current view's line of jagged peaks, like some carnivore's lower jaw. The single spike we had been able to see from our own bedroom window every morning for that last five years in Kenya had no such sublime neighbours.

Beryl at once began to discuss the Petruska situation.

"She delivered on Tuesday, and she and the calf seem to be all right, but I'm worried about her. I was with her just now, feeding her some buns. She seems fine, much brighter than yesterday, when she wouldn't even look at food. She did have a good drink from the bowl I took to her last night, but the calf still looks very shaky. I'm not sure if she has had a suck. When our daughter Clio's friend Ann, who is your student Roger Bates's wife, told us about you and your wildlife interest I thought we should give you a call."

"What's the story behind this moose?" I asked. "Bottle-raised wild animals can be pretty dangerous, especially when they have a new calf. Can you approach her safely?"

"Petruska is special," she replied. "She and I are completely bonded. It all started when a farmer found two abandoned calves. One had died and we got the little female to look after. That was Petruska. I raised her from a tiny baby on milk, and then we added some alpha concentrate to increase the concentrations of solids. We got Peterkin a few weeks later."

"Well, I'm happy to try and take a look, but is she going to let me anywhere near her?" I asked.

"Let's go and see, and I'll show you the weird thing she delivered. It's down below," said Beryl, obviously keen to get on with the job at hand. I found out that she was not one to waste much time on niceties. She walked toward the stairs and lunged forward as if falling. Not so. She simply grabbed the fireman's pole with both hands, wrapped her legs around it, and slid out of sight.

Somewhat gingerly I tried the pole after Miles had also gone down the quick way. By the time I had made a safe landing Beryl had moved over to the window and extracted the bag and its contents from the freezer. I pulled on a pair of surgical gloves and examined it.

"This looks exactly like a textbook example of a bovine mummified foetus," I said. "I have seen one before, but often they are not delivered and remain in the female, creating a sort of long-term pregnancy effect. The animal thinks she is pregnant, so there is no cycling or coming into heat. I can only guess that this one was delivered because the live calf triggered parturition, and the uterus did the rest, expelling this one as well."

"Maybe we can do one more thing before we go to see the moose,"

I said after we had finished turning the mummy over and trying to identify more anatomical parts. "I think we need a back-up plan in case I can't get up to her and she needs to be immobilized for examination and possible treatment. I have brought my blowgun along and maybe Miles can have a go with it to see if he can dart her."

I had by now had seven months to master the art of blowdarting, and at ten metres or less I had found that I could routinely hit a fist-sized target, but it had not happened overnight.

In 1980 Miles published *Completely Foxed*, the last of his nine books. In it he tells the story of what happened when he tried to master the use of the blowpipe:

> In case Petruska objected to his near approach, he suggested that while Beryl talked to her, I might use the blow pipe to tranquilize her. He gave it to me for one or two practice shots. Full of confidence that I could blow the dart for at least thirty feet, I filled my lungs, pointed the blow pipe at a door about thirty feet away, and blew a great blast. To my surprise the dart trickled out of the end of the pipe and fell to the ground.
>
> "You have to sort of spit into it, as you do when blowing a hunting horn or a bugle," said Jerry, laughing.

It took Miles several more efforts to get the hang of the system, but he was soon hitting the door more or less in the middle. I figured that if we had to resort to his marksmanship his target was going to be big enough that he could be off-centre by a foot or so and we would still get a satisfactory result.

I pulled the last embedded dart out of the door and looked at the bent tip of the needle. "Don't worry," I said. "This is just a practice needle. Let's head out and look at Petruska."

CHAPTER SIX

SIMPLICITY

*Examination of Petruska; discretion as
the better part of valour and common sense.*

Beryl delved into one of the cardboard boxes next to the freezers and pulled out half-a-dozen buns.

"We get these from the bakery in town. They've no use for them once they get past a day old, so it's just a question of us picking them up," she said. "We're out of bananas, which she also loves. If she hasn't moved, it should be easy to find her. Let me go first. You follow with Miles, but stay well back, at least fifty yards. I'll see how she's doing, and then we can go from there."

"I'd much prefer it if we can manage without immobilizing her," I said. "Before we make any decisions, I'd like to have a good look at her. It is possible that she might have a uterine infection? We might be able to see some discharge from her rear end if that's the case. I wonder if you, Beryl, could go up to her as you usually do and talk to her. Then I'll come up slowly, talking to you, and perhaps she won't mind me coming up, but we will have to tread carefully, as new mothers can be possessive and dangerous."

Moose on the defensive can deliver powerful blows with their long legs. Gary Wobeser, the wildlife pathologist at the vet college, told me about some wolf carcasses he was studying that had been brought in by conservation officers in the Department of Natural Resources. Many of the bodies had healed or healing broken ribs, almost certainly caused by kicks from the long legs and powerful hooves of moose. One wolf skull even had a big indentation right in the middle. I did not want to be on the receiving end of a blow that could do that.

We had walked no more than a hundred metres before Beryl almost disappeared into a group of tall spruce trees and stepped out into a wide shallow hollow. I had to strain to see her, and I edged forward very carefully until I saw a moose cow standing right beside Beryl, who was stroking her nose and feeding her a bun. Miles and I stood next to one another for what seemed like ages, and then Beryl called softly for me to go forward.

Making sure that I kept a large tree between us, I took small steps to what Miles wrote was forty-five metres from the group. I moved forward talking quietly all the while so as not to alarm Petruska with a sudden appearance. Everything seemed to be going smoothly.

Then, suddenly the situation changed. My memories of the next few moments are a bit clouded, but, in my version, the first sign of the change came when Petruska, who had been looking at us men in the trees, put her ears right back and raised the hackles over her shoulders. This is a really bad sign in many animals. Miles, watching from the side, had his own view:

> Jerry halted, and the ears came forward again. He set off once more, but Petruska had had enough. She pinned down her ears and paced angrily towards him, leaving Beryl with the calf.
>
> Jerry had chosen his route with one eye on a large spruce tree, which he now made haste to get behind. Petruska followed round and then doubled back to meet him, but Jerry, used to similar adventures with rhino, was too quick for her and kept the tree between them. Petruska then made an attempt to dive through the tree, her head coming out of the branches on the same side as Jerry, but since the branches were low and

spreading, her legs failed to make similar progress, and she was temporarily hung up. Jerry took his opportunity to reach the other side of the hollow, doing the fifty yards in about five seconds. Petruska extricated herself from the tree and returned to Beryl and her calf.

There is one slight piece of imaginative hyperbole by Miles in that second paragraph. There is no way that anyone in his or her right mind would hope to use a tree, any kind of tree, as a physical barrier against a rhino.

My recollection of the event has one or two other components. Petruska let out a loud snort as she set off at a full charge, and then I could hear her breath as she crashed through the underbrush, her hooves pounding on the hard ground. It became a sort of Mexican stand-off. Petruska looked at me between the fortunately thick branches of the spruce and tried to get at me, first by stamping her feet, much as she would if she were killing a predator, and second by trying to move around the tree to get a clearer run. Of course there was nothing I could do about the stamping except be glad that it was occurring six or so metres from me, but I could and did move around the tree to make sure that we remained at exactly opposite sides. Not that she came round all the way. That would have put me between her and her calf, which would have been quite an unnatural manoeuvre: she presumably viewed me as some sort of predator that was going to get the most precious thing in her world.

Some people say that the popular children's nursery rhyme and game "Ring Around the Roses" sprang from the grim time of the Black Death. "Ring around a Spruce Tree," as played by me and an irate mother moose intent on reducing me to a thin layer of pulverized flesh on the ground, is quite another game. While she was determined to protect her new calf, I was keen to protect myself.

After what seemed an age, but was probably less than half a minute, Petruska responded to Beryl's gentle call—"Petruska, Petrooska"—and went back to base. I backed off, all the while keeping the tree between us, moving as quickly as I could to the next tree in line.

From a safe distance I watched Beryl and Petruska as they stood next to one another in an atmosphere of complete trust. The little rust-coloured calf stood next to its mother, looking like a chocolate bundle on stilts, and Beryl leaned over to touch it while Petruska munched on a bun and showed not the slightest concern.

"You know," said Miles, "Beryl is the only mother Petruska has ever known. Unlike most moose, she has never been kicked out by her mother."

The complete failure to make any sort of an examination was a bit of a letdown. As we walked back to the house I tried to reason it out. I had travelled all this way, about seven hundred kilometres, and I was not going to do much unless I took the big step and immobilized her. As I tried to work through the options in my head, it seemed to me that there were more potentially negative outcomes than possible benefits from doing so. My thoughts were interrupted when Beryl asked, "What about Petruska, is she all right?"

"It may be that she did have some sort of uterine infection, but perhaps she has overcome it. Did you see any discharge from her vulva?" I asked.

"No, she was clean back there."

"As far as I can tell from our very limited long-range acquaintance, she seems fine. If this were a zoo, and we had a fence, I would probably immobilize her, check that her uterus was properly cleansed, and treat her with antibiotics. I'm obviously not going to be able to examine her properly without immobilizing her, but from her reaction to me I think she may be on the mend. I don't want to intervene if it's not necessary, and I don't want to put the calf at risk or separate the two of them needlessly. If I dart her here in the open she might take off, and it's pretty thick in these woods."

"Fair enough. I wouldn't want to make things worse," replied Beryl.

"'Diagnosis normal' might sum up it up. There's a sometimes-useful treatment called 'Masterly Inactivity,' which just means leaving well enough alone. In Rwanda I once had to do that with a young elephant with a broken leg, and he was walking sound in six weeks," I said.

"What about the stillborn calf, and what about the future?"

"Again, I can't really tell. It is possible that the mummy is the result of inbreeding, as I assume that Petruska's son, Pollux, was the only animal around to mate with her, but I don't really know. The other calf is standing, and you have lots of bottle-raising experience if you need to fall back on it. What's more, Petruska trusts you implicitly, so you can obviously get right up to her and handle the calf if you need to. As for the future it is quite possible that she will not conceive this year," I said. "I know that a cow can sometimes return to breeding if she delivers a mummified foetus, but that doesn't always happen. You will have to wait and see on that one."

We were back at the house by now, but instead of climbing the staircase Beryl said, "Would you like to see the foxes?"

When we arrived at the house I had noticed some wire mesh pens near the house, but we had all been focused on the moose to the exclusion of anything else. We left the storage area–cum–garage by another door, and there, not ten metres away, was a dainty little fox-like creature, with short reddish-grey fur, not much bigger than a domestic cat, sitting near the fence grooming itself. I guessed that it weighed no more than two or three kilograms.

"I've never seen one before," I said. "It reminds me a bit of the bat-eared fox of Africa, but it may be a tad smaller, and of course doesn't have the big ears. What's the species?"

"It's a swift fox, also known as a kit fox—or did you mean his name? That is Napoleon. The other adults are Josephine, Nelson, and Emma."

Beryl was as keen as anything to share the foxes' story with me and talked solidly for at least twenty minutes. There was no need for me to do more than prompt, and Miles hardly got a word in.

"We started this place as a wildlife reserve with our daughter's encouragement. It took a bit of time to get organized, but the Canadian Wildlife Service approved our license in 1970. After that, and the usual go-round with bureaucrats, we did finally get it registered as a charity in 1971. Our first lot of foxes arrived from Colorado in '73. We had wanted desperately to start with muskox, but would have had to pay

$6,000 each for two, which was way out of our budget. We got two trumpeter swans in '74. They are down in the big pond at the end of the reserve. If we get time, we'll take you down to see them."

After a welcome cup of tea we headed out in an ancient Land Rover to the southern end of the reserve to see the swans, which were squatting regally on an artificial island. They were much bigger than the whistling swans that we had at the Forestry Farm zoo in Saskatoon. Little did I know that within seven months this same pair of swans would be shipped to Saskatoon for us to care for after Miles and Beryl were told that they must pay a ten-dollar fee to keep the birds. As the birds technically belonged to the wildlife service, and the Smeetons were only keeping them in the hope of helping with a captive breeding program for this endangered species, they refused, on principle, to pay for what they did not own. It was another example, for Beryl, of what she termed the "hopeless breed" of bureaucrats. This opinion of bureaucratic process was one she held throughout her adult life, starting with her experiences in England after World War II; she opined that it was postwar officialdom and government interference in everyday life that destroyed the country she had known as a girl.

At 6 p.m. we headed out in the little truck, all three of us crammed onto the bench seat, for a twenty-minute ride to the dinner party. There were two other couples there, our host and hostess and other friends. As we enjoyed an excellent meal that included a really good rib-eye steak, Miles recalled an amusing time when he had helped at a cattle round-up soon after having a second bout of surgery on his knees.

"I wasn't much use as we tried to push the mob through a gate, and I was well at the rear. Then they broke back and started to come right over us. Everybody turned and ran, and of course I was luckily now in front."

In reflex mode, remembering the words of the Gilbert and Sullivan opera *The Gondoliers*, I said "Just like the Duke of Plaza-Toro." Miles and I shared a brief grin as our eyes connected, but I don't think anyone other than Beryl caught the reference, and we let it drop. All three of us had been raised on G & S, and Miles and Beryl came from the same generation and social group as my own parents, so the songs were a part of our inner dictionaries.

The words from that opera that match Miles's situation go like this:

He led his regiment from behind
(He found it less exciting.)
But when away his regiment ran,
His place was at the fore, O
That celebrated,
Cultivated,
Underrated
Nobleman,
The Duke of Plaza-Toro!

In order for me to get to the airport in time for my flight Miles had to break away from what was a great evening. The trip passed all too swiftly as I learned more about the amazing adventures of my new friends. Being Miles, he spent most of the time telling me about Beryl, whom he still obviously worshipped after thirty-eight years of marriage.

In 1991 Miles's godson, Miles Clark (named for his godfather), published a wonderful book called *High Endeavours*—a must-read for lovers of adventure—that manages to squeeze a portion of Miles and Beryl's story into 417 spell-binding pages. Clark's last paragraph in the chapter about Beryl summarizes her journeys before World War II, when travel was not what it is today. He titled the chapter "No Ordinary Woman": "In just five years she had driven clockwise around North America; ridden through Portugal; traveled overland across Eurasia in both directions; crossed South America and ridden 1,000 miles among the Patagonian Andes; driven 10,000 miles across North Africa and India; climbed higher in the world that any woman before her, and walked for 500 miles through the sodden jungles of Burma and Siam."

And that was just the period before she and Miles set off on their sailing trips! What is also evident from Clark's account is that Beryl made almost all of these journeys without a companion from her own culture, relying extensively on the good nature of the local people— from peasants to diplomats—for help, hospitality, and good will.

I rang Miles and Beryl a few days after I returned to Saskatoon and was delighted to learn that Petruska had recovered quickly and that the calf was now drinking feverishly, as if to make up for lost time. They called her Simplicity.

CHAPTER SEVEN

SCALES AND WEIGHTS

Moose walking, or walking moose; scales and weights; venturing into a neighbouring province; similar work on a different species.

Moose capture season came around again the following autumn. After the initial success with our December and February trips, Bob Stewart and I had both been keen to improve and refine our methods and results.

"Do you think we can get real weights, instead of just estimates, on the moose this time?" I asked. "I have to get some articles out there to satisfy the university and their 'publish or perish' approach to things. I want to publish the data on our captures, and if I can quote doses based upon weight it makes everything much more meaningful."

"No problem," said Bob, "but we don't have a scale. Can you get one?"

The data I wanted to collect could be used in several ways. If I could get weight values linked to the data we collected about body measurements it would allow those lacking a scale to use simple high-school equations involving things like body and leg length to calculate the weights of their captured moose. Knowing the weight of the animals we captured would also tell us something about seasonal changes in weight.

Within a couple of days of that conversation with Bob

I found myself in the post-mortem room at the university, checking on one of my patients that had been in the bird ward. It was here that I had one of those light-bulb moments. My patient was a crane that had been brought to the college from a roadside menagerie in the province and had arrived almost dead and unresponsive and looking like a box of feathers glued onto a skeleton. I knew it was unlikely to survive when I picked it up and found that it had no muscles. It died overnight, and I wanted to see what was what.

While I was standing next to the student who was opening up the carcass, another student hooked up a dead cow that had been stored in the cooler and lifted it on a chain hoist. Between the hook on the hoist and the body was a large scale that would measure up to one thousand kilograms.

It took a little tact to get permission to borrow the scale for ten days, but in the end I solved half of our problem relative to weighing captured moose.

We solved the other half in Bob's office, on Saskatoon's Eighth Street, where we put a sling together with lengths of the heavy-duty webbing that we used for the identifying collars, riveting loops at each end through which poles could be threaded. The whole contraption, poles, ropes, and all, weighed just over forty kilograms. We were all set—but we still had to try out the system. Before we went any further we had to contact our pilot, Cliff Thompson, to see what he thought of the idea.

Bob called me a couple of days later. "I phoned Cliff," he said, "and he isn't 100 per cent sure, but he thinks it might be all right. He wants to take a look at our equipment when we get to Bainbridge."

Bob had another nice surprise for me.

"We've got our radio collars! Ten came in yesterday, and I've got another ten on order," he said.

Now we would be able to gather a whole new bunch of data about the Saskatchewan River Delta moose, particularly about their home ranges.

When we arrived at Bainbridge Lodge we at once talked to Cliff about the weighing apparatus.

"Will the chopper lift a moose?" asked Bob.

"I think we can manage, as long as it's just me in the machine and we don't have too much fuel in the tank. We can probably hoist five hundred kilograms."

"We'll need to get the animals into clearings," he added. "If not clearings, at least places where I can get down low enough for you to attach the scale onto the cargo hook. I obviously can't get so low that the tail rotor touches anything, so you may have to miss out on weighing animals that go into the spruce trees."

There was one problem. How could we get the animals away from the heavy bush? My experience in Africa allowed me a possible solution: I had, on one spectacular occasion, seen how a darted bull rhino of something over nine hundred kilograms had completely ignored the helicopter as it hovered about a metre above its back. Our pilot had tried to turn him as he headed for a dry river course, but even when he almost touched the rhino's back with his skid the rhino took no notice. After that I realized I might be able to approach smaller animals like impala, even eland and wildebeest, in the same spaced-out condition and grab them.

I related this information to the crew and suggested we try it by hopping out of the machine when the moose looked suitably disoriented.

"What happened to the rhino?" asked Cliff.

"Oh, he was fine. Luckily he went down at the edge of the gully, and not into it."

In the end the "hopping out" was not quite as easy as it sounds. It was more like jumping out of a hovering helicopter into snow of unknown depth and hoping we wouldn't turn our ankles or spear ourselves in the groin on a bush. Then it was a question of ploughing through possibly deep snow after the animal, which might be moving with its high-stepping drug-induced gait fifty or more metres away,

The author (at left) and Bob Stewart get some exercise. A drugged moose can be led into the open and then pulled to the ground.
JERRY HAIGH

catching up to it, and then trying to guide it. A moose's long legs allow it to walk through a metre of snow with no trouble at all. Twenty centimetres slow a human down considerably, unless that human is a tall basketball player.

Once we caught up to the animal its unusual anatomy became a real boon. Dangling from under the chin of every adult moose is a flap of hair and skin called the bell. It resembles the dewlap seen on some breeds of cattle and dogs and is a straggly piece of skin that hangs down beneath the chin and looks like a tag of material that a seamstress forgot to trim. At that time no one knew for sure what it was for, but it was an ideal lead rein for the would-be moose walker.

Bob soon got the hang of the technique, and together we refined it. (You can see a video of the whole process if you search "Moose Bulldogging" on YouTube.) I would go first and grab the bell. Bob would come in behind and goose the moose by lifting its stubby tail. In this way we sometimes walked moose as much as three hundred metres out of heavy tree cover to spots where Cliff could approach.

Then it was time for a rest.
JERRY HAIGH

Then we simply moved to its head and pulled down, sometimes putting a rope hobble on its front legs. The animal would usually subside gracefully and sit up on its chest.

After all the blood samples had been collected, the collar bolted on, and the sling placed under its body, we weighed the moose.

We had tied a couple of aspen poles to one of the skids in order to save us the bother of chopping down new ones each time we had a moose immobilized, so that was not a problem. We took them off the skid and threaded them through the loops in the ends of the webbing, and then I tied on the ropes that we would attach to the cargo hook under the chopper's belly. My Boy Scout skills—especially the ability to tie a bowline at speed, wearing heavy gloves—came into their own. The bowline is the only knot that one can be sure of loosening easily, even with wet or frozen rope.

This was unquestionably the coldest part of the procedure. One of us had to stand right next to the animal and hook the ropes of the scale onto the helicopter. The other had to stand back and signal Cliff when to lift and when to come down again. The guy under the machine had to deal not only with the weather, however cold it might be, but also the downdraft and blowing snow. It gave a whole new meaning to the phrase "wind chill" that one heard each morning on the radio during really nasty winter weather. The Abominable Snowman had nothing on the apparition of a man who emerged after the helicopter pulled away.

As we gathered the information I was able to refine my drug regimes; choose appropriate doses for bulls, cows, and yearlings; and build a body of information that I could share with other moose researchers at the annual moose workshops held in various cities across the U.S. and Canada. Having material to present made it much easier for me to get funding from the university to attend the gatherings and so meet like-minded folks and have some fun while learning much more about moose from an amazing and dedicated group of people.

By this time I was not only doing moose work in Saskatchewan but also in Alberta. Other opportunities to cooperate in research began near Rochester, Alberta, and spread much farther north, to Fort McMurray and Fort MacKay in the heart of the Alberta oil sands. It was here that I also got my first chance to work on a new species.

In the late 1970s a study called the Alberta Oil Sands Environmental Research Program (AOSERP) was underway across a vast swath of the northeastern part of the province. Somehow the word had got out that I was doing some capture work with moose near Rochester, and having great success when working with a young graduate student named Randy Frojker. Randy allowed me to join him in his study, which involved radio collaring of a considerable number of animals, and we worked together for brief periods—ten days or so at a time— for a couple of years. Randy was a big, tough chap, fit as a flea, and seemed to be able to trek in a straight line through deep snow and thick aspen bluffs to a downed moose without fail.

"How do you find them so quickly?" I asked.

"I think it's a question of putting a horseshoe up my arse and using it as a compass" was his memorable reply.

Randy left the program prematurely after he was diagnosed with cancer. The diagnosis turned out to be incorrect, and he went on to study law. However, he did not leave before telling me about one of the collars we had put on. It had disappeared from the area, and because the region was a strictly enforced no-hunting zone, he made an effort to find the collared moose with a radio receiver–equipped light aircraft.

"It didn't take long, although we were getting a weak signal at first," Randy said. "We flew out of the Rochester area, quite a few kilometres, and then got a very strong signal from a farmhouse. When the conservation officers arrived they found the collar in the basement, still sending out its beeps, and a bunch of moose meat in the guy's freezer. Not the brightest star in the sky."

Bill Mytton, with his dark, neatly trimmed, Crusader-styled beard, took over work in both Rochester and the oil sands. (I have posted another YouTube video that you can find under "Leading a Wild Moose" that shows Bill and final year vet student Jack Williams walking a big bull out of some trees into a field.) It was Bill who introduced me to work with woodland caribou in the northern parts of the study area. Bill told me that the team was running into a few problems with the caribou collaring. Too many were succumbing to the effects of capture. It sounded like a stress-related situation, but I could not tell for sure.

Now was the time to call on others who had experience with caribou, and so I called Dr. Bob Patenaude in Quebec City and Merlin Shoesmith in Winnipeg. Bob is a heavily bearded, Alberta-born francophone whom I met when I first attended the annual American Association of Zoo Veterinarians convention. We had hit it off at once and shared experiences as we both worked part-time in zoos and part-time with free-ranging animals. I only got to know Merlin from our telephone conversations,

Unfortunately, I was not able to get any directly practical advice because neither Bob nor Merlin had used drugs to capture caribou. They had no need for drugs because their techniques involved capturing the animals from canoes or motor boats as they crossed lakes and rivers in the summer. In the winter, Bob drove small herds across frozen lakes into hidden nets with a helicopter, keeping a human crew on hand to do the processing. These were not going to be options for us in Alberta because of the different terrain, which consisted mostly of stands of somewhat stunted spruce interspersed with a variety of woody shrubs. I would have to figure out the situation on my own.

I had a stroke of luck when I first headed up to Fort McMurray as I was offered a ride right from the Edmonton municipal airport in the AOSERP helicopter. Fred Wistar, the dark-haired string bean–shaped pilot, met me at the company office and we were soon on our way north. In the late 1970s Fort McMurray was already a growing maze of new developments, hardly able to keep up with the influx of newcomers, who were mainly housed in trailers. Of course this was nothing, a mere hamlet, compared to what came later in the bitumen boom years of the early twenty-first century.

The AOSERP researchers were also housed in a trailer, or rather two trailers latched together side by side. One half had the sleeping cubicles and bathrooms, the other the dining area and lounge.

Every morning we flew out over the tar sands production sites north of the town and carried on past Fort MacKay to the Birch Hills. While the moose work with Bill and technician Tom Hauge, a former college football lineman from Wisconsin who was still trim and fit at about 1.94 metres, was routine, the caribou work had some interesting wrinkles. The technician on this leg of the project was an Albertan, Jon Jorgensen, who sported a straggly beard beneath an impressive mop of curly hair and was at least twenty centimetres shorter than Tom.

I knew from Bill that about 25 per cent of the caribou they had darted had died—which is way too many—and that the researchers were looking for some answers. They were not long in coming.

After two attempts at chasing these fleet-footed animals across snow and through trees, it seemed to me that we needed to change tactics.

As we gave the antidote to the second one we'd captured and watched it jump up and run off, I said to Bill and Jon, "These animals are incredible. I have never seen anything jink like that. As soon

Jon Jorgensen holds a bull caribou in the
Birch Mountains of Northern Alberta.
JERRY HAIGH

as Fred gets close enough for a shot they seem to sense it and jump sideways, or even spin back. I wish I'd had those kinds of moves when I was playing rugby. It's taking far too long to get a shot away, and I missed three times, which is wasting darts and drugs."

"So you don't think it's the M99 we have been using?" asked Bill.

"I doubt it. I'll bet the reason these animals are dying is because of stress, but without post-mortems I can't be sure. I think we should try something completely different."

I looked at Fred and said, "Is there any chance that you could drive the herds very slowly past me if I wait in ambush behind a tree? I can shoot out to about thirty metres, but the closer you get them, the better chance I have of getting a good hit."

"I reckon we can give it a try," he said. "Let's develop a signal system in case this two-way radio fails." With that he handed me a small walkie-talkie. "Just use this on channel six to let us know if you've had a good shot or a miss," he said. With that we climbed back into the chopper and started to search the hills again.

Within an hour we had our third caribou down, weighed on the moose sling system that I had adapted with shorter loops, and were up and away.

The work was slow, but no more caribou died. Many years later, a greatly improved method for capture emerged from New Zealand, when a technique of firing nets from helicopters had been perfected. With the New Zealand method, the rate of captures per day went up, the processing was quick, and deaths remained at very low numbers. Capturing also became much less expensive per animal. Net guns have since been used on a wide variety of species, but the one thing that has not changed is the fact that the skill of the pilot is paramount.

The caribou deaths that I had not seen, but had mused about and avoided by changing tactics when working with the AOSERP, were probably due to the condition I was soon to see in a Saskatchewan River Delta bull moose.

CHAPTER EIGHT

CAPTURE PROBLEMS

A setback; a solution from Africa;
athletic moose calves.

The bull moose was stone dead, a nasty shock to our 1976 capture team, which had collared the moose only two days previously. When we tracked the moose down, we were expecting to do a routine check on a healthy animal, but now our helicopter pilot, Cliff Thompson, had to transport the carcass to our truck, which was waiting at the roadside clearing to which technical staff member Don McInnes had driven it. Then the carcass had to go to pathologist Dr. Gary Wobeser at the vet college in Saskatoon. Gary confirmed the bull's death was due to capture myopathy, CM for short. At the time there were almost no reports of the condition in wildlife in North America, although plenty of animals had been captured and released. Without radio collars, these animals could not be followed and nobody really knew what had happened to them after they had been captured, processed, and then sent back into the wild.

The "myopathy" part of the term for this disorder refers to muscle damage, but that is only one part of the problem, which has many elements. In the most rapidly fatal cases wild animals can die of heart failure within minutes of capture.

There are conditions similar to the one that got our bull moose in horses and humans. The condition in horses is called Monday Morning Disease, or tying up. And most people interested in sports are well aware of the lactic acid buildup that can occur in the muscles of highly trained athletes. CM has similar symptoms to both of these disorders. Granted, if you are a moose, or some other prey species, you are not usually considered highly trained, as all you have to do to earn your daily bread is wander from bush to bush or from one lush clump of grass to another. You are, athletically speaking, a bit of a slob. Fitness is not high on your priority list. However, even predators can go down with CM if they are highly stressed, just as an elite athlete can if a warm-up is not performed properly. In humans, the condition goes by a more complex, but scientifically accurate, name. It is called exertional rhabdomyolysis, which means the breakdown of muscle tissue due to exertion. A torn hamstring can also be considered a form of CM.

I sometimes wonder if another form of CM is involved when people die of cardiac arrest after they are pursued on foot at high speed, pinned to the ground on their chests with their arms held behind their backs, and knelt on by burly policemen. If such people are simultaneously high on drugs, or have been zapped with a stun gun, I imagine that their chance of death is rather high.

As we tried to unravel the causes of the CM in our moose, we found ourselves going back to the drawing board. We could not continue with our project until we found out what had gone wrong and learned how to prevent it from happening again. I searched the moose literature and contacted several folks working with the animals. Nobody admitted to or reported anything similar to what had happened to the bull, but I did know that the condition had been seen in Africa. In fact, some Glasgow colleagues who had been translocating antelope in Kenya made the very first report of CM in any species.

At this point several items aligned and helped me to arrive at the solution to our problem. First, Dr. Toni Harthoorn, an old acquaintance from my Kenya days with whom I had worked to repair the broken legs of a tame cheetah, published a monograph on CM in zebra and other animals that explained how the chase affected the physi-ological state of the animals. The piece offered two solutions for cm's prevention and/or treatment. For part of his study Harthoorn used a delicate blood gas machine that could measure the concentration of two vital gases in the blood—oxygen and carbon dioxide—as well as the blood's acidity or pH. Both the correct concentrations of oxygen and carbon dioxide and the correct pH are vital to the well-being of muscles. During the course of his study Harthoorn also tested the effi-cacy of a simple and inexpensive intravenous solution of bicarbonate to treat animals in which the blood had become too acidified.

Armed with this information, I approached the head of the vet col-lege's laboratory services, where I knew that the very machine I needed had just been replaced, the now redundant one not yet disposed of. The real question was the thing's portability and whether, because of its delicacy and fiddly calibration, it could be used in field situations. He was less than encouraging and told me that the main problem would be finding the right person to run it. However, the third element of luck came in line, which was more than I could have hoped for.

As I was investigating cm in the literature and finding out about the blood gas machine, I was keeping in touch with Bob about the problems, wondering how we would overcome the puzzle of using the tricky instrument in the delta.

"Well," he said, "we have a new staff member. Ray Longmuir has just joined the department after retiring as a radio technician with the air force. I'll check with him, but I'd bet that he can manage that sort of machine."

And so it proved. Ray arrived at the vet college and was given the technical work-up by a now interested and enthusiastic group of lab staff members, who never imagined that the routine work they were doing with the blood of all the domestic animals undergoing surgery could be taken into remote corners of Saskatchewan for use with a charismatic wild animal.

With this sort of luck, we found that we could return to the field, and we soon had a nice collection of data that told us how to proceed.

OF MOOSE AND MEN

A cow moose and her calf (held by Don McInnes).
The calf has a tiny solar-powered radio transmitter in its ear,
which allowed us to see how it fared over the next weeks.
JERRY HAIGH

In the end, we knew we needed to limit any chases to a maximum of two minutes from the moment an animal started to run until the dart was fired. If we did that, the intravenous fluids were not needed.

Later, Bob analyzed the hair samples we had routinely collected from every animal and discovered that there was a marked shortage of selenium. Selenium deficiency is a well-recognized component of the capture myopathy complex.

After we had worked out the difficulties with CM in adult moose, we started a new project in the early summer, placing tiny solar-powered radio transmitters in the ears of one- to two-week-old calves.

Catching the calves presented an entirely new set of problems. By the end of May and into early June all the water bodies in the Saskatchewan River Delta were open, so we would have to get wet, whatever we did. The simplest way to capture the calves was to drive them into the lakes that dot the landscape and then land on the helicopter's big rubber floats, taxi up to the little calves, and pull them into

CAPTURE PROBLEMS

The transmitter in a calf's ear.

JERRY HAIGH

the rear cabin. The transmitters were easy to install, and because we used fast-drying epoxy to glue them in place we could quickly release the calves to rejoin their mothers. Once or twice we attempted to catch calves that were well away from open water, and one can see the folly of one of these attempts in a Super 8 video that I later converted to digital format and posted on YouTube as "Summertime Moose Calf Research." Ray and Don, working on this project with us, can be seen floundering about in water up to their knees as the calf, looking like an international rugby centre or Canadian football running back, evades them with ease. The clip closes with Ray doing an elegant swan dive–like face-plant in the swamp.

The apparatus we were attaching to the calves was simple. Solar panels were glued to a cattle ear tag the size of a large button, with transmitters attached on the other side of the ear, around the pin. A copper antenna was wrapped around the button. These transmitters were only needed for a short time, as the study was designed to look at calf survival over the first few weeks of life. Several groups of moose biologists were reporting that they had discovered that bears were a major predator during this vulnerable period in a young moose's life. Our results were no different, although we saw only one bear in the delta during our studies. Perhaps we were just not looking closely enough, but it has been clearly shown that in some parts of North America bears are the major predator of moose, and in the month after calves are born they may take out 80 per cent of the newborns. It is almost as if nature offers a sort of supermarket special, and the bears line up to grab the goodies, knowing that availability is limited and there will be no rain checks.

Sometimes you tag an animal and never see it again, or if you do, it is only from afar. By sheer good luck in this instance, we were able to test the efficacy of our little ear tag transmitters when two abandoned moose calves became part of the zoo collection back in Saskatoon.

CHAPTER NINE

MOOSE AT THE ZOO

Moose calves at the zoo; one develops a problem;
a novel solution is tried; twig eating.

We discovered the first of the orphaned calves near our base at Bainbridge Lodge. On the third day of our trip, as he drove back to camp, a dripping-wet Don McInnes spotted a small brown bundle of hair in the ditch no more than a hundred metres from the road junction of highways 55 and 9 where the lodge was sited. Naturally he stopped to take a closer look. When he realized that he was looking at a very new, curled-up moose calf he quickly left it alone in the hope that its mother would be nearby and would come and pick it up. By evening there was no sign of the adult, and the calf was still in the same spot. This was most unusual. Moose do not hide their calves; instead, their calves are "followers."

We naturally talked about it and came to the conclusion that it must have been abandoned or that its dam had been killed. We could either leave it to die or take action.

To take action we obviously needed some sort of milk replacer. With little optimism, Bob asked Janet Carter if she had any condensed milk in her store. We had forgotten that in remote spots, a supply of Carnation is a must, especially as many coffee drinkers prefer it to milk

Karen and the newly arrived Mickey
at the Forestry Farm Zoo.

JERRY HAIGH

or cream. She can hardly have imagined that it would be needed for anything quite like this, and her supplies quickly dwindled. Don's next-day trip to the nearby town of Hudson Bay, almost seventy kilometres south, solved the supply issue.

We asked Don to call the zoo foreman, Brent Pendleton, when he went into town, and the calf, already and I suppose inevitably dubbed Mickey, headed back to Saskatoon in a custom-built travel crate with two of the keepers, Stu Hampton, a Saskatoon boy from way back, and Gerhard Stuewe, who had emigrated from Finland where he had been assistant director at the Helsinki Zoo.

Within ten days, another male calf, this time and just as inevitably called Bullwinkle, came to the zoo from a farmer. Both of them quickly settled in to the new routine and were much fussed over by all the keepers and ground staff.

In the meantime, tinned Carnation would not suffice forever. My first task was to find out what milk replacement formula would most closely match the real thing. I took some trips to the library and wrote letters to friends and colleagues. The first reply came from Beryl Smeeton. A few days later, Dr. Bob Patenaude, the Alberta-born veterinarian from Quebec City, whose job closely resembled my own in that he worked half-time at the zoo and the other half on free-ranging animals, sent me a three-page letter with a list of references and some personal accounts.

From the facts I had garnered, I soon learned that there are many formulae that have been used successfully but that care and attention, or TLC, is probably the most critical factor in raising an orphaned moose. The earliest account I found recorded how seven milk cows were needed to feed a dozen moose calves that were destined for shipment to New Zealand in 1909. There were surely earlier successes, but no details. Many of the recommended and successful formulae, with the exception of Bob Patenaude's, did not include ingredients to make up for the fact that moose milk is much richer than cow's. Evaporated milk of several varieties—led by Carnation—has been used, but Bob added egg yolk, butter, and a multivitamin to his mix. I decided to follow his advice, and the calves quickly learned that keepers carrying bottles were just what they craved.

Without exception, everyone related that moose calves took readily to the addition of twigs and brush to the diet from an early age, as early as one week in some cases. And I noted one extra thing when observing Mickey and Bullwinkle. The calves lived in a small shed and had free access to the outside. One morning I saw Mickey bent down on what are incorrectly called his "front knees," chewing at an almost-bare patch of ground. He was eating soil. I mentioned this to others who had experience with moose and other deer and learned that all young deer did the same. Quite what they sought, other than the soil, was and remains a mystery, but there is no doubt that moose youngsters do better in pens if offered dirt. Of course, it has to be changed on a regular basis.

Despite everyone's best efforts, within ten days we had a problem.

Each morning I would go to the zoo and get a briefing from Brent. Before I had even put down my drug box that morning, he emerged from his office and said, "Stu tells me that one of the calves is scouring pretty badly. Can you come straight over with me? He's worried."

We met Stu at the food preparation area in the old Dutch barn, and I asked him, "What's up? Which calf?"

"Bullwinkle seems to have it pretty bad," he replied.

We walked over to the pen where the gangly little calves—collections of bones covered in light-brown hair—were kept. Both came straight over to check us out, and it was at once obvious that Bullwinkle was not quite right. The main tip-off was that he had a streak of pale tan muck down his rear end and on his legs.

"This just started today?" I asked.

"First feed this morning. He came over right away, like normal, and latched on to this bottle, but he abandoned it after two or three sucks, which was weird. When I checked his rear end I could see the scour."

As Stu held the calf I got out my basic tools, a thermometer and stethoscope, and gave him the once-over.

After listening to his chest for a while, which let the thermometer at the other end do its job, I stood up, removed the thermometer, and reflexively lifted it to my nose. There was a faint but pungent odour, even the trace enough to make me gag—once smelt never forgotten—that took me back ten years in a flash. There is no doubt in my mind that smell is our most evocative sense, and I could at once see the barn, the Jersey cow, and the bald thickset farmer standing beside me—a newly minted vet, all those years ago—as his cow let loose another stream of diarrhea.

Turning to Stu and Brent I said, "Temperature's normal, lungs and heart sound fine. He's a bit tender over the belly, but I can't find anything else. I'll take a swab and get it to the lab right away. Meanwhile, cut out all the milk from his feed at 11:00 and for the rest of the day. I'll get back to you."

I checked that there was nothing urgent for me, headed back to the vet college, and went to the lab, picking up a small diagnostic tool as I went past the store. This was a kit containing some absorbent paper and a screw-top bottle about the size of a small jar of mustard. I knew that if I rubbed a little of the fecal material from the swab onto the strip and dropped some of the bottle's fluid onto it I might find out something important, for the mixture would tell me if even a tiny amount of altered blood was in the sample, which of course there should not be under normal circumstances. I wanted laboratory confirmation that the pungent smell that had assaulted me when I sniffed the thermometer had indeed been due to blood from high up in the digestive tract that had been altered on its way down.

The test was (and is) known as a test for occult blood in stool, "occult" meaning hidden and having little to do with science fiction, fantasy, or ghost stories. When blood does enter the stool in any large amount, the smell is a real nose curler. It is almost impossible not to rear back when you smell it. Any owner of a dog that has had the virus infection called parvo will know exactly what I mean. As for the rest of you, the old cliché about ignorance and bliss really fits here.

The test was positive, enough for me to take action. If the patient had been a meat eater, I would have had to wait, cut out all meat from its diet, and repeat everything. That was obviously not a problem with Bullwinkle.

The previous year I had run into exactly the same situation in a small group of white-tailed deer fawns that had arrived uninvited at the zoo. (Every year well-meaning but ill-informed members of the public would pick up a fawn they had found "abandoned," not realizing that for the first month or so of life fawns are left alone by their mothers for much of the day.) Two of the fawns that year had had diarrhea, and one soon died. Both had shown the seemingly strange behaviour exhibited by Bullwinkle: coming up enthusiastically for a feed, taking a couple of tugs at the nipple, and giving up. The routine post-mortem had shown that the fawn had a ruptured stomach ulcer, and my reading told me that at least one cause of that was the stress-related secretion of too much acid. All of the fawns, and now Bullwinkle and Mickey, were undoubtedly stressed by what had happened to them, and maybe each reacted differently depending on their individual temperaments.

The puzzle had been how to treat that remaining fawn, and now I needed to follow the same procedure with Bullwinkle. At the time there were no specific veterinary drugs that would get to the guts of the trouble. This was a few years before the ground-breaking demonstration by two Australian scientists that a specific bacterium is the main cause of the stomach inflammation that can lead to ulcers in people.

I knew that a drug trade-named Tagamet had been used with great success for ulcer treatment in people, but of course we had none in the vet college pharmacy when the fawn fell ill. That was soon remedied by a visit to a local drugstore and the writing of a prescription. The pharmacist was at first sceptical when she read the patient's name, and then she was delighted to help when I told her about the fawn. Some of the five vials of Tagamet that I had had to purchase for the fawn were still on the shelves when Bullwinkle fell ill, and so I did not have to go shopping again.

Naturally the instruction sheet that came with the little vials gave doses for people, so I had to do some simple calculations to scale down from seventy kilograms, the assumed "average" human weight in the 1970s (I imagine it has risen quite a bit in the interim), to the five (for the fawn) and twenty-three (for Bullwinkle) kilograms of my patients.

Faye Kernan was the head pharmacist at the college and had always expressed a keen interest in the somewhat unusual types of drugs that I seemed to need for my work, beginning with that very first enquiry about Fentanyl, the capture narcotic we had ordered from Belgium within a few weeks of my arrival from Kenya.

As I waited for Faye to find the Tagamet on a back shelf where it had sat untouched by anyone for a year, she said to me, "Dr. Haigh, you know we can now get generic tablets of this drug. They are not called Tagamet, but they are the same thing, called cimetidine. They're much cheaper than the injectable form, too. Would you like me to order some? I believe we can have them by tomorrow, or the next day."

"Let's wait and see how things go," I said. "I know that we can give this stuff by mouth, so if it works we can probably try the tablets."

Armed with the three remaining vials of injectable Tagamet, I headed back to the zoo, where I found that some of the younger staff members had finished their meals and were enjoying a game of Frisbee in the parking lot.

As soon as the break was over Stu and I walked over to the moose pen, and it took no time at all for me to draw up one third of the human dose and pop it into Bullwinkle's backside. I added an antibiotic injection to cover any possibility of an infection developing.

"Let's see how he comes along," I said. "Keep him on just water for tonight's feed, but I think we can reintroduce some milk in the morning. About half the usual strength, I should think. I'm not lecturing tomorrow morning, so I'll come straight from home to see how he's doing."

The results were electric. I got to the zoo good and early and met the keepers as they headed out from the coffee lounge to their various tasks. Stu, Gerhard, who had been on his day off when I had examined Bullwinkle, and I headed out to the pen, armed with two bottles of milk formula, one at only half strength. The little calves saw us coming and both stood right at the gate, knowing what we had for them. Stu fed Mickey, while Gerhard offered the red nipple to Bullwinkle. There was no hesitation. The two of them seemed to be in a drinking competition, and both litres of fluid vanished as if drawn by a giant suction pump.

I have seldom seen such a rapid turnaround.

"I'll give him one more injection before I head to the college after lunch," I said, "and then we'll try putting the drug directly into the milk."

After that it was plain sailing. As soon as the tablets arrived I took a few of them, cut them up into more or less moose calf–sized doses, and ground them into a powder with a mortar and pestle. In one feed a day for the next ten days Bullwinkle had his drug and did not have to feel the needle.

I was able to parlay this little experiment into a practical tip for others raising young deer, even a muskox calf that came to the college. You can now get cimetidine tablets for dogs and other small pets.

A key to moose management anywhere is to solve the tricky matter of diet. Moose are highly specialized eaters that ingest a wide range of plant species, up to 150 by some accounts, requiring an environment that is impossible to duplicate in a fenced area as the huge intake would destroy all the trees and shrubbery in short order. In summer a moose in Saskatchewan may eat as much as twenty-five kilograms a day, while a big Alaskan bull consumes as much as thirty-six kilograms, 90 per cent of it coming from browse. They will soon strip local vegetation of all twigs and small branches within reach, readily consuming twigs of at least half a centimetre in diameter even when they are not stressed by a short supply of food. In a witty commentary typical of the humour of the province, a film about Newfoundland moose describes them as "a one-thousand-pound rabbit on stilts." The damage to vegetation done by imported rabbits in England, New Zealand, and Australia immediately comes to mind.

Twigs, or browse, are an essential part of moose's daily intake. They can manage other foods, and for a brief period in summer one will see them grazing on protein-rich plants like clovers, and most famously partially or completely submerging in their search for aquatic vegetation that grows up to about two metres below the water surface.

One solution to the problem of keeping moose and offering a suitable diet has been to keep them in a semi-tame environment, and it is the Russians who have been doing this for the longest time, at least since before World War II. They have tried to domesticate their moose for use in cavalry and then, when that failed, as milk animals.

A remarkable film sent to me by Dr. Alexander Minaev, who is a researcher with the Russian Academy of Sciences, tells part of the story. At the Kostroma Moose Farm some 350 kilometres northeast of Moscow, the raising of moose has been integrated with forestry activities. There are no perimeter fences on the farm, and the animals are free to wander into the neighbouring areas to forage. During the winter months the top sections of felled trees, mainly poplar, are transported to yards near the farm where they are left out for the herd. In the film one sees moose stripping the bark with their teeth, much as if they were using a carpenter's spokeshave. On top of that, staff at the farm use real spokeshaves to remove bark, and the strips are fed to moose in buckets. These items are supplemented daily with an oat porridge, which not only serves to flesh out the diet but also, because the moose obviously relish both the bark and the porridge, to keep the animals tame.

Another major captive moose research centre that has been in place since the late 1960s is on Alaska's Kenai Peninsula, where long-term studies operate under the banner of the Alaska Department of Fish and Game. Teams of dedicated scientists at Kenai have studied just about any aspect of moose biology that one can think of. The best way to study moose up close and personal is to bottle-raise calves, and since the centre started up the researchers have played the role of adoptive mothers. In a recent Alaska Fish and Wildlife news posting, staff biologist Stacy Jenkins pointed out, "If you don't have bottle-raised animals you really can't do these kinds of studies, they just growl at you."

While the folks in Russia could let their super-tame charges wander out into the forest because of the diet they were providing, and the Alaskans had also found a solution to the very specialized dietary needs of moose, at the time we adopted Mickey and Bullwinkle the zoo world was still struggling to find a captive moose diet, at least until the Kenai work was published.

The Kenai team came up with a clever solution to the diet problem for captive moose. As Stacy Jenkins said, "The only way to really find what a moose is eating is to watch a moose eat." Kenai observations of eating habits and studies of moose digestion revealed that moose can handle the woody component better than any other ruminant. This is really no surprise when one considers their natural diet. The team incorporated an aspen sawdust product as 25 per cent of a pellet ration that had all the other essential nutrients built into it and found that the animals did really well. They waited a full five years, until 1985, before letting their moose science colleagues know that they had had success with this clever idea.

Scaling down the dietary formula used at farms or large enclo-sures, such as those at Kenai and in Russia, to zoo-sized pens was and is where major problems arise.

The folks at the Charlesbourg Zoo in Quebec City, where Bob Patenaude was the veterinarian, found an ingenious solution to which there were three legs. The zoo developed a contract with the municipal authorities: all the tree branches trimmed under power lines and other areas of the city were delivered to the zoo on a regular basis. All the brush was promptly placed in a cooler kept just above the freezing point. Special feed holders had been built and quantities of brush were taken out and stood in the feeders every day for the moose to devour. All this was extremely expensive; Bob told me that the annual bill, per moose, was around $14,000.

At the Forestry Farm Zoo, where I also had to find a solution, the 14K budget was out of reach, there was not enough browse to go around from Saskatoon's city streets, and there was no walk-in cooler. We tried. The keepers took a tractor and trailer out to the north end of the property as often as they could and cut small quantities of willow, red osier dogwood, and other moose favourites, but these could never satisfy the appetites of the animals. The problem was compounded when more rescued orphan moose calves arrived.

Occasional willow treats were eagerly devoured, and Mickey's love for the stuff allowed me a fun photo op. At the time, Mickey was in temporary accommodation in a pen that had formerly been occupied by a pair of donkeys. These had been moved forward to the children's zoo area for the summer, and the staff had neglected to remove the sign on the fence. I clipped a couple of willow branches and took them over to Mickey's pen, threading them into the wire right next to the sign. Within twenty seconds, Mickey had come over to check things out and enjoy the offering. I collect photos of odd signs, and this one, with the big bull moose, his antlers in velvet, right next to the sign that states DWARF SICILIAN DONKEY is one of my favourites. I sent it off to scientific humour magazine *The Journal of Irreproducible Results* with the caption "Developments in Bioengineering." Now that

Mickey Moose at the Forestry Farm Zoo in Saskatoon.
The original caption in the Journal of Irreproducible Results
read, "Developments in Bio-engineering."

JERRY HAIGH

DNA technology has moved forward from the *Jurassic Park* movie era, and we have had serious scientists discussing the idea of recreating mammoths from DNA, I wonder if I was entirely off the wall.

The willow treats, however much loved, were not enough for the zoo's resident moose. We soon found out that the inadequate diet led to problems. The moose did not thrive and failed to put on the same weight in summer that they would have gained in the wild. They developed chronic diarrhea, and even after the Alaskan sawdust diet information was published and we found a source from a local sawmill, things did not turn around. Perhaps it was too late and the lining of the animals' stomachs had been irreversibly damaged. I did question the morality of keeping an animal that one could not properly care for, but that went nowhere.

Under the direction of veterinarian Dr. Bengt Röken, who shares my fascination with moose, the folks at Sweden's Kolmarden Zoo have developed the most recent successful diet for captive moose. A

key is that they have recognized the need to offer a high-protein pel-
letted diet in summer that matches the natural protein levels of what
the animals would consume in the wild. In his useful pamphlet, published in 2010, Röken describes how the diet is based upon the needs
of another tall browsing animal, the giraffe. The zoo staff also offer
both grass and cut browse. In winter the low-protein diet they offer
is more closely related to that of reindeer. Added to that are piles of
winter-cut pine that are really more for occupational satisfaction than
any real food value. The moose readily eat the bark and pine needles,
as do wild Scandinavian moose during winter months.

There was another problem at the Saskatoon zoo that soon
needed solving. During the routine health and parasite checks that
I had started we found that as the moose grew, they had picked up
worms. One of those light-bulb moments gave me the solution to the
problem of treating the worms. I saw one of the keepers offer each of
the moose a banana. The entire thing, skin and all, disappeared in a
couple of gulps.

I soon found out that a moose will do almost anything for a
banana. The question is why? Why bananas? They are, after all, very
much a tropical fruit. When reports appeared of petrified trees in the
High Arctic, and the possibility of a very warm climate in that region
way back when, I had fun speculating that moose and bananas might
have met naturally at some time in the distant past, and that a genetic
memory might persist in today's moose; but it is, of course, nonsense.

However, I was able to parlay the banana addiction to the benefit
of both the moose and myself. After cutting the skin carefully, one can
scoop out a little flesh and replace it with a carefully calculated dose
of medication. A few stitches with light cotton and a Trojan horse of
de-wormer-filled fruit can be offered and scoffed. No stress, no mess.

CHAPTER TEN

MOOSE INVADER

More visits to Cochrane and
meetings with moose.

The summer after my close encounter of the moose kind with Petruska and her calf, Jo and the kids and I visited the ranch, the moose, and the Smeetons on the way back from a family vacation in the Rocky Mountains. Ever gracious, Miles and Beryl looked after us and took us round the ranch to meet the moose, especially Petruska, who had either forgiven or forgotten me. That evening I found Miles just by the garage door giving Pollux, Petruska's son, a thorough going-over with a dandy brush and curry comb, something he had no doubt done hundreds of times to horses, during and since his military career as a cavalry officer. Pollux was no different than most horses and was lapping it up, obviously relishing the attention.

After a welcome cup of tea Beryl asked, "Would you like to see our newest arrivals?"

"What have you got?" I asked, intrigued.

"Just the other day we collected two wood bison calves from Elk Island National Park. We've just got them used to the bottle, but when we got them they were a bit too old to adapt easily, so we were having a bit of a struggle.

We're over the worst of it. It's feeding time so why don't you come and watch?"

We trooped out of the split side door, a more-or-less exact replica of a stable door, built out of pine boards, with its upper half held by a wooden latch that could be lifted from the outside by a piece of rope that passed through a hole above it and hung down.

Jo and I and the children stood outside the bison pen and watched the proceedings. The show didn't take long. The calves vacuumed their milk in seconds flat.

In late summer a year after that family visit, and two years after Petruska had encouraged me to leave her newborn calf alone and chased me around a spruce tree, I got a somewhat urgent call from Miles.

"Jerry," he said, "we have a problem here again. A wild moose jumped into the ranch a couple of months ago and it now has a calf with it."

"How long have you been trying to get it out?" I asked.

"Right from the start. It must have jumped over the seven-foot fence during the winter and it's creating some havoc as it runs all over the place and bangs into fox pens, not doing them much good. We tried to chase it out through the gate several times with the horses and the help of friends, but it has stubbornly refused to take any notice of our invitation to leave."

"So what do you want to do?" I asked.

"Can you get here fairly soon and dart her? I can easily get help from friends and then we can shift her back into the wild. I'm mostly worried about Beryl rather than the Wild One because she might walk up to the wrong moose and get attacked."

There was another reason. As Miles wrote in *Completely Foxed*, "'We've got to get her out,' said Beryl. 'I know that Petruska is upset. I can see that she is. Her place has been invaded first by the bison in the drive and now by this bloody moose.'" The phone call and request may well have been one of those "Yes, dear" things that successful marriages are built upon.

MOOSE INVADER

In all her sailing years and then those on the ranch Beryl had developed very close bonds with just two animals. The first was the Siamese cat Pwe that had shared in the circumnavigation, the attempts on the Horn (including the two somersaults) and all the others. Pwe had lived to be twenty years old and had eventually been put to sleep in a distraught Beryl's arms the year before I first visited the ranch. The second animal was Petruska, and there can seldom have been a closer bond between a human and a wild animal. Beryl was probably being overly motherly but understandably did not want her darling to come to any harm.

For this wild moose visit I was armed with my new dart gun. (This time the blowpipe was not even an option because it could only be used on stationary targets within a ten-metre range.) I also had a supply of the drugs that I had used with such success in both Saskatchewan and Alberta, not to mention some degree of confidence in what I was doing. Confidence is all very well, but it has to be moderated with some luck.

Once again Miles picked me up from the airport, and this time I did have some overnight things with me, as I figured that the challenge was going to be considerable. When we spoke on the phone I had told him, "These things can be a bit of a rodeo. I have tried to capture steers that have escaped at the stockyards here, and mostly it ends up as a circus. We'd better allow a couple of days to get the situation in hand."

There was a wild moose running around in sixty-five hectares of land, at least half of it bush and trees, and I did not have a helicopter. Everything was going to have to be done on foot. One good thing about the situation was that even though there were tame moose in that same space, I didn't think I would dart the wrong animal. Pollux was in velvet, with antlers that would by now be at least fifty centimetres long. I was not going to be darting him. And Miles and Beryl had ensured I would not mistake Petruska for the Wild One.

"We've put a big yellow ribbon around Petruska's neck, so you won't have to worry about her. She's had it on for a couple of days and is not at all bothered with it," said Miles. "If you see a moose without a ribbon, it will be our unwanted visitor, you can go ahead and dart her."

After their several failed attempts to get the Wild One off the ranch, Miles and Beryl had a pretty good idea of how she would respond to being driven by the horses, so they posted me near some bushes by the larger of the two ponds where the swans had lived before they came to Saskatoon.

Miles said, "She should come up along the inside of the new bison fence—we put it up last summer—so if you hide there you should get a decent chance at a shot."

And so it proved. The moose came across the top of the dam at a fair lick, followed closely by its well-grown calf, and I took a shot. As those who have done any amount of darting will know, it sounds a lot easier than it really is to "take a shot" with a dart gun. Rifle bullets move at hundreds of metres per second and so a shot taken at twenty or thirty metres will strike very close to the aiming point. Shooting a dart from a dart gun is a horse of another colour. One can usually see the dart moving through the air. To hit the rump at twenty metres I had to fire at her chest. I was breaking two basic rules of darting: 1. one must never shoot at a moving target; and 2. one must always aim for the heavy muscles of the hind end or shoulder. I have drummed these into many a student, in a "do what I say, not what I do" manner, although under the circumstances I had little choice. If I had not fired, the animal was not going to get darted at all. I swung the gun on her shoulder, instinctively using my twenty-odd years of experience as a bird hunter, and pulled the trigger.

Sadly, the consequences of my moving-target shot would make a fine object lesson in "what not to do" for my students. The dart hit right in the middle of her thigh, but the movement of her hide and underlying muscles caused it to bounce out, despite the barb on the needle. I knew that some of the drug would have entered her system, as the internal mechanism works in a few milliseconds to entirely empty the dart. I had also seen a fine mist of drug arc into the air as the dart left her thigh, so I knew that it was now empty. Previous experience has taught me that the amount actually injected could be anywhere from almost none to quite a lot, with the odds being on the former.

We searched for her on foot and horseback for about an hour, but we saw neither hide nor hair of calf or mother. Pollux and Petruska, with her yellow ribbon, looked on with only the faintest interest as Miles, Beryl, and a conscripted team of helpers criss-crossed the woods and glades to no avail.

We took a break for lunch, and I suggested to Miles that I might have better luck on my own in the afternoon.

When I first started working with Bob Stewart, the Saskatoon biologist who had first got me involved in matters moosey, I learned a useful moose hunting technique called Still Hunting. Still Hunting is a bit of a misnomer because it involves walking very slowly and carefully through the bush. As Bob put it to me, "Take a step or two at the most, then stand still for a couple of minutes and listen." This technique seemed to be the best option for the challenge facing me at the Smeetons', but I spent a fruitless hour and a half and saw no moose other than yellow-ribboned Petruska, quietly browsing on a patch of bush near the ranch gate. By the time my need for a break and a cuppa led me back to the house, the search team had left, waiting to be called if help was needed.

After the brief break I set off northeast, skirting the fox pens and making ultra-slow progress into the aspen groves where I had not yet searched. I had not gone more than about two hundred metres in forty or so minutes when I saw the front half and antlerless head of a cow moose lying down behind a tree. Her rump was entirely out of sight, and her neck was twisted in such a way that I could not see it clearly.

Twenty minutes later I finally had worked my way around to the right, the downwind side, and was treated to a full side view. She was chewing her cud and looking away from me. There was no yellow ribbon, and the heavy muscle mass of her rear end was almost exactly at right angles to me.

Experience has taught me that this sort of opportunity can sometimes only last a few moments, and who knew if she would waken to my presence or if I might make some inadvertent noise. I dialled the gun to twenty-five metres and lifted it up.

The sharp little crack of the .22 blank was followed by another, less audible crack as the dart hit her rump and emptied into her muscles.

She stood up, looked around, and moved off through the underbrush, but not running as I had expected. A tiny twinge of worry brushed my brain, but I followed her slowly and watched her gently subside about four minutes later.

She was lying on her brisket and breathing strongly. Her pulse was steady and normal and all seemed to be well. There was only one worry. She seemed to be particularly well groomed.

I legged it back to the house and found Miles right away.

"I've got a moose down, but I'm not very happy about her," I said. "Can you come and take look? She's fine, breathing well and so on, but I don't know if it's the Wild One."

We were lucky that she was not far from the house, because Miles had, by this stage, had two knee operations and could not walk easily.

"She's got no ribbon," he said as he walked toward her, "but you're right, I don't think it's the Wild One." With that he leaned over and ran a finger along her ear.

It took him no more than five seconds to spot that I had made an error. "It's Petruska," he said. "When she was tiny we were supposed to put an ear tag in to comply with some government regulation, but it tore out at once, and we hadn't the heart to try again. There's a tiny piece out of her ear, but you can't see it for all the hair. Our ribbon must have come adrift."

With an internal sensation of horror I bent to check her vital signs again. After reassuring myself that all was well, I said, "I'll run back to the house and get some more material for a collar from Beryl. I don't want to make the same mistake again. I don't think she will move, and she should be fine for ages yet. I've had them down for at least an hour, and they do fine."

Without giving Miles time to consider any other option I ran back and was quickly able to get a length of an old sheet, although it was not yellow.

Back beside the animal I drew up a good dose of antidote and popped half of it into her leg vein, the other half into her backside.

"The extra is to make sure that she does not go back to sleep. This drug works quickly and the intramuscular injection helps to maintain blood levels a bit longer. She should be fine."

By the time I had finished speaking the moose's ears had come alert. A couple of seconds later she opened her eyes, looked around, and began to rise to her feet. Instead of running off, as wild moose do when they wake up within ten metres of a bunch of humans, she stood there for a few moments and then walked over to a nearby stand of red osier dogwood, a favourite moose food, almost like candy, and began to munch.

"Now what?" Miles asked.

CHAPTER ELEVEN

MOOSE IN A FRONT-END LOADER

More matters moosey as the rodeo continues;
a sad ending and a new beginning.

"I'll keep looking for a while, but maybe you can have another look around on your horse," I said.

We searched for a couple more hours, but time was running out, and I called a halt when Miles and I met near the pond below the house.

"We've had some bad luck, and I have learned that darting in the evening is a sure way to turn a rodeo, which we have already experienced, into a real mess. Like Murphy's Law, things will go wrong, and we'll end up trying to work in the half-dark or worse. Let's call it a day and give ourselves a full wodge of daylight tomorrow."

After a relaxed evening over a fine bottle of claret and wide-ranging conversation, I once more took the quick route down the fireman's pole (this time with rather more control than on my first attempt two years previously), walked across the sitting room, and after a rather cursory skim with the toothbrush at the sink, hit the sack and passed out.

After breakfast we set off on our quest again. Miles saddled up and headed west. He was on his horse El Cid, named for the eleventh-century Spanish nobleman and military leader. In his namesake's day the gelding would have been classed as a charger. Of course El Cid's size and height was what Miles needed in order to accommodate his extraordinarily long legs. I set out on foot toward the dam, and Beryl took the old Land Rover up near the gate to the north of me.

I had only been in position for about ten minutes when I saw the moose and her calf coming up between the perimeter fence and the new one that held the bison safely away from the boundary of the ranch. The two fences were about ten metres apart and I could see that this would create a new problem.

As Miles put it in *Completely Foxed*: "Jerry was positioned so that he could shoot at the moose through the bison fence, if she came between the fences, but he also had to be hidden from her if she came along the dam bank. He could not, therefore, put the muzzle of his gun through the fence, which runs along the top of the dam. . . . She gave him an easy shot as she trotted past, but the dart hit one of the wires of the fence and never reached the target."

Beryl was standing a couple of hundred metres up the fence, near the gate, and saw the moose stop only a few yards from her, no doubt alarmed by the car and the human, and head back my way. As Miles describes it, "Meanwhile Jerry had reloaded and was showing a fine turn of speed in pursuit. He met the moose on her way back and she turned again and jumped over the fence back into the park, but he was close enough to get a good shot and the dart went home."

We met up near the fence. "I think we've got her this time," I said. "We'll give her a few moments to let the drugs take effect and then we can try to find her. Once she's down, we can move to the next phase. Maybe you can phone for some help."

Easier said than done. I walked through that bush every which way. I met up with Petruska a couple of times, her new white collar giving her away easily. Pollux gave me the once over and moved off. Miles took his horse along every path, as well as through a few spots where no semblance of a path existed. He complained that El Cid, true to the reputation of his nine-hundred-year-old namesake, had shown no fear, which was all very well for the horse, but hard on his rider's already dubious knees. The intruder was nowhere to be found.

Eventually I went back to the house and met up with our limited and dispirited crew.

By then John Stewart-Smith and his wife, Avki, both ex-Tanzanian and neighbouring beef ranchers, had appeared with a tractor and front-end loader. Two other friends, whom I had not met, Lilian and Garry Gingles, also answered the call for help, no doubt delighted to be involved in a rather unusual quest. Garry was also mounted. Miles changed horses to an equally impressive palomino named Tøsen, and we set off again, this time in a somewhat structured line abreast.

About twenty minutes later, when I had almost given up and was beginning to worry that the drugs might have worn off, Avki suddenly called out, "There she is!"

We looked up and there was the moose squatting in the small pond near the east fence, right out in the open. The only thing visible was her head, and if it had not been for the two ears sticking up she would have looked for all the world like a log.

Miles and I had a quick council of war.

"I'll try and get another dart into her. I think I can if she doesn't move too much. Let's see what happens. We may still need your horse, so if you are willing . . ." I let the implied question trail off, but Miles did not hesitate, despite his dicey knees. I did not know that at this time he had also had one kidney removed, so he was not fully fit.

Within four or five minutes—I can't be certain because time always moves at an altered pace under such circumstances—the dart was ready and I had managed to get within about thirty metres of her. She started to get out of the water, and as soon as she was clear of the edge I fired again, hitting her cleanly in the hip. She hardly changed her gait, but continued to high-step with a collected trotting gait like an Olympic dressage horse across the field toward the house.

I could catch up to her, but each time I touched her, on the bell or anywhere else, she jumped forward a stride or two, and I felt in danger of being trampled. But I was determined to succeed. There seemed to be no way I could pull her down, so my "Walking with Moose" technique was not going to work. She had gone a couple of hundred metres when Miles and John reappeared with their mounts. We waited a full ten minutes more, but the animal was obviously not going to go down on her own. I did eventually manage to get hold of her, and even wrestle her to the ground, but I could not hold her there alone and she soon got up, once more seeming to seek the perfect ten from the dressage judges, moving only about fifteen metres in the space of a couple of minutes.

"Can you catch her?" I called to the horsemen. Miles at once rode up alongside her and dropped a lariat around her neck. He cinched it up to the pommel, and our moose was caught. I topped her dose up with an intravenous injection, and John went back to the house.

Meanwhile I had had a chance to examine her. As I checked her vital signs I realized that she was completely blind in her left eye. She must have injured it quite some time before, as it was a mass of white scar tissue. It was pure luck that we had chosen to move her around that fence in a counter-clockwise direction to dart her that second time. She had probably not seen me at all. The blindness may also have accounted for her blundering into the fox fences and generally creating a nuisance of herself.

John reappeared, his tractor's diesel engine growling away as he crossed the uneven ground. The end of the adventure was soon accomplished. We jointly grunted the four-hundred-odd-kilogram moose into the bucket on the loader and drove to the house. I left my drug box by the garage, and after filling up a couple of syringes of antidote I climbed up alongside my patient in the bucket and we headed out the gate. A couple of kilometres from the Smeetons' front gate the road petered out in a patch of forest reserve. John gently tipped the animal onto the ground and I gave her the standard injections, with a little to spare. Within five minutes she had vanished from sight, heading for the hills at a fast trot.

The whole saga had indeed been a rodeo, but at least we had

succeeded. Miles reported that the Wild One's calf became tame and soon joined the resident moose for their food. When he was two years old they released him to the wild.

The success we had in safely removing the Wild One from the Smeetons' ranch was unfortunately followed by a sad turn of events. Three weeks after my visit I got an agitated call from Dr. John Quine, the Cochrane vet who had helped Miles and Beryl (gratis) with many aspects of their fox program and had come quickly when one of the little vixens had had difficulty whelping just a few weeks before my visit.

"You've heard what happened here?" he asked in a sombre tone.

"No, what?" I replied with a sense of dread.

"Petruska got into the garage not long after Beryl brought a load of buns and stale bread up from town. She ate the lot. Then she disappeared for two days, and they could not find her."

"That doesn't sound good," I replied. "What happened after that?"

"When they eventually did find her she was down and looking very sick. I went out as soon as I could, but she was past hope. Of course, I rigged up a sling and gave her a whole lot of intravenous fluids, but I knew it was hopeless. She had a bad case of grain overload. She died the next morning."

"Beryl must have been distraught."

"That's not the half of it."

By the time this disaster took place, the bison I had met the previous year had grown considerably and had begun to show their intelligent and inquisitive nature. One thing they had learned during this time was about doors. In *Completely Foxed* Miles wrote one telling paragraph that may give a clue about how Petruska made the fatal mistake that led to her death:

> The door of the downstairs living room is a stable door, made in two
> halves, with a wooden latch on the inside, and it is opened from the outside
> by pulling on a thing which passes through a hole in the door. The wooden
> latch does not necessarily fall into place, and the door fits tightly, making it

easy to forget to check that the latch is down. The bison soon learned that if they pushed the door it might open, and if it opened they came inside.

Once the bison had learned the door-opening trick it was something they began to do quite frequently. The door was indeed tricky to close, and I suspect that the bison opened it on that disastrous day. Maybe they even walked into the house, as they sometimes did, but of course they did not close it on their way out. Petruska would have had no hesitation in entering a room where her surrogate mother Beryl had fed her countless times. The bread would have been far too tempting to leave alone, too.

Petruska's death affected the Smeetons immensely. No mention of it appears in anything Miles wrote. *Completely Foxed* was published in 1984, six years after the event, but he chose not to include mention of it in the book. When we last saw him in 1980, a year after Beryl's death from breast cancer, he referred to the sad morning when they had found Petruska on her last legs, but he did not dwell on it.

After Beryl's death in 1979, Miles found that he could no longer carry on the work of the reserve, especially the conservation side of things, and so he sought some help. His daughter Clio was in England at the time, and she returned to take over the reins. Miles lived on until 1988, and Clio continues to run the operation as a non-profit organization, now called the Cochrane Ecological Institute.

Bears, birds, moose, bison, swift foxes, and a variety of other rescued wild animals move in and out of the reserve.

The latest rescued moose is Dolly, who arrived in 2002 and has stayed. "We got a call from a chap in Rimbey," Clio told me when I visited her in 2010. "The young moose, about five months old, had come into his vegetable garden and started to eat his peas, but she was so weak she collapsed. He wanted to know what to do. I suggested he feed her some beet pulp and before long he had loaded her into a horse trailer and brought her to us. Although we didn't bottle-raise her, she is as smart as anything and comes up to be petted from time to time. She loves bananas, of course."

Three years later a newcomer, a "volunteer male," as Clio put it, jumped into the reserve in a reverse of the exit of Castor—one of Petruska's twin sons—thirty years earlier. There are now four moose: Dolly, her volunteer consort, who is very shy and almost never seen, and two of their offspring, a yearling and a young calf.

CHAPTER TWELVE

WHERE MEN WALK WITH MOOSE

Conferences; a meeting with an amazing
moose biologist; a television show.

In 1980 the sixteenth North American Moose Conference was held in the city of Prince Albert, not far north of Saskatoon. This conference, held every year in a different location, was and is the gathering point for leading moose biologists, technicians, and graduate students to exchange information and unwind. In my capacity as a researcher I had two things to present, and in my other capacity as a teacher I was able to bring along a student who had signed up to work with me for her two-week wildlife-cum-zoo rotation.

My first presentation concerned the work we had been doing on the relationship between moose body measurements and weights; the second was to run a Super 8 video that I had edited to show both the goosing and walking needed to be able to obtain the weights of the animals and to alert our colleagues from across the continent to the risks of capture myopathy. cm was something that had not yet been reported in moose, largely, I believe, because radio collars, which allowed people to really learn about the aftermath of the stresses to which the animals were subjected, had only very recently been deployed on them.

The visual collars we had ourselves first used did not always allow us to record the same level of information the radio collars did.

Many of the biologists at the conference were very well-known in the field, and I had a chance to meet several. One was Victor van Ballenberghe, who would go on to study moose and particularly moose behaviour in great detail in Alaska's Denali National Park for thirty-five years and eventually write a beautiful book about his favourite animals.

Another star in the moose biology firmament whom I met in Prince Albert was Tony Bubenik. He is one of the most remarkable men I have ever met, and I was lucky to encounter him several times over the next few years: in Saskatoon, where he stayed with us; at his home in Thornhill, a Toronto suburb; and at conferences around the world.

Tony was highly regarded among all those who studied deer of any species, and he was never backward in coming forward with new ideas or extending discussions. Not all his ideas proved to be correct, but he was the first to acknowledge it when they did not pan out, and to the end of his life at age eighty-two he kept abreast of developments and technology. When we visited him at home, knowing about Jo's green thumb and love of plants, he showed us the greenhouse full of orchids, each one of which had its own computerized drip-water supply. He then took us to his study in which every wall was stacked with natural history texts. He had two linked computers, one full of thousands of scientific references to which he could readily refer for his writing. He was exceedingly prolific in the field, which is all the more remarkable because he only switched to biology at the age of forty-eight after a career as a chemist. His output included something over three hundred articles and contributions in numerous books. He was also fluent in six or seven languages (accounts differ, probably because of differing definitions of fluency) and wrote in thirteen.

To top it all off, Tony was an accomplished artist, and we have two large watercolour crayon works of his: one of a moose, the other of a wapiti. Both contain more than just their subjects because they also show quietly observed animal behaviour elements that make them extra special. The moose one, which we commissioned and which is reproduced in the colour section, shows a bull looking very surprised when he encounters the head and antlers of a dead bull lying in the snow (see colour section). When I asked Tony about the bull's expression, he told me that this was something he had seen during his field studies.

Tony's early life was not easy. He first suffered persecution from the Nazis in his native Czechoslovakia (as it was then) and then dealt with the Communist takeover after World War II, when he was forced to work as a labourer. He came to Canada in 1970 and was soon recognized as one of the most innovative thinkers in the field of deer biology. He died while walking his Norwegian elk hound in 1995, two years before the publication of the most authoritative book on moose, *Ecology and Management of North American Moose*, to which he contributed two chapters and many illustrations. The editors, themselves leading moose scientists, started the book with an In Memoriam piece that ended with this fitting tribute: "He challenges us all with his enthusiasm, lust for knowledge, and life. Tony was an inspiration to many, and leaves a rich, diverse, and enduring legacy."

The highlight of the social events at the Prince Albert conference where I first met Tony was a moose-calling competition after the evening meal. My student, an attractive and vivacious character, entered the competition for fun, and by means of an informal applause-o-meter was voted winner by a considerable margin, although her actual call of "moose, mooooose, moooooose" bore no resemblance to the real thing. She was like a honey jar to a wasp, and several of the non-monogamous alpha males were obviously attracted (Tony and Victor were not among them).

Tony was one of the many who asked questions about the Super 8 movie of the goosing and walking, which got lots of interest and quite a few laughs, as one might expect, but also led to a television gig. The folks from Mutual of Omaha, sponsors of the popular wildlife show *Wild Kingdom* that starred Marlin Perkins, were in touch with me soon after the conference because big-game biologist Dick Denney, one of the delegates, had told them about the movie. The following year our delta research set-up had to be a little different in order to make a film.

Marlin and two younger men arrived at the lodge ahead of us and were testing out their equipment in the cold conditions of early December. This moose business would be very different than the alligator and python wrestling I had recently seen them indulge in on the box.

We shook hands outside and then headed into the trailer, as much for the warmth as for the coffee.

Marlin, slight, greying, and courtly, much as one would have expected from his television persona, was about 1.75 metres tall. The other two, Peter Drowne and Rod Allin, producer and cameraman respectively, were much the same height, dark haired, and lively. Peter was more extroverted and slimmer than Rod, who had a much rounder head.

They had already been out over the delta in a second helicopter to get some background footage and seen one remarkable thing that ended up in the final product. A bull moose had been running from the machine and had hit his antler on a small bush. Right in front of their eyes, and for the entire world to witness, one antler had fallen off. This may sound like something terrible to the uninitiated, but the antlers of all deer from temperate zones are cast every year, and the transition from a strongly attached appendage that cannot be removed with a hammer blow to the casting happens in a very short space of time, a day or two at the most. The antlers will fall off naturally, without any assistance, but the camera had caught this event at the very brief interval when the antler was ready to fall but had not yet done so.

The captures went smoothly, although there was one small dispute before we even started.

"We need to set some ground rules," Bob said to Marlin and Peter. "We do not chase any moose at a run for more than two minutes. If Jerry has not got a shot away in that time, we leave it alone."

"What's behind that?" they asked, more or less in unison.

"We don't want to stress them. There is a condition called capture myopathy that occurs in animals that are chased too hard, and so we have established that two minutes is the cut-off."

Marlin and Peter, with Rod joining in, tried to negotiate their way past this time barrier, arguing that they would need more than this to make a decent storyline. I had previously spoken to Bob about some other films of theirs I had seen and expressed concern that some animals might have been over-chased; we agreed on the two-minute limit. Bob is fairly hard nosed when he needs to be, and he stuck to his guns. It was a case of "my way or no way."

I was impressed with Rod. It was cold enough for me, sitting inside the helicopter, even with the door off, but he was strapped into a harness on the outside, right alongside me. I not only had to keep the barrel of the dart gun inside the cab until the very last minute, in order to prevent the drugs from freezing in the dart (something I found out the hard way—if you will excuse the pun) but I also had to handle all my solutions with care to prevent anything from quickly freezing in the $-20°C$ environment. I have no idea how Rod managed with the downdraft whipping at him, the howling wind magnified by the forward motion of the machine. I suspect that the two-minute time limit became a welcome component of the exercise for him, but the chill must have been brutal. Peter also used a camera, but when we were in the air he sat in the second helicopter, getting different angles or shooting us shooting moose.

The second chopper was written into the script as being needed for survey. If anyone should ever get hold of the footage, they will see that this is a piece of theatrical license. The only people in that machine were Marlin and Peter (other than when we were ferrying back and forth from the lodge, or when Rod needed to thaw) and, of course, Ernie Jurgens, the pilot.

I have a 16mm copy of the program and was eventually able to get hold of a copy of the film on a DVD. My children, after seeing it run through the spools a couple of times, stated that they thought it was better run backwards. The show is called—you guessed it—*Where Men Walk with Moose.*

When the television show filming was out of the way, we continued our studies. The next time Bob called me to help with a moose project, he and his bosses were responding to public pressure from the hunting fraternity. Apparently the group thought that the letting of large numbers of hunting licenses for bull moose was having a negative effect on the breeding success of the population in the Saskatchewan River Delta.

The simple answer seemed to be to capture a respectable number of cow moose and check if they were pregnant.

"What's the best time to do that?" asked Bob.

"Early December would be fine," I replied. "By then they should be at least ten weeks along, and at that stage diagnosis is easy. Let's not do it after New Year's, because the later we try, the more stress on the cows and the less accurate I can be."

For me this exercise would involve exposing one arm to the cold for a brief while, slipping on a plastic sleeve and glove, slapping some lubricating goop on them, and getting my arm warm again as I felt for the calf inside the moose.

In their theory about a declining moose population, the hunters had not allowed for the power of sex drive. Maybe the bull numbers in the delta were down a bit, but the bulls had obviously covered as much ground as was needed and put on enough kilometres. All of our sampled cows were pregnant, none less than about ten weeks, and certainly not as little as seven weeks. This meant that an important part of our study had confirmed that all cows had likely conceived at their first heat. As Chuck Schwartz, another of those leading moose biologists whom I had met in Prince Albert, wrote, "It is more important to know when a cow is bred and how many fetuses she is carrying than simply to know that she is pregnant." He was referring to the likely date of calving, as late-born calves have a much reduced chance of surviving the first winter of their lives. Because it seemed as if there were no late conceptions in the cows we checked, we concluded that a reduction in overall moose numbers was likely not because of a lack of bulls. At the time, a few researchers were reporting that bears are a major predator of very young moose calves, and perhaps this was the problem.

In this case the hunting fraternity was interested in preserving a population of moose that it thought was threatened. Another aspect, much less palatable, about some hunters, however, was and remains the obsession with antlers and trophy hunting and its effect upon the future of antlers, which have such a pivotal role in moose reproduction.

CHAPTER THIRTEEN

ANTLERS AND SEX

The purpose of antlers; the biggest moose antlers ever;
antlers and sound; antlers and scent; a 1576 book on my shelf.

For the moose, antlers and sex are inextricably entwined. A maxim about sex that applies to most living things, including moose, is: "If your parents don't have it, neither will you." Antlers are all about access to females, and their size can be viewed as the means to that end (as it were). As in that old vaudeville song, "Love and Marriage," immortalized by Frank Sinatra, you can't have one without the other (not quite true, but I'll come to that).

Why have antlers? This question has been posed many times, in many contexts, and is the subject of much debate in the scientific community. The main debate within the "access to females" discussion is whether "antlers are for show and tell, or for fighting." The truth is that they are probably for both, and a fight only occurs if the opponents' displays do not resolve the issue. In this case, size matters. The display is crucial and governs the outcome of encounters, more so if there are considerable numbers of moose in a given area or if they can easily see one another.

Antlers are unique to deer and develop in thirty-six of the world's forty species, playing a crucial role in the mating game. Most of my own deer watching has been in zoos and on deer farms and is therefore clouded by the artificial nature of those environments. However, even these environments have given me the opportunity to closely watch the annual cycle of antler initiation, growth, and shedding. Even with minor differences in timing and of course major differences in architecture between the species, the events are the same.

One has to look at the first set of antlers a male deer grows before considering those he sports at certain times for the rest of his life, which are all about reproduction. This first set is equivalent to the wooden swords and plastic pistols that young boys, including my grandson, seem to want to own even when they are brought up in a non-aggressive environment. Unlike all subsequent sets, to which I will return shortly, the first set of antlers develops independently of external factors. They grow from bony protuberances that develop above and slightly to one side of the deer's eyes when he is still a calf. Every deer species that grows antlers has small, highly specialized islands of cells, one on either side of the skull, from which the protuberances, called pedicles, begin to grow when the calf reaches a certain size. These cells are unique to deer and are so specialized that if a few of them are transplanted to another area of the body, say a leg, a structure resembling the pedicle will grow there. The pedicles are covered in short hair that matches the body hair in colour and make-up.

During growth, when the pressure of the tightening skin at the apex reaches a critical level, the process changes and true antlers begin to emerge from the pedicles. These appear as shiny new bulges of skin with short hair that feels like velvet, the luxury fabric associated with wealth, high status, and emperor's robes. Hence the name "velvet antler" and the description of a deer as being "in velvet." The velvet antler soon begins to sprout and grow like a well-watered weed. After a growth period of a few months the velvety skin will be rubbed off and the antler, known as a spike in these youngsters, hardens. After the deer carries the antlers for a few months, they drop off. These spike antlers follow different rules of growth and development than all later ones and are usually but pale shadows of what will develop in adult life.

Once the first set of antlers has grown and been dropped, antlers develop every year in an annual cycle: regeneration, rapid growth, hardening, casting, and then regrowth the following year. A convenient point at which to begin observing the antler cycle is at the end of winter when life begins to stir in the earth and a few hardy plants begin to show their green leaves. At this time bull moose carry no head adornments.

Daylight directly influences the entire cycle: all cyclical events occur according to the seasons and the amount of light that reaches the bull's eye. Indeed day length drives the entire reproductive cycle in both male and female deer species that originate in temperate zones. From the eyes nerve impulses travel to the brain and stimulate the production of hormones that in turn enter the blood stream. In specialized cells in the testicles these hormones stimulate the manufacture of testosterone and thereby the changes in antler through the year. Some minor alterations in the cycle can happen and are governed by food quality and availability.

At some point in spring, after a period of dormancy since the last casting, the old, fully healed scars of last year's antlers begin a new round of cellular activity. Shiny new bulges of velvety skin begin to emerge. The actual date at which this occurs varies according to the age of the bull, but from my twenty years of recorded observations of captive wapiti, whose diet did not vary, I would say that once he reaches maturity the events for each bull are consistent within a day or two over the long term.

As spring becomes summer the new velvet antlers begin to grow upward and outward at an astonishing rate. Antlers are not only the only organs that regenerate normally every year, but they are the fastest growing organs in the animal kingdom, with a rich blood and nerve supply. Within three or four months they have reached their maximum size. This growth needs fuel, and during spring and summer a bull moose puts on body weight at a furious rate, gaining as much as 25 or 30 per cent from the weight that he carried in winter in a few short months. He loses that weight again in as many weeks, as the rut distracts him from eating and the sex drive trumps hunger.

One extraordinary feature of antlers in general is that for each species there is a defined shape template for adults. In North America the antler shape of most moose vaguely resembles the human hand and is thus called palmate. When a bull is two years old his antlers may only have about five "fingers," but by the time they are mature at age six and up, a few bulls may have over twenty.

If all goes well, and he suffers no injuries, the antlers will take the palm form every year until his senior years, when they begin to get smaller and lose shape. That said, palmate antlers are much less common in Eurasian moose, especially in the southern part of their range, where they tend to have branches but no palms.

The changing shapes of antlers relate to function. In young bulls under about five years of age the antlers are more offensive than defensive, with a few sharp tines. During the bull's mature years they have the defensive palmate form with many tines that will interlock with those of a rival and prevent injury. Later in life the form degenerates, and once a bull is past eleven they may look more like a juvenile set with a few tines or even take on bizarre shapes that hardly resemble true moose antlers.

Each moose antler may be as much as ninety-four centimetres long and thirty-one centimetres across the palm at its widest point, although these sizes are only known from prime bulls, aged from about five or six to eleven years from the northernmost regions and wide open country of their ranges.

The simplest way of reporting the size of a set of antlers that is still attached to the head is to state the spread, the maximum distance between the very outside tips on either side. This may be less than the combined length of the individual antlers as these are usually measured without taking any account of the angle at which they join the skull. The current record antlers reported by the trophy

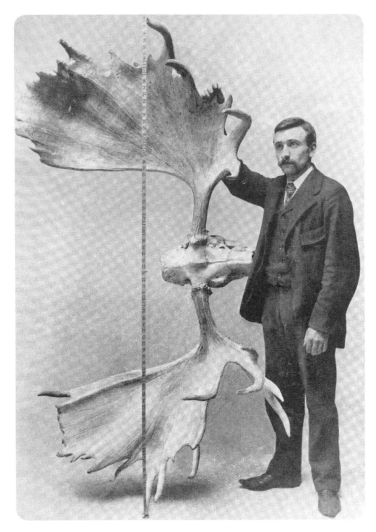

From Sport and Life *by Baillie-Groham. Shot in 1897 in Yukon basin, Alaska, 199.4 centimetre spread, with forty-three points. Owned by W.F. Sheard of Tacoma, Washington.*

GLENBOW ARCHIVES NA-1234-5

hunting fraternity in North America came from a bull shot in 1994 in the Forty Mile River area of Alaska. The Boone and Crockett (B&C) record system is the one by which North American hunters set their standards, and the B&C website states that these antlers had a spread of 65.13 inches (165.4 centimetres). This is completely dwarfed by the antlers of a bull shot in 1897 near the Yukon River, which measured 78.5 inches (199.4 centimetres) and had an even larger spread of 81.5 inches (207 centimetres), reported in Alaska by moose biologist Bill Gasaway and his colleagues. Farther south they are not as large. The biggest ones I ever saw on a hunted moose in the Saskatchewan River Delta were only about 55 inches (140 centimetres) across.

By late summer, in about early August in prime bulls, up to three weeks later in youngsters, when the antlers have reached their full size, the blood supply dries up and the sheen on the velvet fades. Those who have raised moose, or any other deer, in captivity know that at this time there will be a sudden change in the bull's activity. Quite what creates the tipping point is not clear, but testosterone concentrations in the blood reach a maximum. In some cases the bull goes from a mild-mannered individual to a rampaging terror almost overnight, but in Denali National Park in Alaska, Dr. Victor van Ballenberghe sees a different pattern. He has devoted many weeks each year, over many years of field study, to moose in Denali, and he called the autumn "the most exciting time to be in the field" in his beautiful book *In the Company of Moose*. As he wrote to me in an email about the rut, "Bulls remain pretty mild mannered, in fact, more tolerant toward humans than during other seasons." The difference is hard to explain but I wonder if it may be that the bulls in Denali, where no hunting is permitted, are not concerned with mere humans as they know that more important matters are at hand. Other moose biologists have suggested that Denali moose are indeed a bit different.

What does happen across all regions is that a few days after the velvet appears to dry up the bull searches out vegetation, such as trees and bushes, and attacks it, trying to clean the velvet off his antlers. In the zoo Mickey attacked the fence and a barrier cable had to be put up to prevent it sagging like an old skirt and being destroyed. I have often wondered if the rubbing is partly due to a wish to get rid of what is now basically a big, itchy, dry scab. (This is not to admit that I have ever picked at a dried-up itchy scab myself.)

The velvet comes off in strips or even sheets and hangs down around the bull's head, creating a dreadlock look or even a ghoulish appearance if some remaining blood vessels have not quite dried up and blood drips down his face. Over the next few days all the velvet is rubbed off and the bone underneath cleans up. The top of the antler turns white while the underside is heavily stained to a rich dark brown.

At this point the bull is at the start of a full-blown rut. His body weight has maxed out and he has more fat on him than at any other time of year. His neck muscles are massive, which helps him carry the extra thirty kilograms of antler on his head and will be vital in the battles to come. His testes have almost doubled in volume and are full of fertile sperm and fluids. He starts carrying out behaviours intended to attract any lurking females (who are also at the start of their reproductive season) and also to signal to any potential rivals that he means business and that his business is breeding.

He continues to thrash vegetation, creating a din that carries quite a distance. Hunters may use this sound alone to attract animals during the rutting period. Just beating or scraping a stick against a handy willow bush has the potential to act as auditory moose bait for the hunter. Some hunters scrape old antlers against bushes, as such an action may imitate the sound of velvet being rubbed. Both of these sounds may lure a bull to a hunter, or to a rival bull, because he has lost much of the judgment he would normally exercise in an area where predators, either two- or four-legged, are out to get him. Another way of putting this is to say that the bull's brains have gone to his balls, a phrase that has occasionally been used to describe human teenagers. Edinburgh zoologist Gerald Lincoln has described what moose and other deer are undergoing at this time as "seasonal puberty." Although the word "puberty" really only refers to the once-only occurrence in a male's life, the parallel seems reasonable.

There are other sounds that moose make at this time. When he is in full rut the bull can be heard making his low-pitched call, a cross between a grunt and a hiccup, which I can best represent as *Ur-ugh! Ur-ugh!* The call has been likened to a number of things by various authors. Tony Bubenik thought it resembled a hiccup. Victor van Ballenberghe called it a croak. The strangest description I know of came from Frederick Selous, the famous hunter of African big game who came to Canada in the early 1900s. He likened it to "a human being in the throes of seasickness."

First Nations hunters have used this sound for generations, employing a cedar or birch-bark horn to give it resonance. After hearing Cree Elder Barry Ahenakew bring this call from deep in his throat, expanding it with his hands in the absence of the traditional birch-bark instrument, I know that *Ur-ugh!* is inadequate, but it's the best I can do. Darryl Chamakese described a modern representation of the call that is known to work well as we drove back to his office after our meeting with Barry.

"We use a coffee tin," he said. "Take the lid off, punch a hole in the base and thread a string through it. You need a thick string, like a hockey bootlace. Tie a knot in it and leave about this much string hanging down through the middle." He stretched his right hand down to his knee, about sixty centimetres. "You have to wet the string and then pull it sharply to make the right sound." He clarified this later in an email when he wrote, "Did I mention that you have to put your hand into the coffee tin and 'pull-slip' on the string from the inside so it amplifies the sound? Pull-slip; listen; wait three minutes or so for the faintest call." Darryl also told me that most recently some Aboriginal hunters use recordings of the call that they play over loudspeakers.

Darryl's coffee-tin account at once brought to mind my meeting with a hunter in the village of Linyati on the shores of the river of the same name in Namibia many years ago. He demonstrated the use of a hippo caller to my wife and me as we sat in his house. It was made of a hide stretched over a wooden frame and looked very much like a small drum with one open end and a narrow waist. He wetted the thong that was attached to the back of the drum face and emerged from the base and pulled on it. It sounded just like the grunt-cum-roar of a hippo.

"If you want to call a calf," he said, "you pull without wetting."

The bull moose call can potentially carry as far as three kilometres and may either attract cows or challenge other bulls. It is nothing like the musical bugle of the wapiti, or the deep-throated roar of the red deer stag, both of which can set the hairs on the back of one's neck a-tingling. We do not know if the pitch or volume of the sound plays any role in establishing a bull's position in society, which is the case with the roar of a red deer.

A raunchy joke explanation of the bull moose's call was told to me by a Cree hunter near the Saskatchewan River Delta in the days when I was helping put radio collars on the animals. "You know what the sound is?" he asked with a grin. "It's really the sound of the bull reacting to the bushes and frosty grass catching on his pecker as he walks along ready for action."

Joseph Naytowhow, a lanky and charming Cree storyteller and actor who is also a member of the Saskatoon Storytellers' Guild, shared another rude explanation of the bull moose grunt. "Rut time," he said, "is also the time that cranberries are ready to eat and bull moose that have overindulged tend to get constipated. The noise accompanies his efforts to pass them."

Whatever our fanciful interpretations of the moose grunt, if moose sounds are being made, they are also being heard—perhaps with the help of antlers. Three generations of Bubeniks—Tony, his son, George, and grandson Peter—hypothesized, developed, and finally proved the idea that the antlers act as parabolic reflectors and can increase auditory perception by almost 20 per cent. The final proof, shown by Peter, who is a mathematician not a zoologist, was published thirteen years after his grandfather's death.

After Victor van Ballenberghe told me that he doubted the role of antlers in sound collection, because antlers in Denali tend to spread sideways rather than up, I asked George Bubenik about his family's theory. He replied that he had tried three different sets of antlers, including one from Alaska, and had found differences, but he suggested that these differences would be compensated for by the very mobile ears of the moose, which can spin and turn almost 360 degrees. If I think about how I cup an ear with my palm and turn my head, as I cannot do more than wiggle my ears a tad (a trick that impressed my grandchildren for all of ten minutes) when I want to hear better, I feel that there is merit in George's idea.

Another sound that can excite moose during the breeding season is the splash of urine in water, something that females may do when they are coming into heat. This may just be a chance event, rather than a deliberate action by the cow, but First Nations hunters have used this sound to entice amorous bulls for generations. In 1672 Nicolas Denys wrote, "At rutting time the hunting was done at night upon the rivers in a canoe. Counterfeiting the cry of the female, the Indians [Micmacs] with a dish of bark would take up some water and let it fall into the water from a height. The noise brought the male, who thought it was a female making water."

Cow moose also make noises during the rut, and these are sometimes misinterpreted by inexperienced hunters. Best described as a moan, the female's call is not a direct mating call but serves two purposes. It has been known for some time that the moan is a protest to courting bulls, especially youngsters, but, as Dr. Terry Bowyer, now of Idaho State University, showed in his days working with the team in Denali, the moan has another surprising effect. It is used as a tool to attract bigger bulls if a small male approaches. When that happens females moan more and this triggers aggression in larger males. In fact, as Terry said in an interview with BBC Nature reporter Ella Davies, "Male aggression was more common when females gave protest moans than when they did not, indicating that this vocalization incited male–male aggression. Protest moans allow females to exert some female choice in a mating system where males restrict choice of mates through male–male combat."

In this regard it echoes shades of human behaviour and clearly shows that there is a considerable element of female choice during the rut. When I chatted to Dr. Bowyer he told me that one of his colleagues, who read his manuscript, said to him, "This is not unique to moose, I have seen it in bars in Wisconsin." I replied, "Not just Wisconsin; I saw it during my student days in Glasgow." Of course we both acknowledged that this comparison is an oversimplification. As Terry said in that same bbc interview, "Human females have far more opportunities for mate choice than do female moose because of differences in mating systems."

The grunt of the rutting bull and the moan of the cow are not the only sounds that moose make. As we sat over a beer, naturalist and long-time moose watcher Roy Ness of Whitehorse told me of two encounters with moose during which he heard more than just the moans of a cow.

In mid-September 1983, at the height of the rut, "I was in what's locally called the Teslin Burn," he said. "I was camped at the end of Grayling Lake, south of Teslin Lake, an area of regrowth that had the highest moose density in the Yukon."

As he sat on a three-metre tall knoll at the end of the lake in the gathering autumn dusk he listened as a cow accompanied by her calf came to the shore from quite a distance away.

I got goose bumps as I read the graphic description of the next ninety minutes that Roy subsequently wrote. "I was sitting there as it got dark and I heard the cow call. It started high and went down the register for about ten seconds, closely repeated several times, each shorter than the last, until it ended in a couple of short grunts. She would call every five or ten minutes, each time getting closer and each time getting answering grunts from a bull at the far end of the lake."

There was no moon that night and by the time the animals arrived in the meadow just below the knoll only the stars gave any light. It must have been magic.

"Even though they were only a few meters away," he wrote, "I could barely discern their shapes. She continued to call for about an hour while her calf seemed to be playing—fits of running about then standing still for a while."

As we chatted about his experience he told me that she suddenly became aware of him, although there was no wind to speak of. At that point "she let out the loudest sound I've ever heard escape the lungs of any animal. It was a lion's roar with a deep loud belch mixed in. I nearly jumped out of my clothes."

The cow took off at a great rate, down the meadow and through the willows, crashing though the bushes and letting out the same call as she went.

This alarm call is made by both sexes.

On another occasion in early June, Roy watched a cow and her small calf feeding in some willows. "I could not see them a lot of the time," he said during our conversation, "and they certainly could not see each other all the time. However, they both let out a series of high-pitched calls, almost like squeaks, as they stayed in touch. I couldn't tell which was the calf, and which the mother."

Vince Crichton, a moose biologist in Manitoba, has witnessed and videotaped a play fight encounter between two young bulls during which they both made sounds that closely resembled the moan of the cow during the rut. He told me, " If I had not seen them and heard their moaning I would have said it was cows. Quite amazing. I have video of this and I was about twenty feet from them."

Scent is also a vital component of the mating game. Humans, too, are not immune to the power of smell. One only has to watch a few commercials to realize that this is also known to manufactures of many a well-known perfume. I once heard of a social science experiment in which women were able to pick out their partner's unwashed T-shirts by smell alone, but this may have been an urban myth. There are, however, verifiable trials in which women prefer the smell of T-shirts of men with different immune system genetic make-up than their own. Antlers are known to act as scent carriers. Bull moose in rut will urinate in puddles and create pitholes and then stomp in the mess, rather like a child playing in mud. In Denali National Park a bull may make several pitholes in a single day. The urine, especially during the rut, is full of strong-smelling, moose-attracting substances like pheromones, which serve two purposes. If these substances can be wafted downwind they will serve to bring females into his orbit. Watching a rutting bull take a pee into the pithole that he has created, stomp in the fluid mix, and then kneel down and either rub his antlers and his chin in the now aromatic mud, or actively splash it up onto the antler palms with his forefeet, it becomes apparent that he has an ulterior motive. When he stands up his antlers have been nicely anointed and scented. The bigger the antlers, the greater the area upon which the mixture can be splashed, and the better the chances that the wind will pick up and transmit the odours.

Once the female gets close to the bull these same substances will act to stimulate her ovaries and cause her to ovulate. We do not know if the pheromones produced by dominant bulls are more potent than that of juniors.

The moose has its bell, an anatomical feature not shared by any other deer, the "lead rein" that I was able to put to good use when I had to "walk with moose" after darting them. In young bulls and most cows it usually has a long tail, but by the time a bull reaches maturity the tail has often been lost—perhaps due to frostbite—and the bell has grown larger and hangs down like a big semicircular plate. Scientists have long wondered about its function. Van Ballenberghe and his colleagues suggest that it is a simple visual clue to other males, indicating the sex, age, and social rank of the bull. Of course it may also pick up pheromones when the bull is splashing in his pithole, but there does not seem to be a deliberate attempt to use it a scent-disseminating organ.

There is an elegant demonstration of moose in courtship in a film called *High Season of the Moose* that was made in Alaska. Tony Bubenik was the scientific adviser for this work and has explained that the bell of a prime bull is larger that that of either a cow or a yearling and even a "teen," the now widely accepted term that he used to describe bulls that are between calfhood and maturity. Tony went further and classified bulls over several years into calf, yearling, teen, older submature, prime, and senior. He considered any bull under five years of age a teen and wrote that ritualistic courting behaviour was not full developed until at least three years of age. These categories echo the Cree ones, which are based on antler shape and were related to me by Elder Barry Ahenakew. There is no exact equivalent, but the yearling, known as a spiker in English, is *Pipon askos* in Cree. Thereafter the words for the animal change every year and basically describe the antler shapes as the palm enlarges. They are *Iyikïtaw askos, Waskiwichesis, Okini matayésis, Okininatayew, Kiki witéw*, and the seven-year-old bull, *Misi kikiwitéw*. There is no term for a senior whose antlers have regressed. None of these terms relate to the bell, however.

In *High Season of the Moose* a group of half a dozen cows are paying court to a bull and several of them get up very close and personal as they move slowly under his chin and rub their faces on him. Some also wallow in the aromatic mud of the pithole. It's a touching bit of foreplay.

Van Ballenberghe's book also covers the rut and courtship with clear descriptions and beautiful photos, but he has occasionally seen bulls do things that puzzle him. He has seen some of them become quite aggressive toward females and even attack cows or chase them from the pitholes.

Of course scent is a two-way street. The bull uses it to figure out which females are most ready to ovulate and breed. He repeatedly sniffs the cow's rear end and maybe inhales some mucus or other substance. After doing so he may lift his nose into the air to check things out by transferring some of the material to a special organ (called the vomeronasal or Jacobson's organ) that he has on his palate, just inside his mouth. This activity is known as flehmen and virtually all mammals do it, although most authorities seem to agree that the organ has either regressed or become more or less non-functional in people. That is probably a good thing. Just imagine the scene at a party, a big sports event, or the movies!

One of the first people to record this behaviour was a French count named George Turbervile. His *Booke of Hunting*, published in 1576, is one of my favourites on the deer shelves at home. Turbervile was an acute observer of all things related to red deer and the following famous passage gives us the most lyrical description of flehmen ever

OF MOOSE AND MEN

Flehmen, checking out the scents of a cow during the rut.
As Count Turbevile put it in 1576: "When they ſmell the Hynde,
they rayſe their noſe vp into the ayre, and looke aloft, as though they
gaue thankes to nature which gaue them ſo great delight."
GERHARD STUEWE

penned: "*It is a pleaſure, to beholde them when they goe to Rutte and make their vaute. For when they ſmell the Hynde, they rayſe their noſe vp into the ayre, and looke aloft, as though they gaue thankes to nature which gaue them ſo great delight.*"

After the rut, the bull has no further use for his antlers. They may even be thought of as an impediment, as they weigh several kilos that he has to lug around. This hauling around of extra baggage costs him the energy that he badly needs to search for food in order to regain some of the massive weight loss he experienced when in the "*pride of greace*," as Turbervile put it. He may have lost as much as 25 or 30 per cent of his body mass during those tempestuous times, and he has to regain some of that in order to survive the cold months ahead. Who needs a thirty-kilogram mass of useless bone on his head when all he is interested in is groceries?

The solution? Get rid of them. In mature bulls casting is a sudden event that occurs in late November or early December. It was this that the Mutual of Omaha crew caught on their 1982 film when recording our work in the Saskatchewan River Delta. Immature moose drop their antlers a few months later, and it takes a couple of years for them to come into full synchrony with older animals. For the next few months after the antlers are cast, the bull lives quite happily without any head adornment. He doesn't need it. There are no females around to impress or fight over, and, anyway, the breeding season has passed.

The reason for the antler casting is that there has been a rapid change in the hormonal status of the bull. His testosterone levels have dropped sharply and cells that held the big bony structures to his head have died away, making the junction between skull and antler weak. The casting of antlers happens over a very short period of time. It is a case of one being unable to knock the antler off with a hammer on one day and it falling off unaided on the next.

From the time of that antler casting and throughout the spring and early summer, moose bulls are infertile. Their testes shrink in size and there is no sperm production. The reproductive system shuts down while hormonal activity, particularly the all-important male testosterone, is barely detectable, except with very sensitive measurements, in the blood. At the end of winter, however, as the days lengthen, the new antlers begin to grow, and the cycle begins anew.

CHAPTER FOURTEEN

MORE SEX, MORE ANTLERS

Size matters,
and that's the truth.

As well as being useful in both creating and receiving sound and as scent distributors, antlers are involved in two more of the five senses: sight and touch.

As far as sight goes, there is an interesting difference in the mating behaviours of moose living in open areas as opposed to those in forested areas. In the tundra of the most northerly regions like Denali and Yukon, where tall vegetation is scattered or sparse and may only grow in clumps along water courses and near lakes, moose may gather at breeding time in groups of up to twenty-five, although the average is six cows per bull. At the other end of the scale are moose living in boreal forests or taiga that stretch across much of central Canada, like the ones in Saskatchewan. In these areas, a bull and cow may engage in a tending-bonding, a sort of three or four-day moose version of the human one-night stand, with sex the sole objective. Once they have mated the pair will separate and the bull will search for another female in heat. These mating patterns are not absolute, of course. In the Saskatchewan River Delta there are open patches of swampy ground and a few sedge meadows that have

grown in dried-up oxbows alongside rivers. I have seen small rutting groups of four or five animals in these meadows. Victor van
Ballenberghe suggested to me that the larger social groups in the
north may be a fairly recent evolutionary development in response to
living in open areas.

Another open-territory behaviour van Ballenberghe has observed is
bulls using their antlers as beacons: moose may stand in such a manner
that sunlight reflects off their antler palms. Van Ballenberghe recounted
being able to see the glinting over at least three kilometres. The bigger
the reflective surface, the clearer the signal. This behaviour would be
of little use in attracting females if tall spruce or pine, and even three-
metre-tall alder bushes like the ones in the delta, cut the line of sight to
less than a hundred metres. Of course, sometimes the antler beacons
also attract other males.

Regardless of territory, once animals get close to each other the
stakes are raised and the signals are more intense. When two bull
moose approach one other they first take a good look. When they
are in velvet the once-over is about all that happens, unless the pair is
comprised of youngsters. While they are young and still trying to sort
out who is boss, they will often get up on their hind legs and box, or
even "play-fight." However, once the velvet is shed the rules change and
bulls perform a series of stereotypical behaviours, almost as in a well-
choreographed ballet. The first movement is often the showing off of
both body and antler sizes as the bulls walk parallel to one another. In
this way, they can at once see what they may be dealing with. Another
show-off occurs when bulls dip their heads, demonstrating the length
and width of the antler palms, the dimensions of which are less notice-
able in the head-up position and viewed from the side.

If there are obvious differences between the two animals, the interaction may cease right there, and the inferior animal may wander away
in the hope of having more luck over the next hill or clump of bush. If
the junior is very much smaller, say a yearling, and if he behaves himself and engages in appeasement, the champ may tolerate him hanging

Two bulls check each other out. The subordinate (right) turns
sideways and offers no threat. The subordinate bull proceeded
to thrash nearby bushes as if in frustration at his defeat
COURTESY GERHARD STUEWE

around, although the stronger bull may risk the event that happens when large groups of females come into heat at the same time and the mature animal cannot serve them all. This is recognized in red deer and wapiti where these young bulls, hanging on the periphery of the herd and trying to stay out of sight of the herd master, get the occasional chance to breed if a female is receptive and does not get the full attention of the big fellow. This has occasionally been seen in Denali moose, especially when females wander away of their own accord and mate with any available bull, no matter what his antlers look like. They could both be described, in impolite circles, as sneaky fuckers. The fact the moose will "sneak out for a quickie" comes as no surprise when one considers similar behaviour in other species, from humans to red-winged blackbirds. In the United Kingdom, where milk is regularly delivered from a van, there are music-hall jokes about the father of a child in the house resembling the stocky, dark-haired milkman rather than the tall blond spouse. Comic material is often based on fact and there have been plenty of scientific studies about choice and the myth of female monogamy in humans. Overall, in the Western world 10 to 15 per cent of children are "fathered" by men who are not their sires. Across the mammalian world only about 3 per cent of four thousand species are considered to be truly mono-gamous and the same is likely true among birds. Even the swan, long considered the poster child for fidelity, is known to wander. And, as has been clearly shown by DNA analyses of red-winged blackbird nest-lings, this loquacious bird is but one of hundreds of bird species in which both members of a nesting pair engage in regular hanky-panky and actively seek out other partners during the breeding season. In one classic experiment, mates of vasectomized red-winged blackbird males continued to lay fertile eggs.

Younger bulls may also get a chance to mate if the cows do not conceive while the prime bulls are in full rut. The latter become quite exhausted and then the teenagers, whose rut starts later than their elders', have a chance. Count Turbervile put it eloquently in his 1576 observations of red deer, where he has this to say about the changing of the guard (harts or hartes are stags):

> The olde Harts go fooner to Vault than the yong, and they are fo fierce and fo proude, that vntil they haue accomplyfhed their luft, the yong Harts dare not come neare them, for if they do, they beate them and dryue them away. The yong Deere haue a maruellous craft and malice, for when they perceiue that the olde Harts are wearie of the Rut and weakened in force, they runne vppon them, and eyther hurt or kyll them, caufing them to abandon the Rut, and then they remayne maifters in their places.

In well-balanced moose populations over 90 per cent of cows will likely conceive at their first heat, but if bull numbers are low, and the bull–cow ratio dips down to as low as five or twelve bulls per hundred cows, many cows may not conceive first time around, which leads to late calving and downstream effects that carry over to the following years. Late-born calves may not survive the ensuing winter.

The intricacies of moose display are endlessly fascinating. Tony Bubenik carried out a series of experiments related to that pre-fight display, first on red deer in his days as researcher in Europe, and later, after his arrival in North America in 1970 at the age of fifty-seven, on moose and caribou. He established, with the clever use of a feeding pen at the game preserve at Bilje near the town of Osijek in the former Yugoslavia, that stags are acutely self-aware when it comes to antler size. The fence around the feeding station was too high for the deer to jump, so they learned to enter through an open gate. Once the deer became accustomed to this one access point, and their antlers had reached full size, Tony began to reduce the width of the gate little by little, nailing boards on either side. Inevitably there came a time when the space was less than the spread of the antlers of his subjects. Even then they would get into the pen by twisting their heads so that one antler entered ahead of the other. It was rather like a couple of furniture movers getting a large bed through a doorway by tipping it on its side and passing it through at an angle. The boards continued to go up until one day the deer simply refused to try. As Tony put it to me: "They knew it was impossible."

He established that once the antlers had hardened it took about a month for the stag to be fully aware of their exact size, and he reasoned that part of this awareness came from the ground and bushes marked as the animal made his scrapes and thrashes before and during the rut. Taking the experiment a step further, he then cut off part of the hard antler and observed how the stag was unable to recognize the change in the antler size, still acting as if he had the rank and shape that had been present when he was setting his place in society, at least for that particular season. Of course the reduced antler size got him into trouble with other stags, which noted his change of ornament. He was no longer a Mercedes, but more like a vw bug.

In a third experiment that Tony's wife Mary recorded on Super 8 film, Tony built a dummy red deer head that he mounted with inverted padded hooks onto his shoulders, and to which he attached lightweight antlers. As long as he mounted antlers that were smaller

MORE SEX, MORE ANTLERS

Sketch by Tony Bubenik made from Super 8 footage of the
interaction between a bull and Tony's dummy with juvenile
antler shape. Note that the bull appears to accept the
dummy's lack of body length or four legs.

COURTESY GEORGE BUBENIK

than those of a resident stag he could safely approach the real animal and get close enough to establish nose-to-nose contact.

Once he got to Canada he took this idea a step further in a set of experiments on moose and caribou. He called the antlers an "optical supercue" because they overrode signals that might have made a bull caribou or moose wary of the human-mounted dummies that did not smell of anything other than humans. Furthermore they had only two legs, but the wild bulls still reacted to them.

In another Super 8 film shot by Mary, of which Tony gave me a copy, he conducted three antler-size experiments with a bull moose that had taken up residence near a small forest pond in Ontario. He

Tony's sketch of the interaction between a bull and Tony's
dummy with antler shape and size matching that of the
resident bull. The threat gait of the bull is typical.

built a dummy moose head, which he attached to a lightweight frame, and constructed three sets of antlers that could readily be changed.

First, he put on a tiny set of antlers that matched those of a sixteen-month-old spiker and walked out from behind his hiding place when the wild bull appeared. The movie shows the bull lifting his head briefly from the water, taking one glance at the intruder, who was showing the correct behaviour in moving lateral to and not facing the dominant animal, and ignoring him. This was much as expected.

Next, as his experiment escalated, Tony exchanged the spikes for a set of super antlers, far bigger than those of the resident. This time, when the bull saw him, he again took a look, but he did not hang around. He simply retired from the scene and ghosted into the spruce trees.

Then Tony showed his true scientific inquisitiveness. He put on the last set of antlers, a set that he had constructed to match those of his subject as nearly as possible. This time he was neither ignored nor avoided. As Tony's drawing from the film clip shows, the bull came

round the side of the pond and began the ritualized threat that pre-
cedes a serious fight among bull moose of equal rank. He dropped his
head so that the massive palms would show to maximum effect and
rocked his head from side to side, showing off his "stuff." He walked
forward with his forelegs spread wide and locked as if they were stilts,
like Frankenstein figures in early horror films. Again, a fine sketch
from the movie tells the story.

Not surprisingly, Mary's filming technique suffered a bit at this
point as she began to retreat behind a tree. Tony dropped the dummy
head, having no wish to take his proof to its inevitable conclusion.

It was only because he retained his sense of awareness that Tony
was able to override his scientific curiosity and be able to share the
story of a similar test with wild caribou in Alaska. As we sat over
breakfast at our home in Saskatoon he recounted how he had built
a dummy caribou head and, in the interests of science, had placed
upon it a set of antlers that far exceeded anything ever mentioned in
the hunting record books. He waited for a group of caribou to pass
within sight and had then stood to show off the trophy head. As he
had expected, the females in the group abandoned their true consort
and headed toward him, even moving upwind. At this point he noted,
in a corner of his mind, the sound of a light aircraft overhead, but he
soon forgot about the sound as his focused on observing the animal
behaviour. Then he heard a deep-throated roar as the plane turned a
tight circle. At this point he looked up and saw a man leaning partly
out of the side window pointing a rifle at him. Naturally he shucked
the dummy head and ran!

In a different set of trials Tony wrote this about an equally amazing
phenomenon that mimicked the response of those caribou females:
"On two occasions moose cows offered themselves for copulation
even though a short while earlier they were courted by a bull of lower
rank antlers."

As you can see, size really does matter—most of the time—but the
number of bulls in a moose population is also important.

The ratio of bulls to cows varies considerably and if badly out of kilter can have an adverse effect upon the entire population of moose in a given area. The highest bull–cow ratio that I know of was 92:100 in Lake Superior's Isle Royale National Park, which is obviously not hunted. In Denali sex ratios rarely exceed 50:100, which may be because, after the exertions and weight loss of the rut, males are much more susceptible to the effects of harsh winters that occur that far north than are females. There are many areas where this ratio is exceeded but in heavily hunted areas, particularly where trophy hunting tends to eliminate prime bulls, ratios may drop below 10:100, and the females will likely mate with any bull that shows up.

Although moose researchers do not tend to use the word, the group gatherings look very much like the "harems" that are seen in breeding groups of red deer and wapiti. There is a sound reason for avoiding the term: the word "harem" indicates a group in which a single dominant male tries to hold sway over a group of females by herding them. In Denali the situation is different, although, as the research teams there have seen, if a bull can defend a large group from other bulls for the entire rut he gets to mate with most of the cows surrounding him. However, the male does not attempt to herd the females; if he does try to chase one, she may simply move away and outrun him. It almost seems as if she consorts with him by choice, but even that is open to question. Victor van Ballenberghe put it to me this way in an email: "Females do make choices as to which groups they join, but with some groups the dominant bull may change (as fights occur) several times before a female is in estrus. So she can't join a group based on the bull in charge early on because he might not be there when she's ready to mate . . . I think most cows in estrus will mate with any bull that is there when they are ready."

Turbervile made his observations by virtually living among his subjects for days, or weeks, on end. I believe it would be fair to say that Tony Bubenik and Victor van Ballenberghe, equipped with greater technological tools but equal curiosity and insight, are examples of modern Turberviles.

Eventually if all the show and tell has not determined who will get to do the breeding, the antlers become what some believe they were meant to be all along: weapons.

It was none other than Charles Darwin who in 1871 wrote in *The Descent of Man, and Selection in Relation to Sex*: "When the males are provided with weapons which in the females are absent, there can hardly be a doubt that these serve for fighting with other males; and that they were acquired through sexual selection, and were transmitted to the male sex alone."

Those who have quoted this famous sentence may have forgotten that fighting and weapons do not always involve actual combat. The best-known example from modern times is probably the aftermath of World War II. For the best part of fifty years after the atom bombs fell on Hiroshima and Nagasaki, the Cold War raged between the two super powers, the prime bulls of human society. There was a lot of posturing, long-range visual signalling, and noise, but we would probably not be here to tell the tale if the ultimate weapons had actually been deployed.

Having watched male deer—stags, bulls, or bucks, depending upon the species—use their antlers, I have no doubt that they are indeed deployed as weapons between equals, when other forms of interaction have failed to resolve the burning question of sexual access. Victor van Ballenberghe has carefully analyzed fights among prime bulls in the open countryside of Denali, and his conclusion is that a bull may be involved in as many as twelve fights each season. Some fights do not last more than a few minutes; some last for hours.

Antlers are obviously weapons, but even here opinions differ among deer scientists. Some see them as purely offensive weapons designed to drive away rivals and kill or maim them. Others think that their main task is defence.

That male deer are killed and injured in mating fights every year is undeniable, but it is virtually impossible to obtain an accurate figure as to the number of the fallen, let alone estimate the proportion of injuries or fatal encounters to total fights.

The structure of antlers, especially those of moose, makes it difficult for the tines to penetrate as far as the skull of a rival. The multiple forks and branching will be the first thing to make contact as two bulls engage, and these alone are likely to prevent the pointed tines from penetrating far enough to do body damage. Once contact has happened and the antlers lock, a mighty shoving match can take place and may last for many minutes. The cameraman who shot *High Season of the Moose* recorded an epic battle that lasted over an hour and left both bulls exhausted.

As long as the bulls maintain a more or less straight push against one another, the outcome should correspond to the following factors: body size and mass, the choice of the battleground (one bull may be lucky or smart enough to choose higher ground), and perhaps how fit the rivals are. Should a bull have the misfortune to slip or make the mistake of turning sideways, his rival could press home the attack and either kill or injure him. Luck plays a part in the result, as well. In the end one can revert to the old boxing saying: "A good big 'un will always beat a good little 'un."

Of course, interlocking can sometimes go too far and lead to trouble for both bulls. If tines slide past each other and cannot be withdrawn or untangled there may be an unwelcome outcome. In 1983 Ken Child, a leading moose biologist from Prince George, British Columbia, found and photographed the fatal outcome of once such encounter near his home at Summit Lake (see photo section). Carcasses with such interlocked antlers have been recorded from Alaska to Ontario, and there are two sets in the Royal Ontario Museum.

I have not seen such an event in moose, but in the early 1980s I had to deal with two white-tailed deer bucks with locked antlers. The call came in from a conservation officer just after I got home from a farm call and was putting the kettle on. It was too good an opportunity to miss, and as my son Charles's school was only about ten minutes from home I knew that if I moved quickly I would be able to pick him up before the school bus departed so he, too, could witness the scene. When we got to the location, just west of Saskatoon outside the community of Asquith, there was a dead buck being dragged around on the ground by another that was standing and trying to untangle

Two white-tailed deer of equal rank have locked antlers.
Coyotes have already been at work on the one that has died.
Near Asquith Saskatchewan, October 1984.

JERRY HAIGH

his antlers from the carcass. I was scared of what might happen if I simply walked up and cut off the dead buck's antlers, so I pulled out my trusty blowgun from the trunk of the car and loaded up a dart. Once the live buck was down I cut through the base of one antler of the dead buck, which instantly released the lock. Once the two animals were separated I gave the live one an antidote and watched him bound off into the aspen grove nearby. Not all entangled males are lucky enough to have an observant farmer, a handy wildlife officer, and an experienced vet available at short notice. It is likely that both animals would have perished if I hadn't showed up; the dead one had been partially consumed by ever-opportunistic coyotes, even as the live one was still struggling with his unwelcome situation. He must have been terrified. The only antler "trophy" I have ever had at home was of this dead buck's sawn-off antlers mounted on a piece of purple velvet above a photo of the two of them entangled. It hung in Charles's bedroom until he went off to university.

There is one record of a successful outcome to a similarly inter-locked pair of moose from western Alaska. As Randolph Peterson recounts in his 1955 book, *North American Moose*, which was the first book written exclusively about these fascinating creatures, a game warden spotted two intertwined bulls from the air. After the plane landed and the team found one bull dead, just as I had with the bucks, the author writes, "Jack and his assistants lassoed him [the live one] and after herculean efforts succeeded in sawing off an antler and thus dislodged the dead bull. Free, but annoyed by the loss of his antler and the whole situation, the great moose took after his benefactors. They were able to escape uninjured."

In this case the animal may not have been have been the only ter-rified individual. Seven or eight hundred kilograms of angry moose bearing down on you would give your adrenal glands a workout.

We should not become carried away by the drama of all this showing and possible fighting by the bulls lest we forget one very important part of the mating game: female behaviour. The female, as she comes into heat, attracts the male by her smell and behaviour. As her maximum heat and probable fertile time gets closer she allows him to stand near for increasing lengths of time, but she moves away in short runs until she feels ready. The runs get shorter over a few hours. She may allow the bull to mount but moves out from under him until she decides that the time has come to let him do his thing. The Denali team has seen bulls mount up to twelve or even more times before a successful mating. Each time the female simply walks out from under him as he mounts until she finally stands and lets him complete his task, which is all over in a few seconds. Whether all this carrying on, which looks like teasing, racks up the bull's ardour is untested, but if one indulges in the dangerous game of anthropo-morphism, it sure looks like it. Another likely explanation is that the female needs to make sure that she conceives and does not let the male serve her until she has ovulated.

Put another way, the female runs away until she catches the male. If this does not make sense, just watch other mammalian (including human) activity that surrounds breeding behaviour. As well, there is an important element of female choice to the moose mating ritual, and in the end a cow may not mate with the winner of a contest but instead with another bull, perhaps the one she was consorting with in the first place, as long as he is up to it, so to speak.

All the behaviours that take place during this exciting time are geared to but one thing: the passing on of genes to the next generation. This leads one to wonder how successful a bull moose may be in his quest to spread his seed as far and wide as possible. In forest environments this is virtually impossible to determine. In the open ground of Denali National Park, however, van Ballenberghe and his team have been able to make detailed studies. In these studies the researchers capitalized on one advantage: the animals there often aggregate. Researchers concluded that dominant males may mate up to twenty-five times in a season, mating three times a day, if they associate with large groups. However, in the studies there were only a few bulls that could hold a group for a week or so and they did indeed get to mate with most of the cows. The most frequent action that researchers observed was a bull that covered three different females in eight hours. This is in stark contrast to the red deer of Europe, which may hold a harem for many days and will mate repeatedly. Detailed studies of farmed red deer in New Zealand have shown that a single stag in a paddock may breed up to ninety or a hundred hinds in three weeks; in one extreme case a stag successfully fertilized 140 hinds in a month. That is an average of just under five a day. One could say that he almost became a life-support system for an erection.

However, not all red deer require antlers to mate. There is the very unusual situation in this species that only seems to have been reported from Scotland. Naturally antlerless red deer (known as hummels) can hold a harem if they have the chops to dominate encounters with antlered stags through a combination of sheer physical size and aggression. Entirely artificial hummels are regularly created on farms and in zoos and research centres, where males that have had their antlers removed for management reasons breed without trouble. Of course these human-controlled environments are artificial, not only because of the lack of headgear but also because the parks' managers will have chosen which females go into a pen or paddock with which male.

Lack of antlers and mating behaviour leads to the question: what happens when a deer's antlers are misshapen, unbalanced, or otherwise abnormal? And this topic needs a chapter unto itself.

CHAPTER FIFTEEN

WEIRD AND WONDERFUL

Effects of castration on antlers;
other abnormal structures.

Normal antler development is a truly remarkable phenomenon. If someone ever tried to list the seven wonders
of the animal world, this process and its outcome would
surely rank near the top. But the extraordinary cycle of
normal antler development pales beside some of the
things that can occur when antlers go off-kilter due to
castration, injury to antlers, or harm done to other parts
of a deer's body.

I have frequently been asked about the effects of castration on male deer. This operation almost always causes
endless problems for the rest of the deer's life. The queries
are of two types: Can I castrate my tame deer? And what
can I do to deal with the weird antlers that my castrated
deer has grown?

The first question usually comes from someone who
wants a pet deer that will not become aggressive during
rutting season, and it is easy to deal with: "If you castrate
him he will grow abnormal antlers for the rest of his life
unless you can get it done when he is quite young and
has not developed his pedicles." This is because castration
removes the cells that manufacture testosterone, and as

I described in chapter thirteen, this is the hormone that drives the antler cycle.

If I am answering the second question and the deer has already been castrated, and it was done after the first few months of his life, he will already be heading for or already will have problems and my answer is different. The kinds of problems that will crop up depend on the time of year the deer was castrated, but only insofar as the timing of the downstream events. If he was castrated when his antlers were hard, the antlers will have fallen off within seven to twenty-one days. If the knife was applied during the resting phase, when there is no growth, antler growth will start at the normal time. If cut when he was in velvet, the velvet will never harden.

From that fateful day on, a castrated deer's antlers never develop properly and may take on some weird shapes, although the effects of castration on antlers vary with the species. The antlers remain particularly sensitive to injury, break easily, and bleed at the slightest provocation. Depending upon the species of deer involved, the affected antlers have been called a variety of names: freaks, perukes, cactus, or, more prosaically, velveted antlers. These terms reflect both the time and place in which they were coined: perukes (from the French *perruque*), for example, were the wigs worn by men in the seventeenth and eighteenth centuries that still are worn by British barristers during court appearances.

I heard one of the most apt names for these antlers when I was working on a project on the Hawaiian island of Molokai in the early 1990s. I had been asked to go there to help remove certain species from a wildlife reserve and leave the main species, the axis deer that originated in India and Southeast Asia, alone. These beautiful deer, with their pale creamy-rust coats and white spots, were considered sacrosanct—and later a major source of meat—by the islanders because eight of them had been sent as a gift to King Kamehameha V in January 1868. The king put them under royal protection. I could not interfere with them.

A normal axis buck has antlers with simple architecture; they grow

Vince Crichton Sr. holding a set of perukes or
coral antlers of a castrated moose.

fairly straight and have only a couple of branches. In castrates, the simplicity is lost and the velvet becomes dimpled. The locals call them coral antlers, because they nicely match the look of the multi-branched staghorn coral that can be seen when snorkelling over the reefs.

There are a few photos of perukes in moose that have been tamed (more on this in Chapter Twenty-Five) and castrated, but one family has the probable distinction of having collected more actual antlers than any other: Vince Crichton and his father, Big Vince, who was also a biologist and was the Fish and Wildlife supervisor in Chapleau, northern Ontario. During his time in Chapleau, Big Vince was given a set that had been collected many years earlier from a bull shot in 1908 near the community of Biscotasing, south of where Little Vince was raised. The Cree man who shot the moose wanted nothing to do with it and called it *weetogo*, meaning devil. Vince vividly recalls certain Saturday mornings, when he would accompany his father to his office, where the antlers were mounted on the wall. He went to help his dad package and seal each set of furs taken by individual trappers so that each set was uniquely trussed up, little knowing that such activities would kick-start his own career in the wildlife field, a career that has spanned over forty years. Little Vince (he is not so little now) recalls being asked by the Aborigines, especially the elderly ladies—who called the perukes on the wall "devil moose antlers"—to "hurry up little Vince, do not like those." The Aborigines would not touch or go near the antlers.

Later, Vince Jr. was given a different set of perukes by the local Cree community, who were convinced that it was from an animal crossed between a moose and a wapiti.

Of course castration can occur under a surgeon's knife or through other human intervention, but it has been known to occur accidentally in nature, even to only one of the testicles (hemi-castration). Two confounding reports from Victorian authors describe how a sika deer stag and a fallow deer buck, each of whom lost only one testicle, grew abnormal antlers on one side. The problem here is that the results were different. One deformity was ipsilateral (on the same side), the other on the opposite side.

While castration impedes hormonal influence, thus affecting antler growth for the duration of a deer's life, injuries to growing antlers can also cause lifelong deformities, major and minor. One thing I have seen a few times in wapiti is the after-effects of trauma, such as a blow or an insect infestation, on one side of a deer's developing antlers. The shape may change, extra tines may appear near the healed site, and the balance may be quite out of whack. This is not madly surprising.

One of my clients, a major white-tailed deer farmer near Saskatoon, had a champion buck that had a fifteen-centimetre-long, downward-pointing, abnormal tine that grew one year after some sort of insect got at a slight scrape in the velvet and must have laid an egg there. The tine emerged beside the pea-sized indentation in the main beam of the antler and hardened up in the fall along with the rest of the antlers.

What is surprising is that the extra tine or other result of an injury may persist over several subsequent years, possibly gradually reverting to match the "normal" side over time. My deer farmer client and I would show the several sets of cast antlers that grew in the next five years to students, whom I took to the farm for work experience, and we would challenge them to explain what they saw.

Of course, an explanation for what happened with that deer, and any other deer with injured antlers, is not easy to come up with. Damaged antlers and subsequent deformities are one of the big puzzles that remains about antlers and their development. The memory of a trauma is not retained by the antler itself, which is "here today and gone tomorrow." The "scar" therefore has to reside in some other part of the body.

In the last fifty years or so some very sophisticated work on antler development has taken place in several laboratories around the world, most recently in New Zealand. No one has been able to explain how this "trophic memory" of antler structure is retained from year to year. George Bubenik, Tony's son, who was himself a leading antler researcher before he retired, has suggested that an antler structure or centre lies in the brain, but no one has been able to prove his idea. The New Zealanders' view differs from George's, and they suggest that the memory is held at the top of the pedicle stump in the specialized stem cells that are the source for the next set of antlers.

Injuries beyond bumps, bruises, and insect bites create even more puzzles for antler scientists, causing oddities that seem to verge on the realm of science fiction. One of these is the effect of accidental amputation, fracture, or other severe injury to a leg. If this happens to a deer's hind leg, then the antler on the opposite side may never develop properly. Injury to a front leg, however, may lead to abnormal antler development on the same side.

My only personal experience with such an amputation occurred in a wapiti that had a septic claw on one of his hind feet. The only medical remedy was to amputate the claw, a procedure that I had carried out for exactly the same reason in numerous cattle during my practice days in Kenya. I did the surgery in the autumn, when the antlers were no longer in their growth phase. The bull lived for several years and developed normal antlers every time. This surgical injury was well down on the leg, and I deduced that perhaps the harm was not great enough to affect antler growth.

Not all asymmetry in antler form is caused by injury, of course. In the first place, the two sides of a moose's antlers are unlikely to be symmetrical. It is only if they are markedly different that we use the term "abnormal." Other deer that do not normally have symmetrical antlers are caribou and reindeer—which have distinctive antler shape—in the North, in the South, and on males and females alike.

Antlers of male reindeer and caribou have a unique feature in that most of them have a large branch that comes down over the forehead and face and flattens from side to side. This is called the brow tine or shovel. In the northern hemisphere, where these animals occur naturally, the shovel occurs on the left about twice as often as on the right. Reindeer have been moved to the southern hemisphere on a couple of occasions and have established themselves on the islands of South Georgia and Kerguelen. In these populations the dominant brow tine is on the right about twice as often as it is on the left. This more or-less exact reversal can only be due to geophysical forces, which is almost certainly more verifiable than the bathtub draining business that may be more urban myth than fact.

Reindeer also differ from all other deer in that females normally grow antlers. However the appearance of antlers on all other female deer (which can occur) is not normal but has occasionally been seen in moose. Some of these animals can be fully functioning cows, producing calves and rearing them. The reasons for female antler development vary and are sometimes the subject of guesswork, but most often these female antlers grow directly from the skull, without the benefit of pedicles. As an injury to those specialized islands of cells on the skull, which male and female deer both possess, can cause spontaneous antler growth, injury may well be the cause of these anomalies in fertile female deer.

Mammals with anomalies of sexual organ development may have features of both sexes, and often appear to be female on the outside

Moose will allow a very close approach if not alarmed by engines or talking. This picture, taken by the author, was obtained with a fifty mm lens at about fifteen metres. It has not been enlarged. (JERRY HAIGH)

Miles Smeeton grooming Pollux, summer 1977. (JERRY HAIGH)

The 1770 painting by English artist George Stubbs of the moose sent to the Second Duke of Richmond in England by Guy Carleton, Governor General of Canada. The animal had only his first set of antlers, and those at bottom left were included to show what a mature set would look like. (© THE HUNTERIAN, UNIVERSITY OF GLASGOW 2011)

Part of Mutual of Omaha's Wild Kingdom *crew involved in the* Where Men Walk With Moose *production. From left, Cliff Thompson, Ernie Jurgens, Bob Stewart, Marlin Perkins, Jerry Haigh.*

Tony Bubenik's picture of an encounter between a bull moose and the head and antlers of a dead bull lying in the snow. (In possession of the author.) (TONY BUBENIK)

A close encounter. Tony Bubenik's painting of a black bear attempting to take down a moose calf. (COURTESY GEORGE BUBENIK)

September 6, 2008. A bull moose in Riding Mountain National Park starts to shed his velvet. (VINCE CRICHTON)

Down to the river for a swim. Calves at the Kostroma Moose Farm.
(ALEXANDER MINAEV)

Tatiana Minaev with a cow and newborn calf at the Kostroma Moose Farm. (ALEXANDER MINAEV)

December 1983, Summit Lake, near Prince George, B.C. When two mature bull moose of nearly equal social rank come together, they may test their fitness and breeding rights by making intimidating gestures or by sparring and antler contact. In some instances, antlers lock together and both combatants die. (KENNETH N. CHILD)

An example of moose hair tufting on velvet. No dye has been used and the brown and white are simply trimmed from different parts of the hair. The "stem" of the flowers is braided hair. (TRUDY JANSSENS, PHOTOGRPAHY ONE2ONE)

Alexander Minaev and Luchik. (ALEXANDER MINAEV)

Early morning run at the Kostroma Moose Farm. (ALEXANDER MINAEV)

but have internal testicle-like organs that, in deer, explain the antler development. Called intersexes, these animals are unlikely to breed.

Then there are some real oddballs. One of my clients sent me a photo of a young wapiti whose spike antlers had grown straight up normally for about ten centimetres and then seemed to have forgotten what they were about. The tops simply drooped straight down like wilted flower stems, but there was no break in the skin. This was before the days of Viagra jokes; however, at the time I did imagine that the animal needed a medication of that sort, although I doubt the drug would have worked in this case. Wrong end of the animal. I was completely foxed, so I sent the photo on to Jimmy Suttie, another transplanted Scot who was leading the antler research team in New Zealand at the time. He, too, had no explanation, but, never short of a quip, he replied that maybe the stag wanted to move to the southern hemisphere and was showing the way by pointing down through the earth!

CHAPTER SIXTEEN

WHEN IS A MOOSE NOT A MOOSE?

Big, Biggar, biggest; Irish or not;
the greatest monument in Christendom.

Ninety kilometres almost due west of Saskatoon lies the small country town of Biggar, which is known for three things: bragging rights to being the birthplace of the late World and Olympic champion curler Sandra Schmirler, a quirky welcome sign that proclaims "New York Is Big but This Is Biggar," and local area farmer Milo Hansen's world-record white-tailed deer buck shot near the town in 1993. I have seen the last of these celebrated a number of times when passing through the town, where it is impossible not to notice the oversized statue of a leaping buck.

The antlers of Milo's buck, a true monster for the species, had a spread of almost sixty-nine centimetres. Of course, even Milo's buck's antlers cannot compare to those of the moose, which often reach one hundred and fifty centimetres. The biggest moose ever recorded had a spread of 207 centimetres. As the moose subspecies that come from Alaska and northern parts of Canada is one of the three tallest deer species to have ever lived, it would be reasonable to think that it also carries antlers to match. Not so.

If an antler spread of just over two metres in an Alaskan moose is big, then the four-metre spread of the antlers of a deer fossil in Europe is definitely "Biggar" (except with an "e"). This monster spread is recorded in my favourite book on deer, which, at forty by thirty-one centimetres it is also the biggest deer book in my collection. Published in 1897, it is called *British Deer and Their Horns* and was written and beautifully illustrated by J.G. Millais. Right in the first chapter Millais writes about several extinct British deer and includes both illustrations and photos of what he calls the Gigantic Irish Deer.

When I acquired this book fifteen years ago the page-four illustration of these deer took me back just over thirty years to a Glasgow Veterinary College trip to Dublin. The main activities of this jaunt had been both social and sporting and I had found myself playing rugby sevens, hockey, table tennis, and bridge, all of which required liquid refreshment, a need that my colleagues and I were able to satisfy with Guinness, either after the game or during it. A particular highlight of this trip occurred during the Friday evening dance, which was held in the anatomy room: an Irish student wheeled out the well-preserved and partially dissected teaching specimen of a horse. Only in a vet school among vet students who might have indulged in local brew!

One thing I did not do in Dublin, probably in part because I had no idea where my career would take me and mainly because of the social activities that took up most of our time, was visit the National Museum of Ireland's Natural History building. Had I done so I would have seen the remarkable skeletons of three huge deer and many more sets of antlers mounted on the walls. The museum continues to display two antlered males and a female, all just over 1.9 metres at the shoulder. Their stature reminds me of the Clydesdale draft horses that once plied the streets of Glasgow. I remember watching these majestic creatures pulling the flat-bed carts that were decorated with black and white checking and two little dogs, a Scottie and a West Highland White, the logo of Black and White whisky produced by Buchanan's, the firm for which my father worked after leaving the army. But the Irish museum's deer, with their majestic crowns of antlers, surpass even these massive, glorious horses.

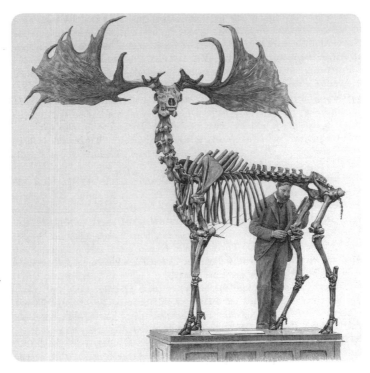

*"Complete skeleton of the Gigantic Irish Deer. From the specimen
in Sir Edmund Loder's museum at Leonardslee. The owner, a man
of 1.85 metres, is seen behind the figure of the animal, and gives the
reader some idea of the grand proportions of this great deer."*

FROM *BRITISH DEER AND THEIR HORNS*. JOHN GUILLE MILLAIS, 1897

The most striking things about those deer are indeed the huge
antlers on the males, far bigger than anything I have ever seen on
Scottish red deer, which also have hefty racks. Millais' illustrated antlers did not stretch four metres across, but they did stick out a good
1.5 metres on either side of their heads. This measurement, and where
their fossils were originally found, of course contributed to the name
given to the deer in the late nineteenth century: gigantic Irish deer.

This same name, also used in Millais' book, has undergone a couple
of changes since 1897. At some point it became the "giant Irish elk" and
now the name "giant deer" seems to be generally accepted, except by
the Irish, who naturally like to hang on to their own and call it the

"Great Head of the Gigantic Irish Deer Found at Tullamore, Ireland.
In the possession of the Duke of Westminster."
FROM *BRITISH DEER AND THEIR HORNS.* JOHN GUILLE MILLAIS, 1897

giant Irish deer. The removal of "Irish" by many scientists has much
to do with the fact that specimens of this deer have been found far
and wide throughout Europe and into Russia, and so the Irish cannot
really lay claim to it anymore. Stephen Jay Gould addressed the naming
problem when he opened an article with these amusing words: "The
Irish elk, the Holy Roman Empire, and the English horn form a strange
ensemble indeed. But they do share a common distinction—they have
completely inappropriate names. The Holy Roman Empire, Voltaire
tells us, was neither holy, nor Roman, nor an empire. The Irish elk was
neither exclusively Irish nor an elk." One would think that this really is
a case in which the taxonomic name for the giant Irish elk would be the
gold standard, but even that does not apply. Millais called it *Megaceros
hibernicus*, which was quite incorrect because the world of taxonomy is
properly concerned with precedent and long before he used this name
others had dubbed it *Megaloceros giganteus.* Of course the *hibernicus*
tag, used by a very influential figure of the time, one Sir Richard Owen,
brought "ownership" of the creature back to Ireland as Hibernia was
the Roman name for the island, which they knew but never conquered.

There is no record of a date when the first set of giant deer antlers was discovered, but it is not difficult to imagine that they were occasionally found by men and women who set out from their homes to cut peat as fuel. This is because the fossils were found just beneath the peat in the so-called shell-marl clay layer that is made of pulverized limestone.

An early record of the perceived value of such antlers lies in the fact that sets were sent to three English monarchs: William III, Charles II, and Elizabeth I. The first known illustration was made in 1588 and has survived. It is now kept in that same National Museum of Ireland, where Nigel Monaghan is keeper of the Natural History Division. The illustration carries the following caption.

> About the year of our Lord God 1588 there was found by certain labourers (by occasion of the making of a ditch about some new enclosure) near unto a great bog within the county of Meath in Ireland the head of a Deer of this form and quantity here described, blemished in diverse parts by the breaking off of sundry tines (as herein appeareth) before it was conceived what the same might be, for that the same was overgrown with the said bog — wherein it had lain beyond the memory of man: whereby and by reason of the hugeness thereof it could not be taken up whole. Nevertheless the broken parts being conjoined to the main and fastened thereto with plates of iron: The head carrieth the form therein expressed.
>
> The head is to be seen in the house of the Right Noble Adam Loftus Lo. Chancellor of Ireland, called, Rathfarnham about 4 miles distant from the city of Dublin and is fastened to the screen of the hall there.

In an email to me Monaghan wrote that Loftus was one of the most important men in Ireland, being not only Archbishop of Dublin, but also the Queen's Money Man—basically the top civil servant in Queen Elizabeth's administration in Ireland. Loftus had a remarkable notion of the value of these antlers when he wrote to the Queen's Secretary of State, calling them "the greatest monument in Christendom."

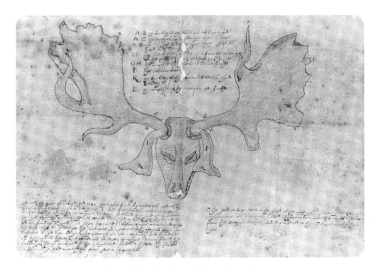

*The 1588 sketch of the antlers found
by a labourer in Meath county, Ireland.*

COURTESY NIGEL MONAGHAN

The one missing piece in the historical puzzle is the name of the artist. Was it Loftus himself or a member of what was almost certainly a large body of staff? Of course the missing parts of the antler are also intriguing. Nigel Monaghan explained that to me as well.

These specimens are typically buried in layers that differ from the skull up to the antler tips. The upper portions of antlers are often in peat, which has a fluctuating water table. This acid environment with fluctuating water levels is not as good for preservation as sand of lime clays that typically house the lower portions of antler. It is not unusual, therefore, to have a line above which tines or parts of antler palm are very delicate and break off or disintegrate completely during excavation. The text refers to repairs made in iron.

As I read his email I could not help imagining the scene in an age when the bulk of book learning and art lay with the church.

It might have gone like this: Finbar O'Malley, out cutting peat for the family hearth as winter approaches, gets a surprise. His slane (a special peat spade) hits something hard as he drives it into the sod. A couple more prods and a thing that looks like bone begins to emerge. He digs frantically. Lifting up the skull, he shoulders it, antlers panning down on either side of his back, and walks back to the cottage he shares with his wife, Brigid, and their five small children.

"Would you look at this now?" he says to her (in the Gaelic of course, which I can't do).

"What would that be?" says she. "Some sort of devil is it?"

"No, surely not," replies her husband. "Remember I told you that Carrig MacLiam found one like it, but with one side missing, last year, and told the factor of it? I think I'll take this one to the big house to see what he makes of it."

It took over a hundred years from that 1588 find before the news filtered through to the scientific community. In 1697 an Irish doctor (later a baronet) named Thomas Molyneux, who lived from 1661 to 1733, wrote an essay with the gob-stopping title of "A Discourse concerning the Large Horns frequently found under Ground in Ireland, Concluding from them that the great American Deer, call'd a Moose, was formerly common in that Island: With Remarks on some other things Natural to that Country." The name of the journal in which the article was published—*Philosophical Transactions of the Royal Society of London*—shows nicely where science fit in 1697. Molyneux was what was then called "philosophically" minded, of a scientific bent.

In both the Irish specimen and the real moose the antlers look like huge multi-fingered hands, so one can see how a relationship between the two might have been concocted. But there was also almost certainly a religious reason for Molyneux to link it to the moose, which he had never seen, but which he would have heard of in the accounts of travellers returned from North America. As Monaghan told me: "Before the discovery of dinosaurs giant deer were classic fossils involved in debates regarding extinction and the effects of Noah's flood. Molyneux's original article had as its central thesis the assumption that the giant deer of Ireland were the same species of deer as the American moose and the fossils became known as the "Irish elk." His limited knowledge of moose allowed him to satisfy his religious conviction that none of God's creatures could become extinct."

Molyneux's idea, however, did not stand the test of time and science. As Millais stated exactly two hundred years later: "Today, however, hundreds of the heads and a few good skeletons are in existence to prove how erroneous his conclusion was."

Almost two hundred years after Molyneux's report to the Royal Society, a prominent Dublin naturalist and giant deer enthusiast named W. Williams employed a man to search for specimens under the peat bogs where they lay preserved in the shell-marl layer. Of all the jobs related to deer none can surely be more unusual than that of this unnamed Irishman whose technique was to use a long (almost twenty-metre) iron pole to probe through the peat into the shell-marl. Apparently he was so good at his job that he could not only pick out likely spots to search, but could also then tell, simply by feel and sound, whether he had hit stone, wood, or pieces of the deer for which he was searching.

As a result of these and many other searches there are hundreds of heads now stored in a variety of museums and private collections. Most have come from Ireland, but this is not because the deer was limited to that island so much as there was widespread deposition of the limestone marl (an excellent bone preserver) in Irish lakes at just the right time, and the peat bogs that developed above them covered the skulls and a few complete skeletons. Other forms of rock and soil are far less kind to archaeological specimens, and in other regions only parts of the deer's skeletons have been found, as opposed to the full sets. The first complete skeleton was found on the Isle of Man, between England and Ireland. The Scottish Duke of Atholl presented this to the Edinburgh museum, and there is another specimen in the Manx Museum in Douglas, the capital of the Isle of Man.

From complete specimens retrieved by Williams's talented hired man and others it is certain that this species of giant deer was one of the two largest deer ever to exist in the British Isles, although most authorities agree that its body was probably not as heavy as the largest

Showing mode of finding the heads, their position,
and the strata in which they are generally embedded.

FROM *BRITISH DEER AND THEIR HORNS.* JOHN GUILLE MILLAIS, 1897

of our modern North American moose, the aptly named *Alces alces gigas,* which may weigh almost eight hundred kilograms.

However there is no doubt that the giant deer stag carried enormous antlers. They would dwarf even the largest set of moose antlers. Most of the specimens on record are about three metres in spread, and one remarkable head spans an enormous 4.26 metres. Some of these antler pairs, now long dry, weigh as much as forty-five kilograms and most are over thirty-two kilograms. Neither of the specimens illustrated by Millais were more than 2.85 metres across so a 4.26-metre specimen would have been quite a sight.

If we assume that, like modern deer, the giant deer annually cast their antlers and redeveloped them to full size from nothing in the space of about one hundred days, then they must have grown at quite a rate. One can almost imagine sitting and watching them sprout up and out.

Considering the weight that had to be carried, it is hardly surprising that the giant deer's neck vertebrae were exceedingly well developed. At the onset of the rut, modern deer from temperate zones morph into massive carriers of fertile sperm and their neck muscles enlarge to such an extent that the circumference of the neck more or less doubles. The increase in size serves well to carry the huge extra weight of the antlers, but just as important, it changes their physical stature and ability to show off both to would-be rivals and females around them. If show and tell does not work to establish dominance in the mating stakes the heavy muscles enable them to effectively use the antlers as weapons.

Like those of moose, the palms of giant deer antlers would have caught and reflected sunlight, sending signals across great expanses of territory, a sort of ultimate version of me showing my grandchildren how Tinker Bell dances on the wall as the light reflects off my watch glass.

The huge spread of the antlers makes it more or less certain that these giant males in hard antler could not have lived in dense forests, although females might have done. If you had two-metre masses sticking out on both sides of your head a dense forest might slow you down as you tried to escape from predators. However females might have spent part of their year in forested areas. In many modern deer the males and females spend large parts of the year in separate locations, only coming together at rutting time. The evidence from pollen samples indicates that this deer was not purely a grazing animal either, but more of a cafeteria feeder, relying on browse species from open woodlands and high-quality grasses and shrubs when available. In this regard it differed from the moose, which is a highly specialized feeder and needs woody plants. So, despite its palmate antlers, the deer's closest parallels are Canada's wapiti and Eurasia's red deer.

Apart from moose there is another species of deer alive today that has the same palm-shaped antler construction. This is the European fallow deer, and recent DNA work has suggests that the gigantic Irish deer, giant Irish elk, giant deer, or whatever takes your fancy, is, according to Julia Sigwart of Queen's University Belfast, basically a great big fallow deer. It all depends upon your point of view. Professor Adrian Lister, a leading paleobiologist from University College London, has even suggested that instead of calling the giant deer a giant fallow deer, as some people did in the nineteenth century, we might consider the modern fallow deer as a diminutive form of what is now known as the giant deer. Of course the change of name and losing the "Irish" may be scientifically accurate, but it is not very romantic. If you are of Irish descent, or reading this on St. Patrick's Day while quaffing a green beer, you might agree.

Whatever you call it, people today who like to adorn their walls with trophies would go bananas for something that big over the fireplace. Biggar's Milo Hansen parlayed his white-tailed deer trophy into what amounted to a second career, with tons of spin-offs for hunting guides in Saskatchewan. Imagine what he, or anyone else, could do with a specimen of the giant deer, assuming he could prove he shot it. Of course the bragging rights of the landed gentry in Europe from the time of Queen Elizabeth I and onwards up to at least Victorian times did not require evidence of the hunt. Imagine a set in the billiard room, or even in what some of those great homes had, a trophy room. A conversation piece, for sure. Then there are other uses. Giant deer antlers have also been used as gateposts to the homes of Irish gentry and as temporary bridges to span rivulets.

Today's avid collector would no doubt mount a set above the mantle shelf, as long as the room was at least four metres wide.

There was some debate among Victorian-era naturalists about whether this deer co-existed with humans, or had become extinct by the time that they came on the scene. We now know that people and the giant deer did occupy the world at the same time: they certainly existed at the same time as many of the other huge mammals that inhabited the globe between the last two glaciations, having first appeared on the scene about 400,000 years ago.

So why did this creature become extinct? From Molyneux's time on, quite a variety of authors have speculated about the demise of the giant deer. He himself suggested "an epidemick distemper" caused by "a certain ill constitution of air." In answer to that same question, others came up with "some overwhelming deluge," "Celtic tribes," and "the slaughters of the Roman public games." Equally strange are suggestions that the antlers cause the animals to become "mired in ponds," "tangled in trees" and "sterilized." Weirdest of all was the suggestion in 1830 by one J. Hart, quoted by Gould in the paper about the inappropriate names: *Megaloceros* died of "epilepsy or apoplexy" when the copious blood supply that nourished the growing antlers "rushed in upon the brain when the velvet was shed."

There are several more modern notions related to the giant deer's extinction. At one time it was thought that the onset of the last ice age and the increasingly cold conditions caused the deer to run out of food. The most recent studies by several people, including Professor Adrian Lister and his colleagues, have shown that the deer survived at least three millennia longer than previously believed.

In fact, the youngest specimen known from all the modern radiocarbon dating techniques died out about eight thousand years ago, well after the ice age had come to an end. By this time its range had contracted to the Ural Mountains that divide Europe and Russia.

In an important article in the prestigious journal *Nature*, Lister's team reported that the animal's smorgasbord-type diet, with its mixture of "of grass–shrub vegetation and open woodland with larch, spruce, pine, and birch trees" would have existed on the eastern slopes of the Urals, but not in surrounding areas. Subsequently the spread of closed forest in the mountains would have excluded the deer and likely pushed them out onto the plains, where the diet was much less suitable.

They further speculated "it is possible that while *Megaloceros* survived in the Ural foothills it was relatively safe from human predation, but when forced onto the plain by vegetational changes, it became critically vulnerable to increased hunting pressure." In a *National Geographic* article about that report and the observed changes in the landscape, Lister was quoted as saying, "In combination with human pressures, this could have finally snuffed them out."

Lister made one other telling point. By this period in human history nomadic herding was by no means the only way of life, and farming for crop production had spread widely from its roots in the Middle East. Did competition for resources and crop raiding by huge deer lead to the same results we see in Africa today, where farmers cannot tolerate elephant, buffalo, and warthogs decimating their annual food supply? Were these crop predators exterminated by snares, pit traps, arrows, and spears just as they are today in gunless cultures? Split bones, stone tools, and in one case a stone axe buried in a skull seem to indicate that in some areas at least early humans exploited this animal when they could.

The next time you go to Europe, and particularly to Ireland, it would be well worthwhile to visit one of the many museums in which skeletons of this magnificent animal are displayed. A first choice might be the ones in Dublin, where the two fully set-up males and one female are on display and entrance is free. On my next visit there I will make up for my deficiency of forty-odd years ago and visit Nigel Monaghan as well as the deer.

CHAPTER SEVENTEEN

MOOSE ACROSS WATER

Trips to New Zealand for me
and for moose.

It wasn't quite like the Dali painting of semi-liquid pocket watches draped over a branch, a box and an unidentifiable object, but waking up on a bed of straw, as hay dropped from the mouth of a thoroughbred horse above me, was a pretty surreal experience. I was with Jo on our first trip to New Zealand, and we were at thirty-something thousand feet above the Pacific Ocean in the back of a DC8 stretch that had no passenger seats. When we did sit, it was on old bench seats rescued from some car-wrecker's yard. Even though we could slide the bench around at the back of the plane, we were required to wear safety belts. On this air-borne ark of animals—which carried pigs; three breeds of cattle; thoroughbred, standard-bred, and miniature horses, as well as others—I was in charge of a shipment of elk (the North American variety) from our home in Saskatchewan to New Zealand's South Island. It was the second-ever shipment of wapiti to New Zealand, the first having been in 1908 when President Roosevelt sent some as a gift. Those had gone to the Fiordland region in the southwest. My charges were going to Tim (later Sir Tim)

Wallis, to be farmed near the town of Wanaka with its majestic view of the Southern Alps.

Little did I know that this would by no means be my last trip to that fabled country. I would later attend conferences and carry out research in artificial breeding of red deer and wapiti in New Zealand. In fact, only one year after delivering the elk from that DC8, in February 1983, I was back again, this time to attend the first ever international conference that was exclusively about deer. As Chris Challies, a biologist with New Zealand's forestry division, got into his talk about the history of deer in New Zealand, I could not stop myself from leaning forward and studying the maps he projected onto the screen. According to him the so-called Acclimatization Societies of the late nineteenth and early twentieth centuries had decided that deer would enhance the New Zealand landscape and make things seem more like home to European settlers. Challies's map showed that seven species had been imported from various countries between 1861 and 1905. But in 1910, marked almost as a footnote, the word "moose" lay alongside a tiny dark-blue square located in the bottom left-hand corner of the map of the South Island.

Challies was talking mostly about red deer, but he made a quick reference to the moose as he moved the tip of his long wooden pointer across the map. "The moose came from Saskatchewan, in Canada," he said, mangling the name of my home province, just as so many people do.

We chatted during one of the coffee breaks, but Chris did not have much more to offer about the moose, and there were so many like-minded people to meet or meet again that I almost forgot about his presentation and our conversation. Almost, but not quite.

A month later I was back home—still grateful for the break from winter and the trout fishing that I had piggybacked onto the trip—dealing with the animals at the zoo and the bitter winter wind and short days.

As soon as I got the chance I tried to dig up more about those New Zealand moose, but in those pre-Internet days this and other similar research attempts were often not fruitful. Enquiries at the head office of the Department of Renewable Resources drew a blank, and the Provincial Archives propelled me no further in my quest.

I gave up for a while as other projects captured my attention, but every now and again my mental Rolodex would flip to "M," with the catchwords "Moose" and "New Zealand" coming together like two pieces in an unfinished puzzle. Somebody, I forget who, suggested I contact the Hudson's Bay Company, which had so much to do with commerce and settlement at the turn of the nineteenth century, and archivist Judith Hudson Beattie got me on the right track. It seems as if the very first moose to reach New Zealand did not travel in 1910, but ten years earlier.

The first shipment, right at the century's end, took place after negotiations at the highest political level. The premier of New Zealand, the Honourable Richard John Seddon (popularly known as "King Dick" Seddon) and Sir Wilfred Laurier, Canada's prime minister, exchanged letters. Subsequently the Hudson's Bay Company sent Chief Factor Archibald Macdonald to New Zealand along with what are variously reported as fourteen moose, or thirteen moose and one elk (which died before shipment). They were gathered at various points on the Manitoba and Northwestern Railway, and transferred to Canadian Pacific at Portage La Prairie, which lies at the southern end of Lake Winnipeg, on December 23, 1899. The only Saskatchewan connection was that the train passed thought the province on its way to Vancouver. In early January 1900, the SS *Aorangi* sailed with the animals on board. Most of the unfortunate moose died in a storm soon after leaving Vancouver, but the remaining four, two bulls and two nine-month-old heifers, arrived in Wellington on February 8 and were later released in the Hokitika Valley on the west coast of New Zealand's South Island. By 1903 only a cow remained, and over the next eleven years she was occasionally seen wandering alone in a local settlement.

In 1907 a Mr. Thomas Donne of the New Zealand Tourist Board tried again to import moose to New Zealand. The trail becomes a little murky here. Donne's own account states that the animals came from

Saskatchewan, and he even cites correspondence between himself and the provincial Lieutenant-Governor of the day, the Honourable A.E. Forget. However, Mr. Forget turned the correspondence over to Mr. Howard Douglas, who was the commissioner of Dominion Parks. This time the animals were rounded up in Alberta and never even travelled through Saskatchewan.

Records from a local newspaper, the *Fort Saskatchewan Reporter*, show clearly that the moose calves were captured by a number of different people and held for hand-raising. A Mr. Webb of Belmont, Alberta, delivered the first of them to the community of Good Hope, Alberta, on June 3, and others came periodically thereafter. A Dr. Archer and a Mr. R.J. Torrie captured one each somewhere in northern Alberta and these were delivered on June 24.

On August 5, 1909, the herd of moose, now seventeen strong, was moved from Good Hope into what is now Elk Island National Park, where Superintendent El Simmons and his wife took over their care. Seven milk cows were required to keep them supplied, and they were fed with brush and saplings. One report states that they were "thriving well in their partial captivity." This almost certainly means that they were allowed to forage during the day. As is the case in many other instances of moose-raising in both Europe and North America, the Simmons family found that the moose became quite tame and could be handled much the same as pet lambs.

The animals were then sent to Banff. The *Edmonton Daily Bulletin* of November 2, 1909, reported that the animals had been corralled, principally by Mr. Ed Carey of Lamont Park, and that there would be a probable shipment of fifteen moose to what was then called Rocky Mountain Park on the next day, a Wednesday. On the other hand, the *Fort Saskatchewan Reporter* said that only nine moose were moved. The Department of the Interior report states that ten moose were secured and sent to Banff. The official report from government and two different newspaper correspondents managed to disagree on the critical matter of numbers. It seems that some things never change.

At the time there was a small zoo in Banff, and it is possible that some extra moose did travel there but did not go on to New Zealand. There is a record of two moose from that zoo being exchanged for a polar bear in 1912. The zoo reached its zenith in 1914, when it housed fifty mammals and thirty-six birds. In 1937 it was closed down and the polar bear went on to the Calgary Zoo.

Fred Moorhouse, inspector of the New Zealand Tourist Department, was sent to the park to receive the moose. The animals were loaded at Banff on December 29, 1909, together with about a ton of baled willow brush, and railed out. Ten crates had been made in Vancouver and the animals were placed on board the ship on January 1, 1910. They travelled via Sydney, where they were transferred to another vessel and shipped to Wellington. Finally, they were taken to the southern part of the South Island and released in Fiordland National Park, in a very inhospitable area where annual rainfall is about 7,600 millimetres. Richard Henry, a conservationist who lived in the park, questioned the choice of this park for release of both these moose and the earlier wapiti shipment. He described it as "a place where it rained three hundred days a year and where sandflies went about in mobs of 30 million and ate everything that the mosquitoes overlooked." Makes me cringe just to think about it, and I have worked in Canada's North, where, it is said, the mosquito is the national bird and if the insects were only to organize themselves they could carry you away. Up in northern Canada horseflies are called bullfrogs, and it is a brave man who spends time out of doors in the summer without the covering of a bug jacket. Shorts are not advisable.

Only three moose trophy heads were ever acquired in the New Zealand release area. Numbers were estimated to have reached a peak of sixty to seventy animals by the mid-1920s, but declined to between thirty and forty by the late 1940s. The last confirmed shooting of a bull was in 1952, when a Mr. Percy Lyes shot one with a 1.2-metre spread in Wet Jacket Arm (even the name makes me feel soggy). Considering that the terrain is mainly steep-sided valleys, and that the browse species would be quite different than what moose are used to "at home," it is hardly surprising that the animals never thrived.

Nonetheless, there are a few dedicated individuals who are convinced that a small remnant population of moose exists today. Ray Tinsley, in his 1983 book *Call of the Moose*, gives an entertaining account of moose hunting in Fiordland and reports numerous sightings of footprints in the late 1970s and early '80s.

My trail went almost dead for several years after I found the above facts and put them together for a magazine article, but then, when I started looking at the story again, I realized that I had missed out on one critical person. Ken Tustin is a New Zealand biologist with a Canadian connection. He did his post-graduate studies at the University of British Columbia and then returned to his native country, where he held a variety of jobs in his field, including one flying helicopters with Tim Wallis. All the while Ken retained his fascination with the Fiordland moose story. His forty-year addiction has almost become a New Zealand version of the search for the Loch Ness Monster or Canada's Sasquatch, but with better results. He took his search to new high-tech levels and spent many days and weeks camped in the soaking valleys of New Zealand's southwest. Ken has written two entertaining books about his addiction: in 1998 *A Wild Moose Chase,* and then in 2010 *A (Nearly) Complete History of the Moose in New Zealand.* In reading his accounts and considering all the time he spent in the rainforest, I sometimes wonder how he did not come to sprout those plate-like fungi that one sees on the trunks of old growth trees.

Most New Zealanders are downright sceptical or simply dismiss Ken's several bits of evidence, but there are enough threads in his research to establish, in my mind, that a remnant population of moose has hung on until the early twenty-first century.

There are several pieces of circumstantial evidence that point to the existence of a small moose population on the South Island. There are far more sightings and successful hunts that is generally recognized. Popular accounts have it that only five moose were ever shot. Ken has tracked down credible evidence that the actual number was twenty-five.

Ken and others have repeatedly seen both the distinctive boat-like footprints of his quarry and places where branches and leaves have been cropped at heights above the ground that would be well beyond the reach of any red deer, even one reaching up on its hind legs. Only a moose would be able to reach that high in those forests.

Most convincing are the findings by others hunting for red deer in the region near the original moose release site of two different tufts of hair that have been confirmed, in a Canadian laboratory, to carry moose DNA. As DNA would deteriorate in a matter of months in that area's climate, there is no chance that these hairs are relics from the past. Still, sceptics have suggested that the tufts were planted.

The pièce de resistance in the gathered evidence is a photograph of a cow that Ken managed to get with one of his early remote-sensor cameras (he really is dedicated and determined in his efforts). The image, which he has shared with me, is blurred, and the head is obscured by vegetation, but the creature cannot be anything other than a moose, or at a long stretch, a dark horse in a place where horses could not survive on their own. Naysayers in New Zealand have not been convinced and call it a red deer or a wapiti. To anyone familiar with both species, this is simply nonsense. Ken has more modern cameras in place but has not yet obtained another undisputable photo.

The saga of the New Zealand moose took a new twist when in early 2011 businessman Graeme Popplewell, the CEO of Hallenstein Brothers, a well-known Auckland clothing retailer, put up a prize of NZD$100,000 (about CD$75,000 at the time) for the first incontrovertible proof of the Giant Swamp Donkeys' (as he called them) continued existence in Fiordland. The project is called "Where's Bullwinkle? 'Proof of Life' reward for New Zealand moose."

In an entertaining interview on April 13, 2011, with the Canadian Broadcasting Corporation's morning program, Popplewell apologized for the nickname but explained that the prize had created quite a buzz on the company's website. "It's going nuts. It's just going crazy," he said in the Skype session with host Heather Hiscox. At the Hallenstein website one can see a fascinating interview with Ken Tustin as he explains the history behind the story.

Unfortunately, I have a feeling that even if Ken were to get a clear picture of a bull moose in full antler, in an obviously New Zealand setting, there would still be sceptics who would suggest that he had taken an advanced Photoshop course. If Ken were to return once more to Fiordland with a bishop or two, a high-court judge, a camera crew, and a couple of North American moose biologists (dare I suggest a wildlife vet?) as witnesses and then find a moose, he might, only might, win over the naysayers. He would certainly deserve the $100,000!

CHAPTER EIGHTEEN

TRANSLOCATIONS SHORT AND LONG

People moving moose;
international, national, local.

The shipment from Alberta to New Zealand will likely continue to hold the record of longest journey for moose, but shipments to New Zealand do not hold the record of "only translocation of moose." Other shipments have also been international—across oceans or very large bodies of water—national, and even local. Some have been more successful than others.

A common reason for species translocations world-wide over the last hundred years is local extinction, or extirpation. In the mid-1980s, for example, an attempt was made to bring the moose back to Michigan's Upper Peninsula. The story caught my imagination immediately when I heard about it at the annual gathering of zoo and wildlife vets in East Lansing. Dr. Steve Schmitt, a lanky, quiet-spoken wildlife veterinarian with the Michigan Department of Natural Resources, was presenting a slide-show about the peninsula's moose. As he performed his show-and-tell presentation about the project, a photo of a moose in a sling under a helicopter grabbed my attention. It brought me back to the days when I was weighing moose in the Saskatchewan River Delta.

As in other regions, moose had all but disappeared from Michigan by the late 1800s, and even the protection afforded by the government in 1889 did not result in species recovery. An attempt was made to reintroduce animals in the mid-1930s, when sixty-three head were brought in, but they did not thrive. Then in 1985, after what were no doubt interesting negotiations, the international translocation project started. Dr. Schmitt was in charge of the project and carried out the immobilizations that took place in Ontario's Algonquin Provincial Park. The captured animals were moved in slings up to twenty kilometres in the park to a holding area, where researchers put them into individual crates. From there they travelled by truck a thousand kilometres to Michigan's Upper Peninsula, skirting, rather than crossing, the large body of water that is Lake Huron. There were two translocations: twenty-nine animals in 1985 and thirty more two years later. By 2010 the numbers of moose in the region had only risen to 433, indicating a surprisingly slow rate of increase. Schmitt attributes some of the early sluggishness to diseases carried by white-tailed deer, of which more I write more in the next chapter.

While Dr. Schmitt's translocation project avoided a journey across a large body of water, another recent and successful translocation risked a water crossing. Moose once existed in Russia's far northeastern Kamchatka Peninsula, which on the map hangs like a huge lozenge about to drop on top of Japan, but by the 1970s the animals had not been seen for four hundred years. The translocations happened in two stages: the first in 1977–1978, the second in 2004–2005 from the Penzhina River area a thousand kilometres to the north. A total of eighty-nine calves and young adults were immobilized, crated, and moved by helicopter, skirting the Sea of Okhotsk—a journey that took from six to nine hours. These moose fared better than the ones in Michigan; by 2008 an estimated two thousand head existed in the region.

One of several translocation programs ongoing for several years, with mixed results, has occurred in the state of Utah, where *shirasi* moose were not recorded until the very early part of the twentieth century. After that first recorded sighting, in 1906 or 1907 (there seems to be some debate among state officials), a few more animals migrated to Utah from neighbouring states (Idaho and Wyoming). By the late 1940s there was a small resident herd. Of fifteen translocation attempts between 1973 and 1995, only two were deemed a success and only eighteen head were involved. Then in 2005 the first of five successful shipments totalling over one hundred animals came in from Colorado. Meanwhile the small resident herd had been engaged in basic Biology 101 without any help from humans. As a result, the state's moose population began a steady rise in the early 1970s, despite the letting of limited hunting permits beginning in 1958. The latest moose population estimates for the state exceed 3,100.

Back in Canada, two other translocations to islands have taken place: one in-country, one international.

By the late 1800s moose numbers had been severely depleted in the province of Nova Scotia and they had been extirpated in Cape Breton Island years earlier. After failed attempts in 1928 and 1929 to translocate moose across the narrow channel that divides the island from the mainland, Parks Canada officials reintroduced eighteen head from Elk Island National Park, Alberta, to Cape Breton Highlands National Park, in 1948 and 1949. This meant that the *A. a. andersoni* sub-species made a leap of almost four thousand kilometres. They still thrive there in high densities—especially as they have no wolves to deal with—and they cause concern to park managers because their overbrowsing damages the forest. Currently, there are thought to be about five thousand head in the region. But this number is nothing compared to the results of another Maritime translocation.

I knew little about what surely ranks as the most successful moose translocation ever until Jo and I visited Newfoundland in the summer of 2009, she to attend a medical conference, me to get some fishing done. The project took place before Newfoundland joined Canada in 1949, so it ranks as an international exercise.

I knew there were moose on the island, but I had not really concentrated on their history or thought much about them. That changed rapidly and in unexpected ways. As we settled into our bed and breakfast room in St. John's, somewhat jetlagged and exhausted from the long flights and hanging about in airports, I turned on the television and found myself watching a Canadian Geographic film called *The Moose: Canada's Most Dangerous Animal*. It was all about moose and their history on the island, as well as the real risk they pose for drivers. Reminders about moose's presence did not end when the credits rolled, however, as one of the main things the clerk who arranged our hired car told us next morning was "Please be careful on the highways as moose are a major cause of traffic accidents and the rut is coming up. They get a bit daft at this time of year."

There were no moose on The Rock, as Newfoundland has long been known, until two were brought from nearby Nova Scotia in 1878 and released at Gander Bay on the northeast coast. There seems to be no further news of these two, but in 1904 two bulls and two heifers were captured in New Brunswick and shipped across the Gulf of St. Lawrence to a release site near Howley, about twenty kilometres from what would become, seventy years later, Gros Morne National Park.

The story of how and why the animals went to Newfoundland contrasts sharply with the New Zealand saga. The account mostly comes from the recollections of John Nowlan, who was raised by the nephew of the leader of the team that caught the moose. It begins when the Newfoundland government of the day, still a British colonial government, requested some moose. One John Connell, a well-known hunter, hunting guide, and fisherman in the Miramichi area of New Brunswick, who was also well known for his tame saddle-broken moose Tommy, persuaded some friends to get involved in the capture. John thought that the men who were involved were paid $50 for each moose. "That was a lot of money in those days!"

The team set out on snowshoes in the winter of 1904 and surrounded a group of moose that were yarded up and more or less stranded in the deep snow in the vicinity of the Bartibogue River. According to Nowlan, "Then they lassoed them—just like cattle." Six captured moose were tethered to sleds and taken to the town of Chatham, where they were put on a train. Surprisingly four of the animals survived the trip all the way to their new home across the water.

The wolves on the island had by then been extirpated and so the moose had no predators. They must have thought they were in a sort of paradise. By 1920 good numbers were spotted over eighty kilometres from their release site, and by 1935 they were known over much of the island. In about 1941 they crossed the narrow isthmus east of Conception Bay and entered the Avalon Peninsula. By 1972 there were thought to be at least 40,000 head, and current figures put the number at something between 120,000 and 150,000: two moose for every square kilometre of forest on the island. Anything above two per square kilometre is considered a management issue.

Of course it is not that simple. Since 1945 moose have become the major resource for hunters in Newfoundland, and since then an estimated half million have been shot, except, naturally, in national parks. It is there that the populations have increased to such an extent that they have altered the makeup of the forest as their numbers have increased more or less unchecked.

In beautiful Gros Morne National Park there has been no hunting since 1973, when the park was established. With nothing except bears—which prey upon calves and adults but do not seem to affect moose population statistics—to stop them, the number of moose has exploded. In 2009 there were around 5,000 of them in the park, and we, like almost anyone we talked to, saw several as we drove up the west coast.

In an email on January 10, 2012, Tom Knight, an ecosystem scientist with Parks Canada, wrote that:

In Gros Morne National Park we have approximately 5,000 moose— roughly five to six moose per km² in our lowland forests. The intense browsing by moose at these high densities has had considerable impact on our native forests. The most visible impacts are in areas where the canopy has been disturbed by insect outbreaks. Moose browsing has essentially halted forest regeneration in many of these disturbed areas, converting them to open grassland landscapes with many non-native "weed" species. Even in areas where the canopy remains intact, understory plant species diversity is declining and plant species preferred by moose are now hard to find in our forests.

Some areas of Gros Morne have what amount to herds of about nineteen moose per square kilometre. According the Parks Canada website, "In 1977, the most important sources of browse for moose in Gros Morne National Park of Canada were Canada yew, mountain maple, balsam fir, white birch, and chuckley pear. Between 1977 and 1996, the availability of Canada yew, mountain maple, white birch, and chuckley pear within Gros Morne National Park decreased from 14.6 per cent to 2.2 per cent."

The moose are obviously not daft and seem to have concentrated where they are safe. The availability of vegetation outside the park appears to be unchanged in the same time period. If there is one iconic tree species that could be the flagship for what has happened, it is the balsam fir. In areas where moose abound, these trees never grow above one metre, unless they are fenced into small areas called "exclosures."

As I sat with park wardens at the Gros Morne Park headquarters in September 2009, I mentioned the possibility of trying to bring balance back to the park by allowing a controlled hunt each year. It turned out that the idea had been talked about, but of course the subject is fraught with all sorts of politics, never mind bureaucracy. Finally, after what must have been some lengthy and complicated discussions, it was announced in the spring of 2011 that a cull of moose in Gros Morne and Terra Nova national parks would take place in the 2011/2012 hunting season. The program was run jointly by Parks Canada and the Wildlife Division of the Government of Newfoundland and Labrador, and qualified resident hunters were invited to participate. Tom Knight told me that of the 500 licenses on offer, 382 were issued, but no results are yet available.

Of course, as I learned when watching the Canadian Geographic film that day in St. John's, Newfoundland, moose are not only affecting the balance of nature in Gros Morne Park. Nowhere in North America do moose create such a road hazard as they do in Newfoundland.

CHAPTER NINETEEN

MOOSE AND TRAFFIC

*Road hazards; rail hazards;
fencing; speed limits.*

Wherever moose have access to roads, they cause carnage. They are a major driving hazard, and in Canada the island of Newfoundland has the sad distinction of leading the field in moose traffic accidents. In a typical year, there are between thirty and forty moose-related accidents on the roads in Gros Morne National Park, and across the island there are between seven and eight hundred collisions every year. On Monday, August 9, 2010, the Canadian Broadcasting Corporation carried a story of six moose/vehicle accidents in a single day! A further twist to these numbers occurred early in 2011, when victims of moose collisions launched a lawsuit against the government of Newfoundland and Labrador.

Traffic accidents with moose are often serious because of three factors. Not only are moose very large objects for a driver to hit, but also their long legs often allow unfortunate cars or small trucks to shoot under the belly or hit the legs, which leads to the massive body being catapulted onto or even through the windshield. Finally, moose's very dark colouring makes the animal an extra hazard at night, and although the moose's eyes do gleam in headlights, they are so high up that a driver may not see them.

While motor vehicle collisions with moose occur right across North America, from Newfoundland and New England to Alaska, it is in Sweden that the problem may be worst of all. At one time moose were the second most frequent cause of accidents, exceeded only by impaired driving. Viewed another way, police reports of moose killed in traffic accidents in 1999 accounted for some 6 per cent of the country's annual minimum of 100,000 hunter-harvested animals each year. That is at least six thousand dead moose!

As if that was not enough, Mats Lindquist, who is a master of mechanical engineering and has a Ph.D. in surgery from the University of Umeå, is also heavily involved with a non-profit organization devoted to moose damage control, wrote to tell me of some changes in the reporting system for accidents. It is now compulsory for drivers to report any kind of moose/vehicle collision, even ones as trivial as those involving damage to a wing mirror. After having told me this, Lindquist said, "In 2010 there were 7,227 police-reported collisions with moose in Sweden, which is the highest number in over 30 years, an increase of 77 per cent since 2005." That is almost twenty accidents a day.

In neighbouring Finland, some five thousand vehicle/ungulate— including deer and moose—accidents occur each year, and almost all of the ones in which humans are injured or killed are caused by moose. In the 2000s there were an average of 240 human injuries and eight deaths per year related to moose/vehicle collisions.

When Jo and I travelled in Sweden in the early 1990s we were struck by the hundreds of kilometres of both main and country roads that were lined on both sides with fences that stretched up over two metres. In 1999 there were some three thousand kilometres of moose-fenced highways, and by 2010 that number had doubled. As Lindquist told me, "usually all new constructed highways are equipped with fences."

Both Swedish and Finnish studies have tried to show how effective proper fencing can be in reducing accidents. The answers are not as clear-cut or encouraging as one might hope. In a 1999 EU report, the Swedish National Road Association was quoted as stating that fencing of roads with fences over two metres in height has reduced moose movement across roads by 80 per cent. However, the report goes on to say that if the fences cut through important migration routes the moose may jump the fences, and when that happens the risk of accidents rises sharply. This is presumably because the fence-jumping moose are then trapped in what amounts to a tunnel, each vehicle coming through acting like a figure in a violent action video game, with the moose as the next obstacle. One dissenting opinion stated in the report was that accidents on fenced sections exceeded those on unfenced ones.

Milla Niemi and her colleagues at the Finnish Department of Forest Sciences at the University of Helsinki have analyzed the effects of fencing on moose/vehicle collisions. There are now about a thousand kilometres of road in that country that have been double-fenced, and in one short section of twenty-six kilometres (fenced in 1998) the collision rate declined by 61 per cent from thirty-eight in the three years preceding the construction to fifteen in the next three years. Those figures sound impressive, but they do not alter Niemi's main conclusion, which, as she wrote to me, "was that fencing of highways can alter the distribution of vehicle/ungulate collisions. The amount of collisions declined in the main highway, but at the same time the number of collisions on the parallel road increased. In other words: the total amount of collisions was almost the same before and after fencing!"

Of course, fencing highways creates a need for wildlife corridors, either underpasses or bridges, because the animals will seek to move from one location to another, both to search for food and to satisfy normal behavioural needs for new territory. In some regions both types of corridors are built when new highway construction occurs, which enormously increases the cost of road building. The highway fences in Sweden cost the equivalent of CD$19 (1999) per linear metre, but this figure is dwarfed by the cost of bridges at almost CD$2,000 per square metre. If the 1999 figure was CD$19, then surely the 2011 figure would be above $30.

In another one of several email exchanges, Mats Lindquist told me of another interesting factor about moose and roads:

One interesting circumstance regarding the Swedish moose population is that they have different ways of living. In the south the moose are quite sedentary, and could be living their whole life in quite a small area. In the north, though, the moose have a strong seasonal migration where they move toward the coast during winter and the other way during summer. This means that there is a larger need for passes in the north. The most common way of doing this is just to have approximately 500 metres of opening in the fence. The drivers are warned and the speed limit is reduced in these openings.

The use of intermittent crossing corridors has been taken a step further in North America. In October 2011 a Canadian-invented electronic system involving the use of two infrared beams mounted in pairs, one above the other, was tested in Newfoundland. When an animal the size of a moose breaks both beams at once, blinking signs at either end of gaps in the fence notify drivers, "Moose on Highway When Lights Are Flashing." Smaller animals, like rabbits or foxes, would only break the lower beam and no signal would be sent. In addition to the infrared devices, so-called electro-mats placed in the tarmac on either side of the corridors discourage moose from straying up or down into fenced sections and keep them within the crossing. The combined system has already been used in several other areas after successful 2007 trials in Arizona reduced elk/traffic accidents to almost zero.

Fencing has also been deployed in Nova Scotia, where moose/vehicle collisions are reported to have caused five hundred injuries and twenty deaths between 1995 and 2000. However, despite the figures, the Newfoundland government is reported to adamantly refuse to institute this type of fencing.

Recent efforts at reducing the carnage for both moose and people have been the clearing of all vegetation back from the verges for as much as twenty metres, further extension of the fencing program, and the posting of ever more road signs depicting the hazards. Another element has been that Swedish car manufacturers have carried out research to see what they can do with car design to reduced human injury.

The Newfoundland moose hazard road sign makes
the likely outcome of a collision quite clear.
JANE MINGAY

Part of the problem, as most highway signs imply and some government agencies try to enforce with limits, is that people drive too fast in high-density moose areas. In an elegant 2006 study from Ontario it was shown that at night, when the greatest risk of accidents is present, drivers going faster than seventy kilometres per hour are "likely to be overdriving the illuminating capacity of their headlamps for moose encounters." When I forwarded these figures to Lindquist he added a further perceptive insight and suggested that the most dangerous condition occurs when two cars are approaching one another at night, with headlights dimmed. Visibility, he suggested, is so much reduced that the speed limit ought to be fifty kilometres per hour.

In Saskatchewan, one interesting component of the road-hazard issue has been the steady southward extension of moose range. The face of prairie farmland has changed steadily, even since we came to Saskatoon in 1975, and there are many more small patches of bush, mostly trembling aspen, scattered across the land. Although I was familiar enough with warning signs about white-tailed deer posted along the main north–south artery of Highway 11 near our home, I was astonished in 2009 to suddenly see not a leaping deer but a striding moose.

I have seen very similar signs wherever moose are present. The bright yellow signs usually carry a simple black picture of a moose. In Newfoundland the signs are more graphic: the designers pull no punches. These show a cartoon version of a collision between an animal and car, with the car hood and windshield looking very much the worse for wear. They at once reminded me of a brief but pithy road sign we had seen in New Zealand's South Island on our last trip. Right next to the speed-limit sign at the edge of the small village of Waihola, south of Dunedin, a sign read, "No Doctor, No Hospital, One Cemetery." Point taken. Slow down.

Statistics about traffic accidents in Saskatchewan that involve moose are not available from any government agency in the province, but we do have figures for all wildlife encounters and some anecdotal moose information.

For the twenty years leading up to 2009 there was an average of over 6,000 collisions a year, with a peak of 12,624 in 2008. The vast majority of these accidents were collisions with deer, and most of them only involved property damage. However, almost two hundred people were injured every year in ungulate/vehicle accidents, and in the worst years some of them died.

Darryl Chamakese, who had helped me with the origins of the word "moose," was raised on the Pelican Lake First Nation in central Saskatchewan, and he recalls a time from his youth when he and his family were very lucky:

> I remember telling my mother once about an incident I remembered as a child. It was a bright sunny day and my mother, brother, and I were driving down an old road back home. The trees were a bright green, the sky was blue, and the sun was shining brilliantly. We were rounding a corner and all I could see was black. Our red truck came to a complete stop. I used to stand on the seats of the truck, as it was not mandatory at

that time to have child-restraint seats. I remember my mother pushing me down to the foot area. I looked up and saw a huge moose crashing through our front window. And then, like that, he or she was gone.

Around three years ago I asked my mother about this and her eyes widened. *"E-kiskisiyan ci anima?"* (Do you remember that time?) she asked. "You were only two years old when that happened!" It happened when I was two years old, but to me it could have happened yesterday because it is one of my most vivid memories. I marvel at how the moose crashed our truck and still managed to run away as if nothing happened.

A much more tragic collision story came to me via our lawyer in one of those six degrees of separation incidents. The lawyer's son-in-law, Jeremy Markwat, was the first person on the scene near Tisdale when he was following members of his hockey team, the Tisdale Ramblers, home from a game in the town of Hudson Bay. It was late at night, just after midnight, when he saw the truck in front swerve and then head for the ditch. Naturally he stopped to see what had happened, at which point he saw a truck and trailer overturned on the other side of the road.

He managed to get a message through on 911, despite the weak and intermittent signal on his cell phone. Later, as those on the scene reconstructed the accident, it turned out that his friends had struck a moose with a glancing blow. The impact had driven them into the path of the oncoming truck, which had been hauling a load of cattle. Two of his teammates died and the entire load of cattle had to be destroyed.

Train collisions with moose are a bit different than those with motor vehicles. Trains do not normally travel at high speeds, but there are times when moose get trapped on the tracks in deep cuttings through the mountains and cannot get away. Worse yet are those times when snow makes the situation even more hazardous for the animals as they cannot even escape to the side. I have also come across occasional reports of encounters when rutting bulls, which have no doubt lost any sense of scale and safety under the influence of all that testosterone, think they can take on all comers, including trains. The result is inevitable.

An example of this comes from Norway, where some 1,500 to 2,000 moose are killed in traffic each year, with 30 per cent of moose fatalities happening after encounters with train. That is at least five hundred train-related deaths a year.

These rather depressing statistics about the accidental deaths of moose come from virtually all parts of the world where humans and moose meet. In Germany's Bavaria, where a few moose have entered from the Czech Republic, most have been killed in traffic accidents. I am not sure quite how many kilometres of autobahn there are in the region, but, having driven there a bit, I know that even with no legal restrictions the recommended speed limit is 130 kilometres per hour. Even when I was driving that speed, Porsche and Mercedes cars, and even a Ferrari that flew by in a blur, have overtaken me. Imagine hitting a moose on the autobahn at two hundred-plus kilometres per hour!

CHAPTER TWENTY

MOOSE AND DISEASE

"To talk of diseases is a sort of Arabian Nights *entertainment."*
— *Sir William Osler, 1905*

(Don't worry. This chapter won't take 1,001 nights to relate, just 2,889 words.)

Canadian Sir William Osler has been described as one of the three great physicians of all time, alongside Hippocrates and Galen. He is memorialized all over the Western world, and a street in Saskatoon is named for him. He was also instrumental in founding and naming the Faculty of Comparative Medicine and Veterinary Science at McGill University in 1889. Scheherazade, the legendary Persian queen and *Arabian Nights* storyteller, used partly told stories to captivate her king and avoid execution each night. I will not use such a strategy because I have no intention of relating the intricacies of every disease that has ever been described in moose. That would be boring and more or less useless in a textbook, never mind here.

There are five important diseases that periodically flare up and have had effects upon moose populations over time. These conditions have had, and continue to have, profound effects, at least in local areas.

One disease that would have undoubtedly intrigued

White-tailed deer in the woods. Potential bad news for moose
when the right sort of snails or slugs are also present.
JERRY HAIGH

Osler, because even as a small boy he had a fascination with nature, came to moose via the white-tailed deer. The whitetail, or something much like it, has lived in North America for about three million years and in that time has learned to live with an important parasite that kills moose, caribou, and many other ungulates. This is the so-called brain or meningeal worm whose life cycle begins in deer and involves a sojourn in a terrestrial snail or slug. The adult worms live in and on the nervous tissues and meninges that coat the brain, and they lay their eggs in the associated blood vessels. The eggs travel in the blood to the lungs, where they hatch to larvae, which are coughed up, swallowed, and passed in the feces. From the ground they get into one of a few species of small gastropod (snail, slug), which are then eaten by deer as they cling to vegetation. In the deer's stomach the larvae leave the gastropod and enter the blood circulation, moving to the spinal cord then migrating along the nervous tissue to the brain, where the cycle begins anew. This neat sequence of events allows the parasite to maintain itself, a crucial function for any living thing.

During feeding, a moose can also accidentally eat infected gastropods, and herein lies the rub. Moose have only been in North America for a tiny fraction of the time that whitetails have lived on the continent. They have not yet adapted to the parasite, and when it gets into their nervous system and moves about it can and does kill them as it migrates through their spinal cords and brains, obliterating the nervous tissue. Affected moose often lose their fear of people, move in irregular circles, and may go blind. As the disease progresses the victim becomes disorientated, collapses, and dies. I have twice watched video footage of a cow moose in the terminal stages as she staggered about, fell down, and desperately tried to regain her feet. It was a grim session, and I could not watch all the way through the second time.

Another way to view this situation is that the whitetail's ability to withstand this parasite represents an efficient form of biological warfare for the whitetail, allowing the deer to thrive and spread while gradually wiping out a newcomer and competitor.

The most dramatic example of the effects of the brain worm comes from eastern Canada. Before settlement and the opening up of Nova Scotia's forests, woodland caribou ranged across the land. As forests turned into farmland the white-tailed deer moved north and east from Maine and New Brunswick, bringing the worm with them. Caribou, which are acutely sensitive to the parasite, are no longer found in Nova Scotia. No moose hunting has been permitted since 1981, and Nova Scotia mainland moose were declared an endangered species in 2003, with only about a thousand left.

There are several other areas where local declines in moose populations are at least in part due to the incursion of infected deer. In Manitoba virtually every deer from the Winnipeg River to the Ontario boundary carries the meningeal worm, and moose numbers are in decline. Similar links have been established in areas like Michigan's Upper Peninsula, Northern Minnesota, and much of New England.

There is a strange and partly unexplained phenomenon associated with this disease. For some reason, the Manitoba–Saskatchewan border almost acts as a glass plate that prevents the worm from being commonly found in the latter. In a survey of 1902 white-tailed deer heads in the two provinces and their southern neighbour of South Dakota, just under 0.2 per cent were positive in Saskatchewan (one of 565 heads, and that was a single male worm, which hardly poses a mass breeding threat) while in Manitoba there was marked variation, with the highest rate, approaching 100 per cent, in the east and in isolated more western areas almost up to the Saskatchewan border. In North Dakota the overall rate was 8.5 per cent but again, the highest numbers were in the east. Despite plenty of searching, only seven cases in moose and one in a wapiti have been found to the west of this invisible line since 2007, all in eastern Saskatchewan close to the border. Geographically there is no difference between the forest, farmland, and swamps on either side of the border, which is after all the result of the work of some bureaucrats a hundred or so years ago and only a line on a map. Signs on the roads tell you when you are in one province or the other, but neither deer nor snails can read. At least part of the explanation is related to weather and rainfall, which both influence snail habitat.

With changing climate and farming practices, whitetails have moved into new ranges, often farther north where moose have been relatively safe, and most scientists in this field are concerned about the potential spread of this parasite.

Another parasite with links to the white-tailed deer is the giant liver fluke, so called because the adults that are found in a host's liver are about five centimetres long. Once again, this parasite has gastropods as intermediate hosts, but in this case the snails live in water and the deer or moose ingest them when they eat the immature flukes that have encysted on aquatic vegetation. Once inside the host, the flukes migrate to the liver where, in white-tailed deer, they are soon surrounded by a cyst and do not break out. However, in the moose the flukes continue to wander, like the Flying Dutchman, and can do terrible damage. As their function is compromised, moose's livers react by getting bigger, which of course gives the flukes even more tissue to invade. Researchers have seen livers weighing up to ten kilograms—double the normal. In northwestern Minnesota fluke infection is considered to be perhaps the most common cause of moose deaths. One possible mechanism for this outcome is that the damage to the liver causes a loss of condition and that this loss, allied with the other stresses, may tip the balance between life and death. It is highly unlikely that fluke infestation alone is responsible for so many moose deaths; the brain worm may also play a role. A November 2010 summary concluded that "concurrent significant parasitic infection is highly prevalent in Minnesota's moose population and affects all age groups." A major research program aiming to find out more about the cause of the deaths is underway in the state as this book goes to press.

Along with brain worms and liver flukes, another moose parasite may be taking advantage of climate change. This is the winter tick that I encountered on the very first moose I ever worked on and which, as I mentioned in Chapter Four, the famous naturalist and author Ernest Thomson Seton characterized as the major moose enemy over a hundred years ago. The life cycle of the tick is superbly adapted to bitter Canadian winters. In fall it grabs on to any passing moose and stays there throughout the cold months, nicely tucked in under the insulating hairs and sucking the odd meal of blood when it needs to. In spring adult females, now full of their host's blood, fall off and lay thousands of eggs before dying. The males, no longer of any consequence to the survival of their species, drop and die. The eggs go into suspended animation for the summer then hatch into tiny pinhead-sized larvae that climb up the vegetation, form small clumps, and wave their legs about waiting to grab on to whatever passes by. Theirs are not chance gatherings as the clumps tend to form at the body core height of large mammals, such as moose and wapiti. The very idea of these clumps has potential as a horror movie scene. All you would need to film the scene would be a powerful magnifying lens, say a thousand times, and you would have a writhing mass of what would look like several hundred one-metre-long, six-legged, brown horrors trying to grab you as you walked past a bush (the larvae only have three pairs of walking legs). Take it to 5,000x and you might imagine a new version of John Wyndham's famous 1951 *The Day of the Triffids*, or perhaps Demi Moore could reprise her role in the 1982 horror film *Parasite*.

The major killers for the larvae are desiccation, cold and snow, and exhaustion from waving those legs around and not finding a host. We do not known how cold it has to be, or for how long, to kill the tiny larvae in the autumn, but Bill Samuel of the University of Alberta and his team have shown that most adult females that drop from moose onto deep or crusted snow in late winter–early spring will perish before they can lay eggs. In a warming climate, with beautiful open Indian summers lasting into November and spring arriving early, the chances of the ticks completing their life cycle are much improved, and, of course, they may survive farther north than formerly. Neither situation is good for the moose. Reports from New Hampshire have recently indicated that 41 per cent of moose deaths in the state are caused by this one scourge. This is the same percentage of deaths as those caused by traffic accidents in the state. Scientists in Canada's Yukon and Northwest Territories are very concerned about this. Even the Alaskans are worried that the ticks may spread northward and westward.

Eurasian moose are not subject to any of these parasites from North America, but they do have their own disease problems to contend with. There is a relative of the brain worm that is widespread across the region, and although it is sometimes called the muscle worm it can and does enter the central nervous system. However, it is not seen as a major problem for moose.

Then there is the ked, which was purely a Eurasian parasite until someone introduced it to the northeastern United States on "European Deer" in the late 1800s. It has since been found on white-tailed deer but does not seem to have moved on to moose. Not yet anyway. I first learned about keds and their life cycle in veterinary school, but it was the sheep ked that worried local producers, and in 1965 there were millions of sheep in the Highlands, mainly Scottish blackface and North Country Cheviots. One of my final-year assignments as a veterinary student was to look at the history of treatment for a parasite that had been known for centuries. The first reference that I found to the ked was from Roman times, when a mixture of sulfur and urine had been used as a dip.

The ked's life cycle involves a larva or prepupa, falling off the host where it was born, turning into a pupa in typical insect fashion, and emerging as an adult in due course. The adult fly makes only one flight in its life, from the ground to a mammalian host, in this case moose, but also to other species. Once there it promptly sheds its wings as they are no longer of any use, and soon mates and begins its blood-sucking life. The female lays a series of larvae, one at a time, and the cycle continues.

Nobody knows how long the ked has been around, but a ked wing was found during the examination of the deer hide garments of Ötzi, the iceman found in the Alps in 1991. Ötzi lived and died—was probably murdered—about 5,300 years ago. One of the things that amused me at the time of his discovery was the furor over his "nationality." He was found in the glacier exactly 92.56 metres inside Italy. How far did the glacier move in five thousand years? Did he actually die in Austria? Was he an illegal immigrant? As if Austria or Italy existed that far back.

The deer ked affects moose and has spread from Russia into Norway, Sweden, and Finland, and it is known from other countries east of Fennoscandia, such as Belarus. In Finland moose numbers have recovered from near absence in the 1930s to the present population of something around the hundred thousand mark, and by 2007 the ked had moved almost a thousand kilometres north. How? The flying adults are attracted to large dark bodies, making the moose their ultimate host. Keds were passengers as the moose spread northward.

Keds create problems on two fronts. Up to 10,000 keds have been counted on a single moose, and they can cause severe irritation and hair loss that makes their host look just like the winter tick–stricken ghost moose that Bill Samuel described. They will also attack humans and make nasty red bite marks, causing severe irritation that may last for up to a year. When keds are on the move there are people in

Finland who will not venture into the bush. Worse yet is that they can carry bacteria of public health concern.

The current northern limit of moose and keds in Finland is right at the southern edge of the huge numbers of semi-domesticated reindeer on which the Saami people have relied for their livelihood for centuries. The potential of the parasite to jump to this new host causes concern on at least two fronts. First, if keds do jump ship they will affect productivity directly by causing hair loss that can lead to severe debility and a cascade effect, much as winter ticks do in North America. The cascade would mean fewer calves, poor quality carcasses, and high winter mortality, especially during harsh winters.

Second would be a direct effect upon a specialized retail market. When Jo and I visited Finland in the 1992 we saw how much reindeer are part of the fabric of life in the north. In the town of Rovaniemi, right on the Arctic Circle, we visited Santa's Workshop, which is simply a themed shopping centre. There were several stores offering beautiful reindeer hides for sale as rugs and so on. The ked bite marks would ruin the hides.

There is no way to predict which, if any, of a string of potential disease agents may cause a new problem for deer, or any other animal, but, as Osler realized, "It is appalling to contemplate the frightful train of miseries which a single diseased woman may entail, not alone on her associates, but on scores of the innocent." He was implying that whenever one sees a new case one can wonder about another outbreak. One dramatic example of such a plague occurred periodically from the mid-seventeenth to the mid-nineteenth centuries in the Baltic countries of Estonia, Lithuania, and Latvia when anthrax, otherwise known as the Siberian Plague, reared its ghastly head. This deadly disease affects any species of mammal and is thought to have wiped out most of the moose in the region, not to mention the domestic livestock. These scourges must have created terrible hardship for the people who would have been deprived of their two major sources of meat as well as milk. Even today desperate people will sometimes eat anthrax-riddled carcasses, as repeated reports in the online medical newsletter *Promed*, to which I subscribed for many years, attest several times a year.

In the mid 1990s Swedish scientists may have thought that they were dealing with another disease outbreak when they reported on what seemed to be a new disease that affected old moose cows in one area in the southern part of the country. Large numbers were found dead, much to the distress of moose managers and no doubt everyone else, and a full-scale search was started to see which infectious agent might be involved. In the end it was determined that this "disease" was simply an accumulated incidence of malnutrition caused by too many moose with not enough to eat. It is a thing vets are familiar enough with in many situations and can be called agroceriosis.

Traffic encounters and diseases will likely continue to be important, certainly at local levels, but they are by no means the major causes of changes in moose numbers across the globe. There are natural and human-induced elements that play much bigger roles and these are where I turn next.

CHAPTER TWENTY-ONE

YESTERYEAR AND TODAY

Past and present;
some things that affect moose.

In 2008 my name was lucky enough to be drawn in Saskatchewan's moose-hunting lottery for a chance to hunt in my old stomping grounds in the Saskatchewan River Delta, which I knew well, not only because of the many hours of being helicoptered over the area but also from several hunting and fishing trips.

When I arrived at the delta for my hunting trip, my first inkling that things had undergone big changes was at my first campsite on the shore of Culdesac Lake, where I once fished for pickerel. It was no longer a lake but a waving sea of two-metre-tall reed grass (*Phragmites australis*, an Australian invader) the colour of ripe wheat with what was little more than a stream coursing through it. For two days I paddled gently down the much-reduced Culdesac River, stopping at spots where I had formerly seen moose cross. I left the river edge and carefully picked my way among the willow and alder bushes to marshy areas that I knew to be favoured by moose. I did not find a single moose bed, nor did I see any moose tracks in the muddy riverbanks.

On the third night I shifted my camp twelve kilometres to another site near the now-abandoned Bainbridge

Lodge, which had once been the centre of our moose research program. From there I explored the Carrot River, paddling and drifting between the tall stands of mixed spruce, poplar, and Manitoba maple. Every now and again a beaver lodge jutted into the river and caused a back eddy where the current caught on the dead logs that made up the outer shell of the structure. As I paddled I often heard the sounds of geese overhead long before I could see them through the trees. It was a thrill to hear the honking and then see hundreds of Canada geese veeing their way south. Snow geese in their thousands, in less-organized skeins, babbled across the sky hour after hour in an almost continuous stream.

I did not see a single fresh print, let alone an actual moose, in three more days of hunting, but I was a bit limited by my inability to cover as much territory as I had in my thirties and forties or to portage my canoe into adjacent creeks that meander across the delta. This may have been because in the intervening years the canoe has somehow gained a considerable amount of weight.

In the camp by the Carrot River I ran into a group of four other hunters who had had just as much luck as I had. It turned out that I knew all four of them. One was Dave Brewster, a tall dark-haired man who had worked on the tagging project a couple of times in the early 1980s. All of them had just retired, or were about to retire, from what was once the province's Department of Natural Resources, but, in the true spirit of bureaucracy, has undergone several name changes and is now the Ministry of Environment. As Dave and the rest of us chatted over an evening beer in camp, we mused about the reasons for our failure.

The real outcome of the experience, however, was that it set me wondering about how moose were doing, not just locally, but worldwide. When I returned from my delta expedition, I chased down as many articles as I could and contacted biologists from all around the globe.

One of these, a man who has kept more than just a finger on the pulse of moose biology, is another reincarnation of the sixteenth century's Count Turbervile. Vince Crichton, whom I met at several of the moose conferences in the late 1970s and early 1980s, and who thirty-five years later is the senior moose biologist working in Canada today. With his tall frame and bushy white eyebrows he stands out in any crowd, and he certainly takes his day job with the province's wildlife branch way beyond the standard eight hours.

He and I have discussed the changing status of North America's tallest creature and shared our concerns. Moose in general are not on any endangered species list, although they are protected in some areas where their numbers are low, but like everything else around us, including ourselves, their numbers are subject to change. How could it be otherwise?

There are several intertwined factors that regulate the changing fortunes of moose populations everywhere. The major positive factor is that moose numbers multiply rapidly when times are good and food is plentiful. Once a cow reaches the age of three or four, she is more than likely to have twin calves. Sometimes she may have triplets—and rarely quadruplets—and raise them. She may continue this pattern for as many as eight to ten years. If half of her calves are female, the population will increase rapidly.

Another beneficial factor for moose comes from modern forestry practices. In the last one hundred years the advent of clear-cutting has had a positive effect upon moose numbers in many parts of the world: the young shoots that are the first things to grow in the cleared spaces are like candy to a baby for "Twig Eater."

Over the centuries climate change has affected moose population numbers in both upward and downward directions. My own experience on that nostalgic 2008 return to the delta was certainly affected by this phenomenon. Professor Norman D. Smith of the University of Nebraska, Lincoln, has worked in the area for a long time and tells me that the area has lost about 30 per cent of its marshes and lakes in the last fifty years. The reduced wetlands are likely to have adversely affected the quality of the environment for moose. Similar changes are occurring in Alaska where, under the influence of global warming, wetlands are drying up and fires are increasingly putting people and forests at risk; both of these certainly have the potential to adversely affect moose. At the same time, the animals are moving into tundra regions, so a net effect on moose has not yet been determined for the area.

I must note, however, that none of my other correspondents in North America or Eurasia noted any reduction in the area of wetlands in the face of warming climate. Indeed, in Latvia, wetlands have expanded under the influence of rising populations of European beavers.

On the negative side, wildlife predation has major effects on moose numbers, and there is plenty of evidence to prove that their absence makes a big difference when it comes to rapid population expansion. Such has been the case in Scandinavia where moose numbers have almost exploded since the late 1800s when very few of them were present.

Dr. Bengt Roken, who recently retired after almost forty years as the veterinarian at the Kolmarden zoo and who told me that the moose is his favourite animal, wrote that there are big changes afoot in Sweden at the moment. This is because a new hunting administration system will start on January 1, 2012.

> Land and forest owners and hunters shall on a regional level be responsible for the management of moose populations in order to minimize the damage on young pine forests. We anticipate that the new administration (which is dominated by land owners) will force hunters to decrease the winter populations to 50 per cent (equaling two to four moose per 1,000 hectares in winter). This is challenging because then moose hunting might have to cease completely in middle Sweden, where we now have an increasing wolf population (approximately forty groups, each killing around one hundred moose per year). Biologists calculate that with the present home range of wolf packs there must be a winter moose density of approximately ten animals per 1,000 hectares in order to allow both wolf predation and meaningful moose hunting. The wolf-moose-forestry issue is very much on today's agenda.

OF MOOSE AND MEN

*Despite being chased by twelve wolves, this moose on Isle Royale
escaped. It outran the wolves for a mile and then turned to defend
itself, which was easy after she wore the wolves out.*

ROLF PETERSON

In North America there have been several attempts to increase
ungulate numbers in order to make them "available" to hunters. This
was done by systematically reducing predator numbers through large-
scale culls. In both Alaska and Canada wolf control was widespread
and effective in the 1950s and 1960s. Game (not just moose) numbers
increased, and the regions became known as a hunter's paradise. It
was not until ten years after the end of wolf culling that game herds
began to decline in numbers.

The best long-term study of the relationship between moose and
wolves comes from Isle Royale, the seventy-two-by-fifteen-kilometre
island in Lake Superior, which has not been hunted in living memory.
In this setting, with no brain worm or liver fluke present, moose have
lived in a topsy-turvy balance with their only predator, the wolf, and
the data tell the tale. Moose numbers have fluctuated from as low as
four hundred to as high as 2,200 in fifty years. As wolf numbers have
declined, moose numbers have risen, and vice versa; in the early 1980s

those peak moose figures followed an outbreak of death and disease in the wolves.

Of course, the correlation of moose to wolf numbers is complicated by other factors, such as weather and parasites. After years of steady increases, the brutal winter weather of 1995–1996 and two years of heavy tick infestation caused the moose population to crash. Snow depth can also be added to the mix. The less snow there is, the more readily moose can deal with attacks and the harder the wolves have to work to find a meal.

The other major non-human predators are bears. In Alaska grizzly bears may take 80 per cent of the calves born in the short space of a few weeks. One can almost imagine them slobbering with excitement and checking their smartphone calendars to see when June 1 will roll around and the new calf crop will hit the ground. Farther east, black bears pick up the mantle, and in the 1990s they played a major part in preventing moose population recoveries in my old stomping grounds of the Saskatchewan River Delta. From the other side of North America, in the Canadian Geographic movie that I first watched in my hotel room in St. John's, Newfoundland, comes remarkable footage of a black bear chasing and only just failing to grab an adult moose. In another clip in that film I saw evidence that black bears can and do kill adult moose. In Eurasia the brown bear takes over.

To get an exact number for the world's population of moose would be impossible, but by adding the numbers from each of the jurisdictions where I was able to get figures and where moose exist, I arrived at a global population of something over 2,250,000 animals, more or less evenly divided between Eurasia and North America. The limitation of this estimate is that some of the figures are from 2010 census figures while others date back seven or eight years. Of course each of these counts, with a couple of obvious exceptions, is a "best guess." In 2005, when I learned that there were only thirty-two animals in the Czech Republic, confined to one small park, I knew I could be pretty certain of my facts for that country. Even if that figure has doubled in the intervening years, the overall global number was not going to change by any meaningful amount.

As I collected the information from all my sources I was struck with the variety of ways in which population numbers were collected and the spread of dates involved. Some best guesses were based upon the number of piles of feces in a given area, or density of tracks in the snow; others on actual head counts, but even with head counts, exact aerial counts over large areas of dense forest are impossible. It is important to realize that these numbers are just estimates and at best may vary by as much as 20 per cent in either direction.

With the exception of four jurisdictions in North America and troubled areas in Russia, China, and Mongolia, moose numbers are stable or rising. I could find no information on Belarus and Kazakhstan.

The four problem areas in North America are Minnesota and its bordering provinces of Manitoba and the most western parts of Ontario, and a localized area around Jackson Hole in Wyoming. (Managers in other areas, such as northern British Columbia, have also expressed concern.) The declines in moose populations in the Canadian provinces adjacent to Minnesota are due to a combination of diseases and excessive and unregulated hunting.

In northwestern Minnesota where it marches with Manitoba, moose numbers have nose-dived. In 1984 there were four thousand of them. Now there are less than one hundred. Erika Butler, the Minnesota-state veterinarian with whom I exchanged several emails about this situation, tells me that the drop is linked to disease, mainly a combination of giant liver fluke and brain worm. Recent studies in the northeast of the state, in the Boundary Waters areas where I have canoed with my children and grandchildren, suggest that this population is also declining, albeit at a slower rate. Butler also told me that even in the northeast it is predicted that there may be no moose left by the year 2020. There are some in the region who think that the warming climate also plays a role by changing habitat and heat stressing the moose, but this is not a unanimous opinion. There is no denying, however, that climate change has affected moose, and all other forms of life, in the past.

YESTERYEAR AND TODAY

A rock art (petroglyph) depiction of a moose from the
World Heritage Site at Alta, in the far north of Norway.
The work has been dated between 4000 and 6000 BC.

NICHOLAS TYLER

Although moose (as *Alces*) have been around for about 400,000 years, it is possible to trace something of their distribution only over the last 15,000 years in central Europe. At that time there was a brief, two-thousand-year, warm, moist period when moose established themselves in the region. Then there was a cold snap, known as the Younger Dryas, which came on suddenly over a mere ten years and reduced things back to near-glacial levels. Naturally this had a profound influence on all life forms in the area as food resources changed and cold weather had a direct effect upon everything.

Then, about 11,000 years or so ago, at the start of the period known as the Holocene (which continues up to the present time), came a final retreat of the glaciers as the weather warmed up. At this time humans began to have major impacts on just about everything on Earth, including moose, which were among the first large mammals to recolonize central Europe. It was also at about this time that they entered North America.

In the early Holocene moose ranged from the Pyrenees to Denmark and from Great Britain to parts of central Europe, where they still exist today. As they moved north they disappeared in more southern regions, and by about the start of the Christian era only relic populations existed in western Central Europe, although the Romans knew of them, no doubt because their empire ranged well beyond the Italian peninsula into Gaul and Germany.

At this time moose became widely distributed throughout the northern Eurasian landmass. Dr. Nicholas Tyler, a transplanted Englishman who has made Norway his home and is a deer scientist from the University of Tromsø, tells me that about six thousand years ago moose were probably more abundant than reindeer in the extreme northern regions of Norway.

By about three hundred years ago the range across Eurasia began to contract greatly, and in many regions they disappeared altogether during the period known as the Little Ice Age. For many years there were about twenty totally isolated populations scattered from Scandinavia to the Bering Strait. Another example comes from Dr. Tyler. He wrote, "When a moose was shot near Kirkenes in 1915 it was considered an event so unusual that someone published an article about it in the Norwegian natural history journal *Naturen*. Moose were completely unknown here at that time. Now, of course, there's a regular annual hunt throughout Finnmark."

Since about a hundred years ago the ranges have again increased, and many of those isolated populations have expanded and coalesced except where high mountain ranges prevent migration.

The state of the forests in which moose live also affects how well they do. They need a supply of young shoots on which to browse and a plentiful supply of wetlands. When coniferous forests mature, the availability of young shoots dries up, but when fire takes out mature stands, young trees and shrubs get a chance to grow as sunlight reaches the struggling shoots. Within a few years, there is ample moose food. Fire is not the only factor that can effect this change on forests. The pine beetle infestation of the pine forests of British Columbia has destroyed many thousands of square kilometres. I witnessed a strip of the devastation when Jo and I drove across the province and saw vast areas of the landscape appearing rust-red in colour where dead trees stood, instead of the healthy dark green of conifers. It is expected that within a few years' time moose will benefit when a new crop of trees begins to grow. A human practice that mimics the ability of fire and infestation to level forests is clear-cutting. However, sometimes clear-cut forests are converted into farmland, and moose numbers decline.

Some opine that clear-cutting has had a positive effect on moose numbers in some forested areas; however, sometimes the practice has gone too far. In many cases re-growth and re-establishment of commercial woodlands has been hampered by the fact that too many of growing tips of young trees are chomped by hungry moose and therefore cannot reach maturity. There is some friction between the forest industry and wildlife managers, and many forestry personnel have actually lobbied for a reduction in moose numbers through increased hunting quotas to offset the impacts of moose browsing on young plantations after logging.

From whatever angle you look at it, it is clear that moose populations are in a state of flux. While some populations are declining the very opposite has been happening close to my home. People are seeing moose more frequently than before in the prairie farmland areas of Saskatchewan, Alberta, southwestern Manitoba, and the bordering state of North Dakota south of the boreal forest and the aspen parkland, where small bluffs, mainly of trembling aspen, and hedgerows dot the landscape. Nobody is really sure how it has happened but two ideas seem reasonable. Fifty or more years ago there were about 140,000 small farms scattered across the southern half of Saskatchewan. Couples made a living and raised families on their half-sections (130 hectares), but they worked hard to do so and times were very tough for many of them. If a moose happened to wander into a farmyard or hang out in a patch of willow, it is quite possible that it got no farther than the larder or root cellar and provided a delicious supply of meat. In 2011 the number of farms has dwindled to less than one third of that historical figure.

Major corporations have taken over, and far fewer families live on the land as ownership areas now number in the dozens of sections or thousands of hectares. One does not have to drive far in rural Saskatchewan to find abandoned yards. This gives the moose much more room to live unobserved, and of course they have another huge safety blanket because their other arch-enemies, wolves and bears, have not yet made it out of the forests in any number worth mentioning. With high twinning rates, it has only taken a few years for "pioneer" moose to multiply rapidly and spread across the prairie landscape.

A second theory about the expansion of moose range on the prairies is tied to land management in a different way. A hundred or more years ago the land was subject to frequent wildfires that were sometimes the result of lightning strikes and sometimes caused by deliberate burning by Plains Indians intent on improving the grasslands for their staple food source, the bison. These fires kept the number of tree stands at a minimum and even burned riparian bush lands. Since then extensive fires have been much less frequent and farmers have planted thousands of kilometres of hedgerows in an effort to reduce wind erosion. With increased cover and food sources in the bush, the moose have moved out of the forests and onto the plains.

Another expansion story that caught my imagination came to me from Dr. Lee Kantar of Maine, where moose are doing well, or, as some think, too well. The amusing start to the title of his piece reads, "Broccoli and Moose, Not Always Best Served Together." In the article Kantar wrote that over forty moose have been seen in a single field of broccoli. They particularly favour the crop in the fall when the sugar content is high. This is a sensitive issue in the state, and I don't envy Lee in his efforts to appease the farmers.

While diseases, traffic encounters, climate change, and predation play important roles in regulating moose numbers, the major factor is still to come. It is so important that it gets its own chapter.

CHAPTER TWENTY-TWO

HUNTING AND POPULATIONS

Moose and people;
hunting and its effects.

While four-legged predators play a role in regulating moose numbers, there is no doubt that humans have been, and remain, the major predator of moose, and at times our effects can be catastrophic: hunting moose is not difficult and in winter it becomes especially easy. Rock art and other evidence shows that skis were developed in Asia about five thousand years ago and that while skis remained the preferred method of travel over snow in Eurasia, snowshoes became the platform of choice in North America. Both were used in moose hunting. It hardly matters which one was used, as either would serve well for a hunter to chase down a quarry in deep crusted snow. Moose cannot move easily through such snow deeper than seventy centimetres. In it they quickly become mired, which made hunting them pretty risk-free in the winter months. A quick slash with a sharp knife or jab with a spear and the job was done. In 1274 this efficient and deadly technique of hunting on skis was banned in Norway, but it was not banned in Sweden for almost another six hundred years. Of course, in modern times, with strict hunting seasons mostly set to end before the New Year or even earlier, snow is not usually deep enough for this method to work, and rifles have supplanted the need for a close approach.

Even when snow is not a factor, moose are not difficult to hunt because over aeons they have evolved a strategy to survive wolf attacks by standing their ground. I can hardly think of a worse technique for avoiding death by spear, or bow and arrow.

While moose shy away from vehicles and the noise of machines, which may help them escape hunters using all-terrain vehicles (ATVs), they are remarkably tolerant of a quiet approach. I have often been closer than twenty metres to moose when in my canoe, paddling quietly along. When hunting on foot and making as little noise as possible, I have been able to get within fifty metres on a few occasions and watched them simply look at me.

Given all of the above, unsurprisingly, in the absence of regulation and during periods when there has been a breakdown of law and order, humans have had a devastating effect on moose populations and have more or less wiped them out in local areas.

Cape Breton Island is a case in point. For at least two thousand years prior to European contact, moose were an important spiritual and cultural icon and a major supply of nourishment for the Mi'kmaq people. Then Europeans arrived in the 1500s and brought with them not only their firearms but also an insatiable commercial drive for hides. By the mid-1600s moose numbers had declined to the extent that one Nicolas Denys wrote: "The Indians . . . have abandoned the island . . . finding there no longer the wherewithal for living."

In most North American jurisdictions moose were either rare or almost unknown until the late 1800s, and it has been suggested that the huge numbers of Aboriginal people on the continent played a major role in keeping those numbers low. Charles Kay of the University of Utah has argued, somewhat controversially, that conservation as we think of it today was not part of the culture of North American Indians. He suggests that in pre-contact times there were tens of millions of people on the continent and that they were the major predators of ungulates. They used the available resources to survive and developed cooperative hunting techniques that opti-mized their efforts. One only has to think of the technique of driving bison into corrals or over steep cliffs to realize that the acquisition of food, clothing, and other resources derived from carcasses was more important than any thought of or need for conservation. All animals injured or captured in these events were used, regardless of sex or age. Conservation was simply not part of the picture.

One of Kay's telling pieces of evidence is that there were more ungulates in boundary zones between warring tribal groups than within their traditional territories because people tended to avoid the boundaries and spent less time hunting there.

There were over a hundred different cultural zones and tribal groups in North American Aboriginal societies within the range of moose before European contact, and for them big-game ungulates were of primary importance: in terms of nutrition, they represented the greatest return on investment. The most desirable animals were the adult females. They have more fat at most times of year than the males, and the hides are less scarred by fighting and easier to cure. Of course killing adult females is the worst possible way to conserve an animal resource.

Near the time of contact came the accidental arrival of diseases that began to have disastrous effects on the Aboriginal peoples, who had never been exposed to European pathogens. Of course, the accidental passing on of new diseases was followed by deliberate introduc-tion of epidemics, such as smallpox, and indirect genocide via bison slaughter that led to mass starvation. On top of that, between the late 1600s and late 1800s, Europeans and their descendents perpetrated outright mass murders of Aboriginal peoples. Human population numbers crashed, and moose no longer had to avoid their major predator. Gradually moose returned, and by the late 1800s or early 1900s their numbers increased and then ballooned.

The Eurasian story bears some resemblance to the North American one. In the Middle Ages moose more or less disappeared, and the gen-eral opinion among scientists is that the trend did not reverse until hunting restrictions were imposed in the late nineteenth or early to mid-twentieth centuries.

The next clearly discernable dip took place in many East European countries during and after World War I and after the Russian Revolution, when famine and economic hardship devastated people's lives. Moose became a rarity. The total number of moose in all three Baltic countries in 1920 was probably no more than 125 head. They were slow to recover, but by the 1980s there were about 80,000. Then, because of poaching and predation in the 1990s, the population declined to less than 20,000.

Hunting bans worked for a while under the new totalitarian regimes, but in a bizarre twist, conservation officers in the former USSR were allowed to hunt commercially and even sold moose meat to butcher's shops. These professional hunters, working with packs of as many as ten dogs, and when snow was deep, had a serious impact on population numbers.

There were major disruptions like World War II, the Cultural Revolution in China, and perestroika followed by the collapse of the Soviet Union in 1991. These political upheavals particularly affected moose in China, Ukraine, Mongolia, and Russia. The almost ten years of turmoil during the Cultural Revolution that began in 1966 and the perestroika that started in 1985 both changed things dramatically, with the loss of central monitoring, increased hunting, and a resultant reduction in moose numbers. For instance, in Russia in the period from 1990 to 2007 the populations across all its nine time zones dropped 25 per cent from over 800,000 to about 600,000. The biggest decline was in the European part of the country where the numbers of moose declined by half. Vince Crichton told me that when he was in Siberia in 2008 he learned that high rollers and wealthy foreign hunters have flooded into the country and that guides now use helicopters to fly over the forest and allow their clients to pick and choose which moose they will shoot—invariably a bull, and of course preferably the biggest one they can find. It is an echo of Tony Bubenik's story of the giant caribou dummy that I mentioned in Chapter Fourteen.

While Russia has the largest number of moose in any country and therefore has suffered the greatest overall decline, examples of similar problems in smaller countries tell the same story.

I made three trips to Mongolia in the years 2004 to 2006. My task was to work with the Tsaatan people, nomadic reindeer herders living in the Sayan Mountains close to the Siberian border in the far north of the country. They have been hunters as long as they can remember, relying on reindeer for milk and milk products, and as pack and totem animals, but not using their animals for meat. One of my hosts in camp was Jbat, who showed me his rifle and told me, through our translator, about a desperate hunting trip he had taken with friends. They had ridden for ten days and were getting very hungry when they finally came upon their quarry, in this case a cow and calf moose. Normally they would have left her in peace, but not this time. I was later told that foreign hunters, mainly Chinese, were coming into the mountains and poaching. Of course, this information is not proven hard data, but it does reflect the perspective of the Tsaatan, whose livelihood was changing.

Poland also provides a dramatic recent example of a country whose moose numbers have undergone fluctuations in fortune in the past fifty years. To get at the most recent information, I contacted Dr. Andrzej Krzywinski. I had last met him at the International Deer Biology Conference in Edinburgh. We were at the conference's memorable social, which was held in a marquee at the home of John and Nichola Fletcher of Auchtermuchty in the Kingdom of Fife, which is only thirty-nine kilometres from Scotland's capital. John and Nichola are renowned hosts as well as authors, and a leading deer scientist and chef-cum-silversmith respectively. Krzywinski partook of his fair share of John's fine wine and excellent single malt. The meal, or should I say feast, began with a wonderful spread of salmon and was followed by cuts of spit-roasted stag and all the trimmings, of which a highlight was Nichola's homemade rowan jelly. The evening wrapped up with a Scottish country dancing session in which Dr. Krzywinski became the ninth member of an Eightsome Reel. To those familiar with the structured nature of this dance, which must be performed "by the numbers," this was one of the sights of a lifetime, never mind the evening. Hats off to the band; they played on without a hiccup! Years later I was reminded of that Scottish scene at my son's wedding near the city of Kraków, when almost everyone in the room got up and danced just for the fun of it. The most memorable tune of the night was the Polish rendition of the classic 1960s novelty tune "Itsy-Bitsy Teenie-Weenie Yellow Polka-Dot Bikini," to which I used to dance in my student days in Glasgow.

Dr. Krzywinski told me that in the early 1950s there were only about eighteen moose in Poland. Five were introduced from the Soviet Union in 1951 and some animals migrated in from neighbouring countries to the north and east. Ten years later there were about 160 head in two areas. These animals began to spread out and reached about 450 head in 1965. Twenty years later there were thought to be almost five thousand individuals. Most of this rapid increase was related to human factors: hunting was banned in 1967, there were large areas of excellent crops for the moose to dine upon, and few wolves remained. Those that were still present preferred to prey upon red deer. In addition, the weather was favourable and there was little competition for food. All these factors, combined with the usual high twinning rate of healthy moose, made the increase possible.

Then the crash came. At the end of the 1980s the Polish moose population was estimated at about 1,800. The question is: where had over three thousand animals gone, never mind the natural increase that one would have expected? Krzywinski wrote that a combination of incorrect counting methods in the first place, as well as excessive hunting, poaching, and road accidents, all contributed to the decline. Hunting bans were put in place in 2001, and moose numbers have risen again and are currently hovering around 6,500 head.

A similar story emerges from Latvia, which has only one twelfth the area of Poland or one twentieth of Saskatchewan's. After World War I there were only eighty-five moose in the whole country. Hunting was banned or heavily restricted, carnivores were more or less exterminated, and ideal habitat including young forest stands was available. By the 1970s the numbers had risen to well over 20,000 head. Hunting was again allowed and harvest peaked at close to 10,000 in the mid-1990s. A sharp drop in overall numbers inevitably followed, but today, with tighter hunting controls and natural moose increases, there are an estimated 15,000 head in the country.

Another thing that is happening under the relentless pressure of trophy hunting is a worldwide decline in overall antler size. Virtually none of the visiting hunters who pay thousands of dollars to hunt with professional guides would be satisfied with a non-trophy animal. Most, if not all, hunters who can afford the fees and special hunting season flights into remote destinations like Norman Wells in Canada's Northwest Territories or some corner of Russia or Ukraine are interested in only one thing. "Will it make book?" is a question I have heard directly from hunters and from their guides relating client encounters. In North America they are referring to the Boone and Crockett Club's record book, which focuses solely on antlers.

Those who follow the fate of the African elephant are well aware that a hundred years and more of heavy hunting and persistent, unbridled, gangland-style poaching (with large tusks being the objective), has led to a rapid decline in really big tuskers and a marked increase in the number of entirely tuskless animals. The days of huge ivory, with each side weighing over fifty kilograms, are likely gone forever. A similar decline in the size of bighorn sheep trophies has reportedly occurred over a short time.

The search for the trophy has other effects as it disrupts the normal structure of moose society by taking out mature bulls. Tony Bubenik described populations robbed of their older bulls as dysfunctional, and it is easy to see why. The number of cows per bull rises sharply and most of those bulls are youngsters with small antlers. They are inexperienced, and at the rut they are like a bunch of human teenagers: lots of interest but not quite sure how to go about things. Moreover, some young bulls may not yet be fully fertile at the onset of the rut. The cows are only in heat for a short time, usually about twenty-four hours, and a young bull confronted with half a dozen or more cows cannot always get the job done in time. The cows go on to a second heat period in about three and a half weeks, and if they do not conceive at this time they will go into heat again. The end result is that some cows may not conceive. Calves that are born late the following year because of delayed conceptions do not grow as fast as their earlier-born cousins and often do not survive their first winter. It is not just the late-born calves that die in winter. Those young bulls may spend too much time chasing the cows that return to heat, overwork themselves late into the season, and also succumb to winter's harshness or fall victim to predators.

Swedish managers were the first to come up with a solution to this problem of populations without mature bulls. Their idea involved allowing hunters to take a calf instead of an adult. By fall moose calves are well grown and may weigh nearly two hundred kilograms, which provides a lot of particularly tender meat. There are two clear advantages to this system. First, it protects the vital breeding segment of a population, not only the females but also the mature males. Second, it acknowledges the inevitable loss that occurs when a significant proportion of calves die during the cold winter months.

My own introduction to moose hunting in 1976 came just when my friend and research colleague Bob Stewart had managed to get the Swedish model introduced in Saskatchewan. He recognized the advantages of this management technique straight away and was the first biologist to propose it in North America.

There is another component to moose hunting that concerns many biologists—not regulated hunting under license or illegal poaching. The Aboriginal peoples of Canada have long had the right to hunt wildlife for sustenance and ceremonial uses across the country. Depending on where they live, Aboriginals can hunt almost anywhere at any time of year, except in national parks or on private land, and they take almost any species they wish, although harvest of some species, such as grizzly bears in British Columbia, are tightly controlled. In British Columbia Aboriginal hunting rights are also restricted within the boundaries of traditional territories. When treaties were signed, Aboriginal populations were small in numbers, but in some areas, such as Manitoba and Saskatchewan, Aboriginal peoples are reportedly the fastest-growing human demographic in Canada. As these populations continue to increase, the numbers of moose in many jurisdictions are reportedly declining, and as Aboriginal peoples exercise their right to hunt for food, they are likely having an increasing impact on moose. Moreover, Aboriginal hunting practices have changed with improvements in technology, mobility, and equipment. All hunters have access to trucks, nine-power scopes, ATVs, motorcycles, snowmobiles, two-way radios, and cellular phones. Non-natives are tightly restricted in that they are permitted to hunt only in short and specified blocks of time, and their use of ATVs or snowmobiles is also limited or prohibited. In some jurisdictions non-natives are only allowed to use these vehicles on designated trails at certain times of day to retrieve a harvested animal. Other "tools" like powerful spotlights and the use of digital recordings of moose calls, although illegal for non-native hunters, are available for use by Aboriginal peoples.

It is impossible to know where this will all end up, but for now moose populations are experiencing a continuing downward trend in Manitoba, especially where some people have not been taught or fail to practice a conservation ethic. In some areas where moose were once common a few years ago, they have virtually disappeared. Vince Crichton has recorded a 95 per cent drop in an area east of the Duck Mountains, and Aboriginal hunters are reportedly moving farther afield to exercise their rights, even crossing the border into Saskatchewan.

There are two sides to this situation.

Crichton told me that some bands and individuals readily accept the need for responsible management of the resource, while others take a different view based on "traditional rights." For instance, one band chief has recently asked a senior provincial politician to help him receive government permission to hunt moose inside Riding

Mountain National Park. If permission is sanctioned, a dangerous, "rights-based" precedent is set, and there is only one possible end point for the moose resource.

Crichton and others have taken efforts to involve Aboriginal peoples in the management of moose and other wildlife resources by developing co-management programs similar to the successful ones currently administered in Cape Breton and by the Sahtu and Gwich'in settlement areas in the Northwest Territories. These jurisdictions have learned that involvement and partnership with Aboriginal peoples in the development and delivery of a mutually acceptable management plan that identifies achievable and sustainable subsistence harvest of moose is a "win-win" for all parties. Fortunately for the moose resources, other enlightened managers in Canada and the U.S. are taking the same approach.

CHAPTER TWENTY-THREE

THE HOW OF THE HUNT

The hunt; techniques, problems; the use of the body,
from outside in; non-consumptive use.

Moose have been a vital part of human culture for thousands of years, and wherever they have shared an area with humans there is no shortage of records of the importance of moose in the lives of people. While there were other sources of meat, such as caribou, deer, and small game, the moose is the one that really mattered for Subarctic people. The caribou (or wild reindeer in Eurasia) were nomadic and so could not be relied upon for a year-round supply.

Moose have also been a vital part of Cree, Athapaskan, and other First Nations cultures for many years, and hunters have used every conceivable method of getting at their quarries: from stone tools and various kinds of snares, to spears, daggers, bows and arrows, and finally modern long-range rifles. All of these methods have pros and cons.

Bows and arrows have drawbacks (as it were). While using a bow and arrow did increase the range at which people could successfully hunt moose, in very cold weather the twang of the string was loud enough to scare the target before the missile reached its destination.

Another technique that was widely used in North America was the deployment of snares, usually made of partially cured and braided moose hide, which were set along known trails or even in gaps deliberately left in drift fences. One disadvantage of this system was that a carcass might hang in a snare for a long time and become more or less useless if the hunter was not able to make frequent checks along his trapline.

Another successful hunting method employed Canada's many lakes. When moose are swimming they are easy to hunt because they offer no resistance to the approach of a canoe. It was Samuel Hearne who noted, "When pursued in this manner, they are the most inoffensive of all animals, never making any resistance." We took advantage of the water in our research efforts on the Saskatchewan River Delta and were able to use a helicopter equipped with big rubber floats to land right next to calves and place radio tags in their ears.

Another moose hunting method, this one requiring a great deal of advance preparation, was the use of pits. One can still see old pitfall sites in Scandinavia and Estonia that were in use less than a hundred years ago, but pitfalls do not appear to have been a popular method of capture in North America. I am not sure why.

A detailed account of moose hunting among the Kutchin people of Alaska mentions the different techniques used at each season of the year, making it clear that the short rutting period is the best time to hunt moose. Moose often come to the water at this time, most frequently at dawn and dusk, and bulls are not as cautious as they are at other times, making it easier to approach them.

During the rut, antlers have played a vital part of the actual hunting practice. One feature of rutting moose is that they rub their antlers on shrubbery, and hunters have used a dried moose shoulder blade (scapula), similarly rubbed, to entice bulls within range. Anthropologist and historian Richard Nelson, who lived among the Kutchin and Koyukon peoples of interior Alaska, at the easternmost edge of the state at the Yukon border, has stated this imitative behaviour must be done with great subtlety and involves scraping the scapula up and down the bush "briskly, but rather gently, letting it ride along the branches." The technique involves "allowing the wrist

THE HOW OF THE HUNT

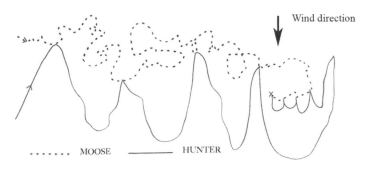

The "semicircling" moose stalking technique.
(Redrawn from Reeves and McCabe, 1997)
JERRY HAIGH

to flex . . . as if the bone were a brush and the bush a wall" being painted. There are records of bulls charging as soon as they hear the sound. Other bones, such as leg bones, it seems, are a poor substitute for the shoulder blade.

Another very successful method that Richard Nelson described can only be employed once there is snow cover and requires considerable bushcraft and familiarity with the local area. This hunting method involves a looping strategy after finding the meandering fresh tracks of a feeding animal.

The hunter moves downwind and makes a series of semi-circular loops in the general direction of the animal's movement. Each loop brings the hunter back to the line of the original track until he no longer finds it. At this point the hunter can assume that the moose has backtracked slightly and has bedded down. The hunter also backtracks, but in much smaller loops, still downwind, until he finds the quarry.

There is plenty of written evidence that moose hunting trips were very dangerous, especially in the days when daggers or spears were the main weapons. A telling example lies with a photo taken in the late 1920s by a Minnesota man named Dr. F.E. Anderson, which shows the skeletons of a bull moose and a man lying together. One can only imagine what led to this tragic scene. Was it a young man out to prove

OF MOOSE AND MEN

Dr. F.E. Anderson's 1920s photo of what would appear
to have been a double fatality: moose and hunter.
COURTESY OF THE WILDLIFE MANAGEMENT INSTITUTE AND RICHARD MCCABE

his bravery but making a fatal miscalculation? Was it a man trying to provide for his family? Was the bull in full rut and did he see the man as a rival to be eliminated? Did the hunter rub the scapula too well and not have time get out of the way as the bull charged? Did his spear thrust miss the target or his dagger break on a bone?

Then the consequences. Was he a dearly loved son or husband who never came home and never received his proper burial? Perhaps he was the father of three small children whom he loved dearly? How did his widow cope?

Moose hunting occupies a special place in Swedish life. This country, about half the area of Canada's British Columbia, has a population of something like 350,000 moose, and roughly one third of these are harvested every year. In 1982 hunters harvested an astonishing 183,000 moose, the largest legal moose harvest relative to population in any country, anywhere, ever. The most common technique involves drives to shooters stationed at known spots along forest gaps and bears little resemblance to the methods used in North America. Large parties of hunters (up to twenty) gather on designated moose grounds. They are usually well-acquainted with one another and have strict rules about protocol, safety, and meat distribution. One of the most interesting components of the Swedish hunt is that it often involves a specially trained elk hound, which searches for moose and bays them up.

In my own dozen or so hunting trips I have had most success when either Still Hunting, the ultra slow walk and stop method I used to try and dart the moose on the Smeeton ranch, and when paddling a canoe.

While I was researching the origin of the word moose and meeting with Elder Barry Ahenakew, I chatted with Darryl Chamakese of the Saskatchewan Indian Cultural Centre about our approaches to hunting, and I told him of my successes and failures. I think he was surprised to learn that I am a hunter, and have been for the best part of sixty years, obtaining almost all of the meat that my family consumes by means of a gun or a fishing rod. He told me that he, too, is a hunter and has been for as long as he can recall. Darryl's response told me not only about his hunting ethic, but also about the spiritual nature of Cree hunting culture:

> I used to be trophy hunter, but one night I had a vivid dream. I'd just shot the biggest deer ever. Great big horns, the biggest I'd ever seen. They'd have been tops in Boone and Crockett. [Darryl stretched his arms out across the passenger side of the car.]
>
> As I was skinning out the head I looked up and there was a huge white moose coming straight at me. I lifted up my gun and fired at him. He didn't stop. I fired again and again until I ran out of ammo. He kept coming and chased me right into a building, breaking down the doors as he came after me.
>
> I woke up in a sweat and later asked my dad about this dream. I also asked Barry. They both told me that I had forgotten the ways of my ancestors and was hunting for the wrong reasons, not respecting the traditions. I should be hunting for food, not horns. Ever since then I've never hunted for trophies.

Moose cow and calf in the fall. The calf is
well-grown and probably weighs around 200 kg.

GERHARD STUEWE

While I lack the spiritual background that Darryl was brought up with, I only hunt for food. I have never collected a trophy of any sort (other than the odd-ball antlers of the locked white-tailed deer that I mentioned earlier), and until someone comes up with a recipe for antler, I have no desire to collect them. For me the hunt is a special experience, and if I am out with a companion, camped beside a river, and absorbed in my surroundings, I am able to enjoy the experience for itself. When the opportunity has presented itself, I have taken a calf rather than its dam or even a consorting bull.

I am not alone in my reasons for hunting. The most important human use of moose has always been food. When fresh it was usually roasted or stone-boiled, but before the days of refrigeration it had to be preserved in some way, and smoking was the commonest method.

An alternative preserved moose product is pemmican, which, if properly prepared, will last for long periods. It was developed by First Nations people across the continent and so bison was the commonest meat, but others, including moose, were also employed. The word "pemmican" is derived from the Cree *pimîhkân*. The meat is thoroughly dried in thin strips in the sun, or over a hot fire, until brittle. It is then pounded until almost powder-like and mixed with fat in an approximately 50:50 ratio. If marrow fat is available, that is the fat of choice. Several varieties of dried berry were added, according to what was available. A popular one was the delicious Saskatoon berry. My experience of this berry's flavour comes from numerous pies, jams, and syrups made from the fruit that we have picked every July for thirty-odd years, and not from pemmican. The meat, fat, and berry product was then packed into rawhide pouches and stored. Pemmican became a vital high-energy food source for fur traders and was even used by Arctic and Antarctic explorers.

Once a moose has been shot and the meat has been taken for processing, most other parts can also be put to good use. Starting from the outside in, these parts include: antlers, hair, hides, bones, sinews, internal organs, including parts of the intestines and even the intestinal contents.

Other than their use as hunting aids, antlers have served two main purposes. They have been employed as tools and in art. In England's Yorkshire there is a famous and much-studied archaeological site called Star Carr, which lies about eight kilometres west of the town of Scarborough, where, at midnight on New Year's Eve, I once joined a group of friends on the castle ramparts as one of us floated the bugle notes of the "Last Post" toward the rising moon and its rippled reflection in the North Sea. Some have considered Star Carr a major kill site, others as an industrial processing location, but either way, while red deer remains predominate the Star Carr findings, a quarter of the bone fragments were of moose, and their antlers were used as mallets.

Moose antlers with large palms also lend themselves to artistic activities. You can find moose-antler cribbage boards, scrimshaw surfaces, and carvings in many a curio shop today. They have also become an important part of the displays at craft shows and have pride of place at the Saskatchewan Indian Cultural Centre in Saskatoon.

Similarly, for centuries moose hair has been used for artistic purposes over a wide geographic region, from Western Siberia right across North America to New England, in a variety of stitched patterns that bound lengths of hair to clothing. This form of embroidery, which is no longer practiced in most areas, was used in many Aboriginal cultures for decoration of moccasins, robes, and accessories, and was even employed to decorate the tumplines women used to carry heavy loads. At first artisans used natural plant dyes that tended to fade over time. In North America, with the arrival of missionaries, aniline and other dyes with more longevity and brighter colours became the norm.

Later, shortly after World War I, a technique known as tufting or brush appears to have been started by Boniface Lafferte, a Métis woman living in the community of Fort Simpson in Canada's Northwest Territories. This provenance is not absolutely certain, and Geoffrey Turner, who published a fascinating eighty-three-page monograph in 1955, suggested that she may have reintroduced a much older skill that died out about fifty years earlier. Small bundles of hair were tufted onto cured hide backed with birch bark or, later, velvet backed with canvas or cardboard.

In 1982 my family and I drove up the fabled Alaska Highway to Yukon and another moose conference and there saw, for the first time, how the Dene people had used their handicraft skills and turned the long moose winter guard hairs, which are only dark at their tips, into attractive decorations.

This kind of tufting was something I at once recognized as I have used it for the quite different purpose of making fishing flies. A small bunch of hair, slightly more than a chef's pinch, but not a clump, is held against the shaft of the hook, near the eye. Standard tying thread is wound around the middle of the bunch and pulled tight. This constricts the hairs, which promptly stand up straight and look like a bad hair day in miniature. Once the thread is tied in with a few rolling half-hitches, the untidy clump can be trimmed to shape.

The long winter hairs of moose and other deer from temperate regions are hollow, which of course makes them a superb insulating material, vital for the moose in extreme winter weather. The hollow

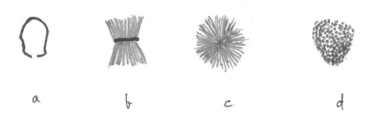

Moose or Caribou Hair Tufting
a. Make a loop on the surface of the backing.
b. Insert a bundle of moose or caribou hair.
c. Pull the loop tight, and the hairs stand up.
d. Trim the hairs with scissors to the desired shape.
(Redrawn from Turner, 1955)
JERRY HAIGH

hair shafts are not simply tubes but have numerous little compartments that are isolated from one another. If a hair breaks, the tube will not fill with water. That hollowness not only provides insulation but also helps deer species that have such hairs float when swimming.

I heard about the hollow hairs well before meeting my first moose as I had read about it in a now defunct magazine called *The Fly Tier*, which I used to receive from England and would leave in my clinic office in Kenya. The article described how the hairs could be used to give both shape and action to the fly as one tried to tempt any waiting trout. The action came from the fact that the trapped air inside the hairs made the fly float. The Muddler Minnow was the first such fly in my collection, and nowadays many dry flies are tied with some sort of deer hair. They are almost unsinkable.

The simplest form is to make it look like the chunky front end of a small minnow. If one is after bigger prey, like the fabled taimen of Mongolian and Russian rivers, or the über-carnivorous northern pike, one can trim the hairs to another shape, such as a mouse.

For hair-tufted flowers, about fifteen or twenty hairs, or as Turner put it "a bundle of hairs about half the size of a little finger," are slipped under a stitch that has been looped through the backing material. The

OF MOOSE AND MEN

Tying a Muddler Minnow
a. Tie the tail, body, and turkey feather wing quills (not shown in fig. a)
in place along two thirds of the shank and then position a small
bunch of moose hair there, holding it on with a loose loop.
b. Pull the bunch of hair tight to the body and wings (now shown). The
hairs will stand up. Add more small bunches forward as required.
c. Trim the hairs to desired shape, but leave
some of them long at the back.
JERRY HAIGH

stitch is pulled tight and then tied at the rear. Finally, the shape is
trimmed. Today it would be hard to visit a tourist shop or gas station
in Yukon or the Northwest Territories and not find a wall hanging or
other decorative item containing moose-hair work.

Just under the hair lies the hide, which was widely used by
Aboriginal peoples because it is the thickest and toughest of all the
deer hides. Moose hunters of several Athapaskan groups used hides
as the covering for boats, often to transport the meat. Richard Nelson
also tells how small boats, about two metres long, with ribs and
thwarts made of spruce and covered in a single hide, could be made
in a day. Larger boats might need as many as twenty hides. These were
stitched with sinew and caulked with fat from the shot animals.

Other Athapaskan groups along the Mackenzie River Basin, among
them the Shotah Dene and the Sahtu Dene, also made and used
moose-hide boats, and in some cases not just for carrying meat. A
National Film Board of Canada (NFB) documentary titled *The Last
Mooseskin Boat*, made in 1982, may have recorded the last building
and use of such boats.

Moose hide has other uses. In particular it was popular for the soles of moccasins and was used in robes of various sorts. Some North American tribes even used it to make shields. In Russia moose hides were once used to make trousers for Cossack cavalry, but the supply could not keep up with the demand, which may have contributed to the decline in moose numbers in some areas.

At home my wife has used commercially tanned hide to make various items, including a very smart waistcoat, mitts, and poufs, one of which she turned into a tortoise about as big as the more famous giants of the Galapagos and Aldabra islands, just for the fun of it. I rebelled slightly at its thick, rather sexy, come-hither eyebrows, an anatomical feature that all reptiles lack, but artistic license won the day, and it makes a nice footrest.

Also in recent times, inventive artisans have taken advantage of the tourist industry and made things like potholders and tea towels that incorporate hides and hair.

The much older and time-consuming traditional tanning of hides involved rubbing brain tissues and other fatty materials like marrow into the hide. Leslie Main Johnson of Athabasca University wrote to tell me that "moose hide is durable and the best hide for moccasins and also widely used for beaded jackets. The skills to make good native tanned hides are disappearing, but this form of hide processing produces a kind of leather that is very different from commercial tanning, much suppler and softer, far easier to sew. It is really more like sewing thick, felted wool."

Moving along on our anatomical journey, people use moose bones in various ways, over and above the subtle scrape of the scapula. Long bones can be cracked and yield the highly nutritious and tasty marrow. Some long bones can also be made into scraping tools for cleaning the hide, and all bones can be put into a pot and used for soup.

My colleague and friend Peter Flood, who was at the veterinary college in Saskatoon at the same period I was, told me of a quite different use of one particular leg bone. He went on a research-cum-hunting trip with a group of Dene people near Fort Good Hope in Canada's

The late Mary Barnaby preparing moose
sinew for use as stitching material.

SUSAN KUTZ

Northwest Territories and brought back a small leg bone (one of the small metacarpals), shaped like a letter opener, just under 20 centimetres long and no more than 1.5 centimetres wide, with a bean-sized bobble at the lower end. It had been used as a "talking stick," giving the person holding it the right to speak at a sharing circle held on the last morning of the trip. As Peter wrote:

This sharing circle was a solemn affair beginning with smudging with sweet-grass. People thanked other people for help, made thoughtful observations, and said many things that I did not understand. I am sure that the Creator was thanked for the bounty of the hunt, and I suspect that there were prayers in North Slavey. It ended with the Lord's Prayer in English. I was very grateful for the opportunity to thank everyone for their kindness, tolerance, and hospitality.

Aboriginal peoples have traditionally turned sinew into a natural sewing thread. An important women's skill in moose hunting camps has been the splitting and spinning of this tough tissue derived from tendons and the sheet of fibre under the skin along the back.

Even a moose's internal organs have found their uses in Aboriginal cultures. The reticulum, or first stomach, is sometimes turned into a carrying container. The Kutchin people usually discard the liver, quite why I do not know, as I make a point of keeping it and using it as a delicious fresh dish, sometimes fried with onions, or cooked with bacon and spices and turned into a pâté. Other First Nations peoples, such as the Western Woods Cree, consume the liver, and the bone marrow has always been considered a delicacy.

To sum it up one can quote Bernard Ross, a long-time employee of the Hudson's Bay Company, who in 1861 gave a succinct list of the use of moose other than for food: "The hide supplies parchment, leather, lines, and cords; the sinews yield thread and glue; the horns serve for handles to knives and awls, as well as to make spoons of; the shank bones are employed as tools to dress leather with; and with a particular portion of the hair, when dyed, the Indian women embroider garments."

While moose have been hunted throughout history, and their parts made good use of, an important development in the last fifty years or so has been the growth of the tourist industry (and with it non-consumptive use of wildlife), epitomized by the African tourist safari, but certainly important in other parts of the world, including Canada. Hunt-free and photographic safaris contribute to the economy. In Alaska the value of moose viewing and photography, teased out from the much larger figure tied to all tourism, has been estimated to be almost CD$4 million (mid-2005 dollars). Of course, viewing wildlife also affects the spiritual well-being of humans.

Thirty-five years after the event my wife and I can still vividly recall a magic moment during an early June canoe trip in Prince Albert National Park with our small children. We had stopped for a break and were sitting on a beaver lodge when a cow and her gangly little calf emerged from the bush across the river about fifty metres away. They came steadily toward us through the bulrushes, waded in among the water lilies, and swam across to clamber up the bank not fifteen metres away. We simply sat and marvelled, and as we had no cameras with us we have retained the memory as a mind's eye image.

CHAPTER TWENTY-FOUR

THE TAMING OF THE MOOSE

Film clips; moose milk;
moose cheese; moose domestication.

The YouTube video opens with a close-up of an ancient loudspeaker attached to a wall made of wooden slabs. A doleful, descending, four-note call moans through the air. The scene cuts to an earphone-clad dark-haired woman holding an oblong grey box from which several wires emerge. The cry switches from four to two notes and continues as she holds the box up. If you were to walk in and join me watching this odd scene, you would certainly wonder what it was all about! You may still be perplexed when the video cuts to a cow moose wearing a radio collar and walking around the side of a barn. The sound changes from the muted trumpet notes, for that is what they are, to a muffled human voice calling out something in a foreign tongue.

The moose goes through a barn door and enters a stall, where a handler puts a halter on her. The woman picks up an ice cream pail–sized bucket, walks around to the side of the stall, and proceeds to milk the cow. I am watching a video about a Russian moose farm where milk is the end product.

The almost seven-minute Reuters clip goes on to

At the Kostroma moose farm. Milking time for moose.
ALEXANDER MINAEV

describe how the farm entices moose cows, which were raised on milk of domestic cattle, to return from the nearby forests each day for milking. I watch the milk as it is processed and frozen, and then, in a sudden change of scene, the film jumps to a hospital canteen where a group of older women are drinking small glasses of milk. The accompanying script and description on the website has conveniently been translated into English, and I learn what I have already suspected: the milk in the glasses is from the moose farm. The Ivan Susanin Sanatorium supplies the beverage to its patients as one form of treatment for a variety of stomach ailments.

After watching the video, I scroll through the English translation of the script, which tells me much more about the operation. This farm, officially known as Sumarokovskaya, lies on the banks of the Poksha River, not far from where it empties into the Volga, famous in song, near the town of Kostroma, which is part of the "Golden Ring of Russia" tourist circuit.

The end shots of the Reuters clip show a mob of new calves being called out of the bush and led to stalls by a couple of young women, veterinary students. The calves stand and stretch out for buckets that they can't quite reach until the handlers are ready. One of the vet students, Natalia Korsakova, tells me more about the calves: "We are like mothers for them. We feed them, we talk to them, we walk with them. The most important thing is to talk to them. They remember our voices. They come only if they hear a familiar voice. They will not come close to a stranger. You see she listens only to me and tries to eat me now."

It's not quite the summer job that Canadian vet students would expect to be doing, but then we have no moose farms in Canada, even though Canadian moose have been tamed.

The mournful calls played in the film sound out every day for four months from late May to early October to attract cows that are being milked. From mid-September they are left alone to go into the forest during the rut, but some still return daily for milking, often accompanied by bulls, some of which are wild, as opposed to farm raised. The wild bulls are standoffish, but the habituated ones may follow a cow right into the milking stalls. Not all of the cows respond to the calls and return for daily milking, but Dr. Alexander Minaev of the Russian Academy of Sciences has equipped every one of the farm's charges with radio collars, so finding them is no problem. Milking tails off during the rut and although some cows may give as much as one hundred millilitres after the peak of the mating season, the yield is not sufficient to justify the effort unless, as Dr. Minaev put it to me, "the cows insist."

I contacted Dr. Minaev as the Reuters story seemed incomplete, and we exchanged several emails. He also sent me a copy of his own ninety-minute film that gives a lot more information and shows not only the farm's management methods but also gives one some idea of the operation's pitfalls. He also cleared up my confusion about names, as he prefers to call the farm by its old name: Kostroma.

In one extraordinary sequence in Minaev's film, moose that are in the throes of delivering calves, and those who have newborn young that are still wet, allow videographers not only to enter their large (four-hectare) calving areas or "maternity enclosures" but also to approach for close-up shots. Over the last forty years, the cows seem to have become more tolerant of the strangers, but some will still not allow a cameraman or other stranger to approach after she delivers. Watching this footage in 2010 reminded me of my 1976 encounter with Petruska, her absolute trust in Beryl Smeeton, and her wish to pulverize me into the dirt.

Perhaps we are witnessing the development of a new domestic species.

I asked Dr. Minaev about the use of the term "domesticated" relative to moose, and he wrote that he would "rather say that Kostroma farm moose are not domesticated at all. Moreover, I say that moose is a 'ready' domestic species that doesn't need any domestication at all. Don't change the nature; change the way you use it."

Another way to view it is that at this point in their transition from truly wild animals, these moose are more habituated than domesticated, as the latter is a very long process that may take many generations, perhaps thousands of years. However, it may already be happening because by autumn it is difficult to distinguish, by behaviour alone, the bottle-raised calves from wild-born ones that join them. There is no doubt, however, that they are remarkably tame and tolerant of humans, especially ones they know and trust.

I cannot imagine that the transition of the ultra-wild, huge, and aggressive aurochs to the domestic cattle of today was an overnight process. It probably took a very long time and involved selection of traits deemed desirable thousands of years ago, when animals that were tamer than others were kept in the herd. Perhaps the ones that were difficult to handle were slaughtered or took off back to the wild. From that probable first step one can speculate that dual-purpose breeds like the shorthorn were developed and then came the individual characteristics of higher milk yield, faster growth, ability to pull a plough, and so on.

The most important factor in the overall moose taming process is that from an early age the moose are trained to recognize the farm as their home. Calves are taken from their mothers a day or so after birth, which, given my experience with Petruska, would be a highly risky business. Minaev explains that he thinks the combination of subtle calf removal by trusted humans and the cow's transference of her maternal instincts to her handler makes the process possible.

After the calf is removed from her mother, two things happen. First, the cow is trained to be milked by a human, although some cows are a bit reluctant at first. Second, and for me this was a real surprise in the film, the cows are trained to be milked by machine. When I saw this in Minaev's film, I realized that Kostroma truly is a moose dairy operation.

Another major undertaking at Kostroma involves ensuring that cows deliver their calves "at home." Once she establishes her own maternity area, a cow will return to it each year and defend it vigorously against all comers, especially other moose and strange humans. In one sequence in Minaev's movie, a reluctant young cow—due to deliver her first calf at any moment—is tranquilized and brought home at the end of a halter and rope.

When the calves are removed from their mothers, they are initially fed moose milk from bottles, but this is soon altered to a milk replacer from a bucket, and then oatmeal gruel is added. Pretty soon the calves have had their first taste of native shrubbery as they are taken in groups into the nearby forest for a feed and to goof off and swim in the Poksha River. They are led there by handlers who call them as they go and bring them back three times a day for their fix of milk and porridge. By this time, they are thoroughly habituated and rush into stanchions for the treats.

There is one more crucial element to the taming process. This is the constant supply of treetop slash, tree bark, and oatmeal that I referred to in Chapter Nine. When the winter snow melts and roads and tracks are an impassable morass of mud, even for tractors, this supply of specialized food is of critical importance.

As for the pitfalls, Dr. Minaev has listed nine on his website. The major ones are: the need for a large area without fences that will allow the animals to roam and find the food variety they need on a year-round basis; the damage to crops, especially if there is any silviculture in the area; the physical risk to people if a moose is either being aggressive or playing; the huge operational expenses; and a steady leakage because not all moose return home each year and they require constant protection from hunters and poachers, who are active year-round but especially so once the first snow flies and tracking becomes easy.

The first scientific report to reach the West about domestic moose use came in 1964, my penultimate year at veterinary school in Glasgow. I had read about it, in passing, as I crammed for my exams, and copied the article out of curiosity. I hung on to this article for over forty years and several changes in country and home. It concerned a spot at the foot of the Ural Mountains in the village of Yaksha in Pechera-Ilych National Park, which was first developed in 1949 and was known as the Pechora Experimental Moose Farm. When teaching veterinary students in Saskatoon I frequently used Pechora as an example of an unusual wildlife utilization activity and went back to search for any updates with a Google search of "moose farm."

That is how I stumbled across the Kostroma operation and made contact with Dr. Minaev. In the correspondence with him I learned that when Pechora was started no acknowledgement of others that had existed before it was ever made, because the information was classified. The classification may have had something to do with the Russian army having long wanted to domesticate moose for military purposes. The reserve and its moose farm were gradually destroyed in the Stalin era but remained a scientific research centre until the early 2000s. Vince Crichton visited the centre in 1990 and not only stood by the milkmaids as they did their work but also drank the milk. Just as at Kostroma the milk goes to local hospitals. Today there is a small tourist attraction where Pechora used to be. As Dr. Minaev wrote, "Now it takes a couple of hours and a couple of thousand roubles to visit that tundra on an excursion helicopter."

When I was searching for more information about the Russian moose farms I also chanced to come across a Google reference to a similar enterprise in Sweden. Of course I followed the link and found out that there is a different sort of moose dairy operation near Bjursholm in northern Sweden. Instead of producing milk for drinking, this commercial operation produces the most expensive cheese on the planet.

The owners, Christer and Ulla Johannson, market the product of three cows named Gullan, Haelga, and Juna—which were found abandoned and which they hand-raised—to upscale restaurants and visiting tourists. At $1,100 a kilo I'm not sure that many tourists would want to dip into their wallets for this item, however delicious.

CHAPTER TWENTY-FIVE

HARNESSES AND HARNESSING

*Moose in harness; photographic records and an unverified attempt
on the world's high-jump record; an unusual means of propulsion.*

As I related in Chapter Eighteen, some Newfoundland
moose arrived in New Brunswick in 1904 after being captured by John Connell. However, I have already told you
that Mr. Connell was no ordinary "moose catcher": he also
owned a young moose called Tommy that he had trained
as a riding animal. While this may seem odd, there is no
shortage of even earlier records from both sides of the
Atlantic about tame moose, particularly as harness animals. There are also archival pictures of harnessed moose
from the earliest days of photography and more modern
ones of moose standing beside or pulling a variety of rigs,
including travois, sleds, and single or tandem moose pulling wheeled buggies. With no verifiably true exceptions
the animals are either females or castrates that exhibit the
characteristic coral antlers of their kind.

The first written records of tamed moose in North
America come from the early 1600s when French priests
reported that there were moose in captivity in New France,
but it seems highly likely that Aboriginal people had
tamed them long before that because those same priests

Moose in harness. Unfortunately the photographer provided only a brief caption to the image: "Moose Yoked." No other information about the location or history of this photo has been found.

COURTESY PROVINCIAL ARCHIVES OF ALBERTA, COPYRIGHT ERNEST BROWN

and later European explorers commented on how easy moose were to train, and many authors and raconteurs mention how remarkably tame a moose can become.

In 1770 Samuel Hearne, who was the first European to reach the Arctic Ocean by a mainland route across North America, noted that moose "are also the easiest to tame and domesticate of any of the deer kind." He went further in describing the details. "I have repeatedly seen them at Churchill as tame as sheep, and even more so; for they would follow their keeper any distance from home, and at his call return with him, without the least trouble, or even offering to deviate from the path."

The deviation, or lack of it, is not constant. In 1910 a man named

D.E. Lantz, who worked for the U.S. Biological Survey, gave a pithy account of this when he wrote the following about a pair of moose that had been trained to pull a buggy, "which they did with great steadiness and swiftness, subject, however, to the inconvenience that, when they once took it into their heads to cool themselves in a neighbouring river or lake, no effort could prevent them."

Also in 1910, author, explorer, and naturalist Ernest Thompson Seton wrote that moose were "much more tractable and valuable than reindeer . . . they are docile, easily trained, exceedingly swift, and, being natural trotters, are well suited for light travel."

There are several even earlier accounts of tamed moose, especially ones that were shipped to Europe, to men like England's King George III and to dukes who could no doubt afford the considerable costs involved. Many of these animals, however, died soon after arrival or even while on board ship.

The year 1770 crops up again in this context because the first bull moose to make it alive to England was sent that year by Guy Carleton, Governor General of Canada, to the Second Duke of Richmond, who later imported two more. The duke must have acted quickly after the animal arrived in order to engage an artist, because that first one is the subject of a work, also dated 1770, by one of the great animal painters of all time: George Stubbs, best known for his wonderful pictures of horses.

There are fewer records or claims of moose being used as saddle animals and some of these may be more fancy than fact. Among others these accounts include descriptions of attempts to use moose for postal delivery and as cavalry mounts in Sweden.

An urban myth has it that either King Karl XI of Sweden, or his successor Karl XII, even went so far as to invade Russia with moose-mounted hussars in the late seventeenth or very early eighteenth century. This story seemed to be too good to be true and the dangers of the Internet soon showed themselves as some entries appeared to confirm it, while others made no mention. I did some digging and received this email from my colleague and friend Dr. Bengt Roken.

There is no documentation to be found in the historic literature about moose used by the ancient military. Not even their use for postal deliveries is true. During the nineteenth century a number of moose calves were reared and got tamed, and some of them could pull a sledge or carry a rider. One farmer, Darelli, published his experiences with a pair of hand-reared moose and speculated about the possible use of trained moose as superior to horses in the cavalry. From his speculations most of the tales about moose cavalries have evolved.

How much can a moose carry, and how far can it go? Difficult questions to answer. There are all sorts of claims on the Internet, but they are hard to verify. Claims that they can pull four hundred–kilogram sleighs for a whole day seem excessive, and the idea that a moose would travel up to two hundred kilometres in a day is equally unbelievable. The Internet is full of hyperbole. Kostroma's Dr. Minaev is sure that a moose would not be able to act as a saddle animal for long periods. One claim has it that moose can carry 125 kilograms—that is a big man.

The images of unusual pack and saddle animals that we see today are intriguing, at least to human eyes: horses may have a different perspective. Whether being ridden or in harness, at one time moose had to be barred from the city of Tallinn, Estonia's capital, because horses became a danger on the streets when they panicked at the sight of the moose. In Finland the private ownership of moose was once prohibited because bandits thus mounted could escape the law with ease, leaving horses well behind. This would certainly apply in winter, as a moose's long legs allow it to run through deep snow in places where a horse would come to a grinding halt. In Russia, one account has it that a group of Siberians escaped from a Cossack army on mooseback. Hoping to erase all memory of the event, General Jermak Timofeitsch, under orders from Tsar Ivan the Terrible, ordered his troops to kill all the moose and impale or otherwise brutalize the people. He also passed a strange edict banning all knowledge of moose-taming techniques. It seems as if armies the world over, throughout history, have similarly brutal behaviour patterns.

OF MOOSE AND MEN

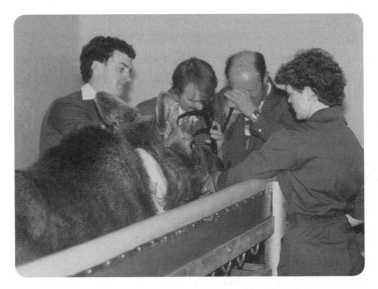

Minnie moose in the examination stall at the Western
College of Veterinary Medicine. The author is checking
the laryngoscope as colleagues look on.
JERRY HAIGH

True or not, these accounts trigger my imagination, particularly the stories of military use. We do know that the Russians wanted to train moose for military duty up until shortly before World War II.

Dr. Minaev thinks that unless proper authentication can be found, these reports may be a joke like the one that was published in the April 1, 2010, Russian issue of *Popular Mechanics* showing a photograph of Luchik the bull, with which Minaev has a special relationship. Luchik is equipped with a heavy machine gun (and Minaev's UHF transmitter on his neck).

My own experiences with tame moose include the visit to the Smeetons' ranch in Alberta and a new arrival at Forestry Farm zoo in 1979. She was brought in by a conservation officer the year after Mickey, and was, almost inevitably, named Minnie. By late summer she had grown like a weed. She had also developed some sort of infection in her nasal passages, and I could not get to the bottom (or should that be the top?) of it. I tried a course of antibiotics, but that proved fruitless, so eventually I suggested to Brent, the curator, that we should take her to the vet college for a more detailed examination. She happily walked into the trailer and out again at the other end with just a halter and rope to guide her. My colleagues made a thorough examination, and we concluded that the next step must be to take a look up her nose with the college's very expensive and brand new fibre-optic equipment.

At this point the cost of the equipment—the flexible rod alone was worth several thousand dollars—became a cause for concern, as no one knew how she would behave. There was no doubt that the best chance for a clear diagnosis would be if Minnie could stand upright and still in the horse stanchion. Any drugs, especially ones that would cause her to lie down, would alter and possibly completely obscure the picture. It was Minnie herself who more or less provided the solution. In the three days she had been in her stall she had been visited by a steady stream of curious students and had behaved like a complete lady, never showing the slightest sign of aggression or discomfort. We walked her from her stall to the examination room, and she stood as if to the manor born while a long black tube was passed up her nose. Unfortunately, all that effort did not yield a more definitive diagnosis and the snotty-nose problem eventually resolved itself with no further intervention.

While domesticating moose is relatively easy, experience tells me that they are not the only deer that can be tamed with a bottle and lots of attention. Jo and I have raised several tame deer over the years. They were not all the same (why should they have been?), but two that happened to be with us at the same time in the late 1980s stick in my mind. Gimpy was a white-tailed deer doe that came to us as a fawn needing help because of a broken leg. That was soon fixed with a cast, and she walked fine after its removal but retained her nickname. She naturally had a passion for milk in a bottle, but quite where she learned to nuzzle into jacket pockets for treats I never knew. In any case, visiting kids loved her gentle ways. Missy was a wapiti that came to us as an adult after a few years at a research centre in Edmonton. In winter she would follow us when we went out cross-country skiing. Visitors would be astonished to see the procession as I broke trail, Jo followed in my tracks, and Missy backed us up, ruining the trail with her hooves. She was so gentle that one day in early June she allowed me to help her deliver a calf that was having trouble arriving, right in the paddock without any form of restraint.

As I described in my story about Petruska in Chapter Six, tame moose can be dangerous when protecting newborn calves. Petruska was however very special and had total trust in Beryl, allowing her to come close. Miles ascribed Petruska's behaviour to the fact that unlike moose in the wild her mother never sent her packing. However, if female moose are readily tamed and can be trusted most of the time (calving excepted), males are a different matter altogether unless they are castrated.

For those who have worked among captive deer, especially ones that have been bottle-raised, the transition of a male from gentle puss that will take a bun from your hand to a raging nutcase that will kill you as soon as look at you can be a nasty surprise. The bull moose at the Saskatoon zoo would attack fences and threaten keepers the day after allowing their noses to be stroked.

My own scary experience with an enraged "tame" bull occurred with three hundred kilos of mind-bent, testosterone-crazed, but luckily de-antlered wapiti. He was part of a research group that I had been working with for several months. I used to visit them almost daily but had missed seeing them over the first weekend in September. On the Monday morning I entered the pen without taking due note of the changes that had happened. The bull came straight for me and pinned me against one of the uprights in a corner of the yard. As long as I stood fairly still he simply leaned on me, albeit with some force, pressing my back against the post so that I could feel each of my vertebrae creating a dent in the wood. If I tried to move he leaned a bit more—quite a bit more. I wondered if I was ever going to get out of this mess, but luckily I was with one of my students, who was outside the pen, and so I called out to him to help me. He had the presence of mind to grab a handy length of two-by-four, lean around the nearby gatepost, and give the bull a good thump on the rump. Happily the bull turned to face this new threat, giving me a chance to break the world's standing high-jump record over the three-metre fence. Once again, those rugby training days paid off.

In 2007 an extraordinary picture of a big bull moose in log-pulling harness, complete with multiple straps and even a bit in the mouth, did the rounds on the Internet. There were several remarkable things about the picture, not the least of which was the full set of antlers he was carrying. For moose scientists anywhere this fact alone would have created a profound level of suspicion, or outright disbelief, but no comments came from this sector. A few days after the image surfaced, a chatty down-home account of how this animal was raised among horses and came to be domesticated appeared alongside the photo. Not long after that, someone with much more computer savvy than me, and an obvious deftness with Photoshop, analyzed the image with great care and declared it to be a fake. By this time blogs and comments had appeared, and no doubt some people still think the story is true, while others admire the picture, which is indeed remarkable, but do not seem to care that it is probably fabricated. Somebody with a sense of humour has even added to the original image by inserting a view of himself on a motorcycle, claiming that he was there when the harness was being fitted.

The main problem with the pictured Alaskan logging moose was his antlers. If the picture had been of a cow moose, or even one with the coral antlers of a castrate, people in the know might not have been so suspicious. With few exceptions, tame male deer of any species can be deadly when the antlers are hard and the rut is on.

A couple of pictures on Alexander Minaev's website are therefore all the more remarkable because they show humans close to and interacting with animals in hard antler, which of course means that they have not been castrated. Indeed the home page picture is of Tatiana, Alexander's wife, scratching the neck of fully antlered Luchik, who is more interested in the feed bucket in front of him than what is going on behind his head. As if that is not enough, another picture on the site shows Dr. Minaev himself lying right beside antlered Luchik, who looks totally chilled out. It is a still photo, but if it had been a movie I imagine the big bull would have been chewing his cud.

Given my own experiences with bulls in rut, I naturally asked about this picture and how it was taken. Minaev said he snapped the picture with a self-timer, and he assured me that he does not go near any bull when a cow is in heat, and it is only Luchik that he can approach at all during the rut. They have a special relationship, and Luchik will allow this closeness right after he has bred a cow, and also late in the rut when his ardour has somewhat diminished.

Unless you know your animals very well, this is definitely one of those "don't try this at home" things.

Another scientist who must have developed a special relationship with a bull moose is Dr. Andrzej Krzywinski (the ninth member of the Eightsome Reel). He is a bear of a man, not particularly tall but shaped like an international rugby prop forward or NFL lineman. My other abiding memories of him relate to red deer. Together with a colleague he was the first person to figure out a safe way to collect semen from a red deer stag. They constructed a dummy hind, which to human eyes was one of the ugliest deer ever seen, but which, when sprayed with the appropriate hormones, was good enough to fool a love-sick or sex-starved stag. The hind was constructed with a hidden artificial vagina and . . . bingo!

I never witnessed Krzywinski's management of rutting deer at the Popielno Research Station where he carried out his studies, but an impressed friend described his technique to me. He dominated all stags (which had their intact antlers) by simply roaring at them and charging if they dared to even dip their heads at him. It is probably a good thing that he never played rugby at the international level. He might have changed the nature of the game.

Krzywinski must have managed the business of breeding tame moose and collecting semen for study in an interesting fashion, but in the sparse language required by scientific journals he simply stated,

*Dr. Andrzej Krzywinski collecting semen from a bull
moose using a cow that has been fitted with a harness
that holds an artificial vagina in place.*

ANDRZEJ KRZYWINSKI

"Great differences in tameability and aggressiveness were found among moose males." He built a harness that he placed over the back of a female and then allowed a bull to mount her and serve into the artificial vagina. The remarkable pictures he sent me do show one important thing. He had removed the antlers of the bull. Nonetheless!

Tame moose have become more than harness animals and producers of milk and cheese. In Sweden, where moose are an iconic animal (apart from being a road hazard) they have also become a popular tourist attraction. There are at least seventeen moose sites tourists can visit up and down the country, and one or two collections for the curious have also appeared in the United Kingdom.

Considering their cultural importance, it is no surprise that moose have featured in various art forms including songs, stories, and ancient rock art. The World Heritage site at Alta, about as far north as one can go in Norway, has a variety of rock art that includes a depiction of a moose that has been dated between four thousand and

Bronze statues outside the Cabela's store in
East Grand Forks, Minnesota, created by
Beverly Paddleford.
JERRY HAIGH

six thousand years ago. Apart from our friend Tony Bubenik, other well-known artists who have done striking works of them are Carl Rungius, who made many trips to the Rocky Mountains in the late nineteenth and first half of the twentieth century to paint wildlife, and Clarence Tillenius, whom my wife and I met in his Winnipeg home. It was here, at aged ninety-two, that he was working away at an easel on a collage of bison that would be digitally photographed and projected onto the side of a local supermarket to be transformed into a huge mural. He took us for lunch to the gallery in Assiniboine Park Pavilion that is named for him and is dedicated entirely to his huge body of wildlife paintings. Then we went to the city's Manitoba Museum of Man and Nature, where he was warmly greeted by the staff, and he showed us the dioramas that he designed and for which he had painted the backgrounds. Among them were a striking moose and calf in an amazing boreal forest setting. We could hardly tell where paint took over from physical structure.

The creatures in the dioramas were made with the skins of real animals, but moose have also been sculpted. At the front entrance of the Cabela's store in Minnesota's East Grand Forks stands a stop-you-in-your-tracks bronze of two moose fighting. The work, about double life-size, was created by Beverly Paddleford, and the setting shows that in about a millisecond the bull that has unfortunately turned his head to one side is going to lose his left eye when his opponent's sharp tine will skewer into the socket. It will hardly matter, as his lower neck and shoulder are fully exposed to the other antler that will drive into him and either disable or kill him.

Moose motifs also appear in heraldry that ranges from the Canadian Air Force to provincial and state emblems, the Hudson's Bay Company, and the International Order of Moose. The moose (as *elch*) is the national animal of Norway and Sweden and the state animal of Alaska and Maine. A bull moose is the featured animal on the twenty-five-rublie note of Belarus.

Moose are used as mascots for a variety of organizations, especially sports teams, and I was delighted to learn that Team Canada had a stuffed moose as a mascot at the 2011 Rugby World Cup.

Ancient evidence of moose in archaeological dig sites is sometimes hard to find, particularly where coniferous forest once stood, because fallen pine needles create acid soil and acid eats through bone. However, some well-preserved remains of *Alces alces* are known across Europe and Asia from about a hundred thousand years ago. They include artistic and totemic representations, especially of antlers.

Among the oldest archaeological sites in Canada is one where the provinces of Manitoba and Ontario meet up with Minnesota. It has been dated to about 7,800 years ago, long before the bureaucrats got involved. Another, dated from about 6,500 years ago, lies on the shores of Wuskwatim Lake in northern Manitoba, west of Thompson. It contained a single antler that had been covered with red ochre and laid atop a small child buried with its mother in what must have been a poignant ceremony.

A much more recent site is near the market town of Nipawin,

Sune Häggmark and his bio-fueled Volvo.
SUNE HÄGGMARK

Saskatchewan, about a four-hour drive north and east of Saskatoon. The Francois-Finlay Post, built in the 1740s, was the first so-called peddler post in my home province. Most of the moose remains there are skulls and antler sets, and the evidence suggests that they were mounted above the wooden buildings used by the people who lived there. As you drive around Saskatchewan and other parts of Canada today you will occasionally see exactly the same thing in many farmyards and above the lintels of trappers' and holiday cabins.

During my personal journey in the company of the charismatic moose, which spans thirty-six years, and my time spent delving back 10,000 years into their history, I have come across many fascinating facts and corresponded with over eighty people around the planet. The final story I leave you with now is one that has captured my imagination and involves the combination of one of humanity's oldest technologies with one of its newest.

Once humans had learned to manage and tame fire for their personal use, they must have discovered that dung would provide a slow-burning and reliable source of heat for both comfort and cooking. I have no idea how long the dung of cattle, bison, yaks, water buffalo, and camels has been used as fuel, but recent findings from Peru have shown how closely the development of the ancient site of Machu Picchu 2,700 years ago was linked to llama dung as fertilizer and fuel. I think that the use of moose pellets, which look like large grapes or small plums, for this purpose is likely much more recent.

This story is an example of harnessing a moose product rather that a case of a moose being in harness. It comes from Sweden, where Sune Häggmark, who owns and runs a tourist moose garden in Orrviken, a village close to Östersund in the centre of the country, dubs himself Mr. Moose. He has adopted that ancient dung fuel technology that goes back into prehistory and has used it to adapt his 1962 Volvo 142. He powers it by using dry moose droppings as a simple and readily available form of biofuel. The heat from the burning turns the cellulose in the dung into gas that feeds the engine. Each load of ten kilograms will take him about seventy kilometres at ninety kilometres per hour before he has to refill the burning chamber.

Häggmark's idea, and his ability to implement it, is unlikely to usurp our addiction to oil anytime soon, but the notion intrigues me, just as moose do.

CHAPTER ONE

Presnell, K.R., P.J.A. Presidente, and W.A. Rapley. "Combination of Etorphine and Xylazine in Captive White-tailed Deer": i. Sedative and Immobilization Properties. *Journal of Wildlife Diseases* 9, no. 4 (1973): 336–341.

CHAPTER TWO

Banfield, A.W.F. *The Mammals of Canada.* Toronto: University of Toronto Press, 1974.

Dr. Eung-Do Cook English-Chipewyan Dictionary. Accessed May 12, 2011, http://archives.ucalgary.ca/private/cookcardlist_m.

Forbes, Edward, ed. *The Zoology of the Voyage of H.M.S. Herald: Under the Command of Captain Henry Kellett. During the years 1845–51.* In a series titled: Vertebrals, including Fossil Mammals by Sir John Richardson. London: Lovell Reeve, 1854.

Hundertmark, K., and R.T. Bowyer. "Genetics, Evolution and Phylogeography of Moose." *Alces* 40 (2004): 103–122.

Reeves, H.M. and R.E. McCabe. "Of Moose and Man." In *Ecology and Management of the North American Moose.* Edited by A.W. Franzmann and C.C. Schwartz. Washington, DC: Wildlife Management Institute, 1997.

CHAPTER THREE

Haigh, J.C., and H.C. Hopf. "The Blow-gun in Veterinary Practice: Its Uses and Preparation." *Journal of American Veterinary Medical Association* 169, no. 9 (1976): 881–883.

CHAPTER FOUR

Haigh, J.C., R.R. Stewart, R. Frokjer, and T. Hauge. "The Capture of Moose with Fentanyl and Xylazine." *Journal of Zoo Animal Medicine* 8, no. 3 (1977): 22–29.

National Geographic. *Ticks Can Kill Moose?* Accessed May 12, 2011, http://www.youtube.com/watch?v=Rsd2i-qFHK4.

Samuel, W.M. *White as a Ghost: Winter Ticks and Moose.* Natural History Series, Volume 1. Edmonton, AB: The Federation of Alberta Naturalists (now Nature Alberta), 2004.

Seton, E.S. *Life-histories of Northern Mammals: An Account of the Mammals of Manitoba.* Volume I. Grass-eaters. New York: Charles Scribner's Sons, 1909.

Welch, D.A., W.M. Samuel, and C.J. Wilkie. "*Dermacentor albipictus* (Acari, Ixodidae) on Captive Reindeer and Free-ranging Woodland Caribou." *Journal of Wildlife Diseases* 26 (1990): 410–411.

CHAPTERS FIVE AND SIX

Clark, M. *High Endeavours: The Extraordinary Life and Adventures of Miles and Beryl Smeeton.* Toronto: HarperCollins, 1992.

Smeeton, M. *Completely Foxed.* Toronto: Key Porter, 1984.

CHAPTER SEVEN

Haigh, J.C. *Bulldogging Moose.* Accessed May 12, 2011, http://www.youtube.com/watch?v=Qugw7JA1cJw.

———. "Capture of Woodland Caribou in Canada." In *Annual Proceedings of the American Association of Zoo Veterinarians.* 110–115. Knoxville, TN: 1978.

———. "Hyaluronidase as an Adjunct in an Immobilizing Mixture for Moose." *Journal of American Veterinary Medical Association* 175 (1979): 916–917.

Haigh, J.C, R.R. Stewart, and W. Mytton. "Relations Among Linear Measurements and Weights for Moose (*Alces alces*)." *Alces* 16 (1980): 1–10.

CHAPTER EIGHT

Haigh, J.C, G. Wobeser, and P. MacWilliams. "Capture Myopathy in a Moose." *Journal of the American Veterinary Medical Association* 171, no. 9 (1977): 924–926.

CHAPTER NINE

Alaska's Kenai Moose Research Centre. Accessed May 12, 2011, http://www.juneauempire.com/stories/112303/out_moose.shtml.

Haigh, J.C. "Cimetidine for Treatment of Abomasal Ulcers in Young Ruminants." *Journal of Zoo Animal Medicine* 13 (1983): 173.

Roken, B. "Feeding and Management of Captive Moose (*Alces alces*): Experiences and Recommendations from Kolmarden Zoo." Three-page pamphlet. 2010.

Schwartz, C.C., W.L. Regelin, and A.W. Franzmann. "Suitability of a Formulated Ration for Moose." *Journal of Wildlife Management* 49 (1985): 137–141.

Spiedel, G. "Care and Nutrition of Moose *Alces alces americana* in Captivity." *International Zoo Yearbook* 6 (1966): 88–90.

BIBLIOGRAPHY

CHAPTERS TEN AND ELEVEN

Geist, V. *Moose: Behavior, Ecology, Conservation*. Minneapolis, MN: Voyageur Press, 1999.
Smeeton, M. *Completely Foxed*. Toronto: Key Porter, 1984.

CHAPTER TWELVE

Schwartz, C.C. "Reproduction, Natality and Growth." In *Ecology and Management of the North American Moose*. Edited by A.W. Franzmann and C.C. Schwartz. 141–172. Washington, DC: Wildlife Management Institute, 1997.
Haigh, J.C., E.H. Kowal, W. Runge, and G. Wobeser. "Pregnancy Diagnosis as a Management Tool in Moose." *Alces* 18 (1983): 45–53.

CHAPTERS THIRTEEN AND FOURTEEN

Abraham, C. "Mommy's Little Secret." http://www.canadiancrc.com/Newspaper_Articles/Globe_and_Mail_Moms_Little_secret_14DEC02.aspx.
Bubenik, A.B. "The Behavioral Aspects of Antlerogenesis." In *Antler Development in Cervidae*. Edited by R.D. Brown. 389–447. Kingsville, TX: Caesar Kleberg Wildlife Research Inst., 1982.
Bubenik, G.A. and P.G. Bubenik. "Palmated Antlers of Moose May Serve as a Parabolic Reflector of Sounds." *European Journal of Wildlife Research* 54, no. 3 (2008): 533–535.
Clutton-Brock, T.H. "The Function of Antlers." *Behaviour* 79 (1982): 108–125.
Darwin, C. *The Descent of Man, and Selection in Relation to Sex*. New York: D. Appleton & Co., 1871.
Denys, N. *The Description and Natural History of the Coasts of North America (Acadia)*. Toronto: The Champlain Society, 1672. (Translated by W. Ganong, 1908.)
Gasaway, W.C, D. Preston, D.J. Reed, and D.D. Roby. "Comparative Antler Morphology and Size of North American Moose." *Swedish Wildlife Research* Suppl. 1 (1987): 311–325.
Hundertmark, K. and R.T. Bowyer. "Genetics, Evolution and Phylogeography of Moose." *Alces* 40 (2004) 103–122.
Lincoln, G.A. "Teeth, Horns and Antlers: The Weapons of Sex." In *The Differences between the Sexes*. Edited by R.V. Short and E. Balaban. 131–158. Cambridge: Cambridge University Press, 1994.
Schwartz, C.C. "Reproduction, Natality and Growth." In *Ecology and Management of the North American Moose*. Edited by A.W. Franzmann and C.C. Schwartz. 141–172. Washington, DC: Wildlife Management Institute, 1997.
Selous, F.C. *Recent Hunting Trips in British North America*. New York: Scribner's Sons, 1907.
Turbervile, G. *The Noble Arte of Venerie or Hunting*. Wotton-under-Edge, U.K.: Clarendon Press, 1908 (originally published in 1576). This book has recently been recognized as probably being the work of George Gascoigne, rather than Turbervile. In any case it is a translation from his *La Venerie de Jaques du Fouillou*, 1561.
Van Ballenberghe, V. *In the Company of Moose*. Mechanicsburg, PA: Stackpole Books, 2004.

CHAPTER FIFTEEN

Bubenik, G.A., and A.B. Bubenik. *Horns, Pronghorns and Antlers*. New York: Springer-Verlag, 1990.

Davis, T.A. "Antler Asymmetry Caused by Limb Amputation and Geophysical Forces." In *Antler Development in Cervidae*. Edited by R.D. Brown. 223–229. Kingsville, TX: Caesar Kleberg Wildlife Research Inst., 1983.

Peterson, R.L. *North American Moose*. Toronto: University of Toronto Press, 1955.

CHAPTER SIXTEEN

Gould, S.J. "The Misnamed, Mistreated and Misunderstood Irish Elk." *Natural History* 82 (1973): 10–19.

Lister, A.M. et al. "The Phylogenetic Position of the 'Giant Deer' *Megaloceros giganteus*." *Nature* 438 (2005): 850–853.

Millais, J.G. *British Deer and Their Horns*. London: Henry Sotheran & Co., 1897.

Molyneux, T. "A Discourse concerning the Large Horns Frequently Found Under Ground in Ireland, Concluding from them that the Great American Deer, Call'd a Moose, was Formerly Common in that Island: With Remarks on Some Other Things Natural to that Country." *Philosophical Transactions of the Royal Society of London*. 1697.

Monaghan, N.T. "From Grave to Cradle, the Changing Fortunes of the Giant Irish Deer." In *Value and Valuation of Natural Science Collections*. Edited by J.R. Nudds and C.W. Pettitt. 144–148. London: Geological Society, 1996.

Stuart, A.J., P.A. Kosintsev, T.F.G. Higham, and A.M. Lister. "Pleistocene to Holocene Extinction Dynamics in Giant Deer and Woolly Mammoth." *Nature* 431 (2004): 684–685.

CHAPTER SEVENTEEN

Challies, C.N. "Establishment, Control and Commercial Exploitation of Wild Deer in New Zealand." In *Biology of Deer Production*. Edited by P.F. Fennessy and K.R. Drew. 23–36. Wellington, NZ: Royal Society of New Zealand, 1985.

Tinsley, R. *Call of the Moose and Other Fiordland Adventures*. Wellington, NZ: A.H. and A.W. Reed, Ltd., 1983.

Tustin, K. *A (Nearly) Complete History of the Moose in New Zealand*. Auckland, NZ: Halcyon Press, 2010.

———. *A Wild Moose Chase*. Dunedin, NZ: Wild South Books, 1998.

CHAPTER EIGHTEEN

Aho, R.W., S.M. Schmitt, J. Hendrickson, and T.R. Minzey. "Michigan's Translocated Moose Population: 10 Years Later." Michigan Department of Natural Resources. *Wildlife Division Report Number 3245*. 1995.

Parker, G. "Status Report on The Eastern Moose (*Alces alces americana* Clinton) in Mainland Nova Scotia." 2003. Accessed May 12, 2011, http://www.gov.ns.ca/natr/wildlife/biodiversity/pdf/statusreports/StatusReportMooseNSComplete.pdf

Sipko, T.P. "Status of Reintroductions of Three Large Herbivores in Russia." *Alces* 45

BIBLIOGRAPHY

(2009): 35–42.
Utah Moose Statewide Management Plan. Accessed May 12, 2011, http://wildlife.utah.gov/
hunting/biggame/pdf/moose_plan.pdf.

CHAPTER NINETEEN

European Co-operation in the Field of Scientific and Technical Research. *Cost 341:
Habitat Fragmentation due to Transportation Infrastructure.* Swedish State of the Art
Report, 1999. Accessed May 21, 2011, http://www.iene.info/cost-341/swedenUKdef.pdf.
Gundersen, H., H.P. Andreassen, and T. Storaas. "Spatial and Temporal Correlates to
Norwegian Moose-Train Collisions." *Alces* 34 (1998): 385–394.
Niemi, M., A. Martin, A. Tanskanen, and P. Nummi. "How Effective Are Wildlife Fences
in Preventing Collisions with Wild Ungulates?" In *Improving Connections in a
Changing Environment.* Collection of short papers from the 2010 IENE Conference.
Edited by V. Richter, M. Puky, and A. Seiler. 79–83. Varangy Akciósoport Egyesület —
MTA Ökológiai és Botanikai Kutatóintézete: SCOPE Ltd., Budapest — Vácrátót.
Parks Canada. "Case Study 2: Too Many Moose on the Loose? Moose in Gros Morne
National Park of Canada." In *True to Our Nature.* Accessed May 12, 2011, http://www.
pc.gc.ca/apprendre-learn/prof/itm3-guides/vraie-true/etu-stuplan3case2_e.asp.
Rogers, A.R., and P.J. Robins. "Moose Detection Distances on Highways at Night." *Alces*
42 (2006): 75–87.

CHAPTER TWENTY

National Geographic. *Ticks Can Kill Moose?* Accessed May 12, 2011, http://www.youtube.
com/watch?v=Rsd2i-qFHK4.
Kaitala, A., R. Kortet, S. Härkönen et al. "Deer Ked, an Ectoparasite of Moose in
Finland: A Brief Review of its Biology and Invasion." *Alces* 45 (2009): 85–88.
Kynkaanniemi, S., R. Kortet, L. Härkönen et al. "Threat of an Invasive Parasitic Fly,
the Deer Ked (*Lipoptena cervi*), to the Reindeer (*Rangifer tarandus*): Experimental
Infection and Treatment." *Annales Zoologici Fennici* 47 (2010): 28–36.
Lenarz, M.S., M.E. Nelson, M.W. Schrage, and A.J. Edwards. "Temperature Mediated
Moose Survival in Northeastern Minnesota." *Journal of Wildlife Management* 73
(2009): 503–510.
Murray, D.L., E.W. Cox, W.B. Ballard, et al. "Pathogens, Nutritional Deficiency, and
Climate Influences on a Declining Moose Population." *Wildlife Monographs* 166
(2006).
Parker, G. "Status Report on The Eastern Moose (*Alces alces americana* Clinton) in
Mainland Nova Scotia." 2003. Accessed May 12, 2011, http://www.gov.ns.ca/natr/wild-
life/biodiversity/pdf/statusreports/StatusReportMooseNSComplete.pdf.
Rehbinder, C., M. Cedersmyg, M. Frolich, and L. Soderstrom. "Wasting Syndrome in
Swedish Moose (*Alces alces L.*): Results from Field Necropsies." *Microbial Ecology in
Health and Disease* 16 (2004): 35–43.
Samuel, W.M. *White as a Ghost: Winter Ticks and Moose.* Natural History Series. Volume
1. Edmonton: The Federation of Alberta Naturalists (now Nature Alberta), 2004.

Samuel, W.M., and K. Madslein. "Are Louse Flies Potential Problems for Moose and Humans of Maritimes Canada and Northeastern United States?" *The Moose Call* 25 (June 2010): 1–5.

Seton, E.S. *Life-histories of Northern Mammals: An Account of the Mammals of Manitoba.* Volume I. Grass-eaters. New York: Charles Scribner's Sons, 1909.

Wasel, S.M., W.M. Samuel, and V. Crichton. "Distribution and Ecology of Meningeal Worm, *Parelaphostrongylus tenuis* (Nematoda) in Northcentral North America." *Journal of Wildlife Diseases* 39, no. 2 (2003): 338–346.

Welch, D.A., W.M. Samuel, and C.J. Wilkie. "*Dermacentor albipictus* (Acari, Ixodidae) on Captive Reindeer and Free-ranging Woodland Caribou." *Journal of Wildlife Diseases* 26 (1990): 410–411.

CHAPTERS TWENTY-ONE AND TWENTY-TWO

Andersone-Lilley, Z., L. Balciauskas, J. Ozolins, et al. "Ungulates and Their Management in the Baltics (Estonia, Latvia and Lithuania)." In *European Ungulates and Their Management in the 21st Century.* Edited by M. Apollinio, R. Andersen, and R. Putman. Cambridge: Cambridge University Press, 2010.

Baleišis, R., P. Bluzma, and L. Balciauskas. *Lietuvos kanopiniai žvėrys.* 3 leidimas. (*Hoofed Animals of Lithuania.* 3rd edition.) Vilnius: Akstis, 2003. 216 pp.

Bartos, L., R. Kotrba, and J. Pintir. "Ungulates and Their Management in the Czech Republic." In *European Ungulates and Their Management in the 21st Century.* Edited by M. Apollinio, R. Andersen, and R. Putman. Cambridge: Cambridge University Press, (2010). 243–261.

Baskin, L.M. "Status of Regional Moose Populations in European and Asiatic Russia." *Alces* 45 (2009): 1–4.

Bridgland, J., T. Nette, C. Dennis, and D. Quann. "Moose on Cape Breton Island, Nova Scotia: 20th Century Demographics and Emerging Issues in the 21st Century." *Alces* 43 (2007): 111–121.

Chapin, F.S., S.F. Trainor, O. Huntington, et al. "Increasing Wildfire in Alaska's Boreal Forest: Pathways to Potential Solutions of a Wicked Problem." www.biosciencemag.org 58, no. 6. (June 2008): 1–10.

Crichton, V.F.J. "Co-Management: The Manitoba Experience." *Alces* 37, no. 1 (2001): 163–172.

———. "Moose and Ecosystem Management in the 21st Century: Does the King Have a Place? A Canadian Perspective." *Alces* 34, no. 2 (1998): 467–477.

Jia, J. and Y. Ma. "Moose Conservation in China: Challenges for the 21st Century." *Alces* 34, no. 2 (1998): 269–278.

Kantar, L.E., "Broccoli and Moose, Not Always Best Served Together: Implementing a Controlled Moose Hunt in Maine." In *Proceedings of the 45th North American Moose Conference and Workshop: Moose in a Warming World* (2010): 28.

Kay, C.E. "Aboriginal Overkill and the Biogeography of Moose in Western North America." *Alces* 33 (1997): 141–164.

———. "Aboriginal Overkill: The Role of Native Americans in Structuring Western

BIBLIOGRAPHY

Ecosystems." *Human Nature* 5, no. 4 (1994): 359–398.

Kuznetsov, G.V. "Moose and Forest Problems in Russia." *Alces* Suppl. 2. (2002): 65–70.

Lavsund, S., T. Nygrén, and E.J. Solberg. "Status of Moose Population and Challenges to Moose Management in Fennoscandia." *Alces* 39 (2003): 109–130.

Marshall, J.P. "Co-Management of Moose in the Gwich'in Settlement Area, Northwest Territories." *Alces* 35 (1999): 151–158.

Peek, J.M. and K. Morris. "Status of Moose in the Contiguous United States." *Alces* 34, no. 2 (1998): 423–434.

Rea, R.V., and K.N. Child. "Featured Species — Moose." *Wildlife Afield* 4, no. 2 (2007): 285–317.

Riordan, B., D. Verbyla, and A.D. McGuire. "Shrinking Ponds in Subarctic Alaska based on 1950–2002 Remotely Sensed Images." *Journal of Geophysical Research* III (2006): G04002, doi:10.1029/2005JG000150.

Schmölcke, U., and F.E Zachos. "Holocene Distribution and Extinction of the Moose (*Alces alces*, Cervidae) in Central Europe." *Mammalian Biology — Zeitschrift fur Saugetierkunde* 70, no. 6 (2005): 329–344.

Sipko, T.P., and M. Kholdova. "Fragmentation of Eurasian Moose Populations During Periods of Population Depression." *Alces* 45 (2009): 25–34.

Stewart, R.R. "Introduction of Sex and Age Specific Hunting Licenses for the Moose Harvest in Saskatchewan." In *Proceedings of the North American Moose Workshop*. Lankester, M. ed. Lakehead University Press. 14 (1978): 194–208.

Timmermann, H.R. "The Status and Management of Moose in North America circa 2000–01." *Alces* 39 (2003): 131–151.

Zheleznov-Chukotsky, N.K., and E.S. Votiashova. "Status of Moose (*Alces alces*) in the North East of Asia Before and After Perestroika (1985)." *Alces* 33 (1997): 125–127.

CHAPTER TWENTY-THREE

Crichton, V.F.J. "Hunting." In *Ecology and Management of the North American Moose*. Edited by A.W. Franzmann and C.C. Schwartz. 617–653. Washington, DC: Wildlife Management Institute, 1997

Gwich'in Elders and G. Raygorodetsky. *Nành' Kak Geenjit Gwich'in Ginjik; Gwich'in Words about the Land*. Inuvik, NWT: Gwich'in Renewable Resources Board, 1997.

Legge, A.J., and P.A. Rowley-Conwy. *Star Carr Revisited*. London: Centre for Extra-mural Studies, Birkbeck College, University of London, 1988.

"Moose Hunting." Nordic Way. Accessed May 12, 2011, http://www.nordicway.com/search/Sweden/Sweden_Moose%20Hunting.htm.

Nelson, R.K. *Hunters of the Northern Forest*. Chicago: University of Chicago Press, 1986.

Pitts, M. "Hides and Antlers: A New Look at the Gatherer-hunter Site at Star Carr, North Yorkshire, England." *World Archaeology* 11 (1979): 32–42.

Reeves, H.M., and R.E. McCabe. "Of Moose and Man." In *Ecology and Management of the North American Moose*. Edited by A.W. Franzmann and C.C. Schwartz. 1–75. Washington, DC: Wildlife Management Institute, 1997.

The Value of Alaska Moose. Prepared for the Anchorage Soil and Water Conservation

District and the Alaska Soil and Water Conservation District by Northern Economics Inc. 2006. 33 pp.

Turner, G. *Hair Embroidery in Siberia and North America.* Pitt Rivers Museum Occasional Papers on Technology, 7. Oxford: Oxford University Press, 1955.

CHAPTER TWENTY-FOUR

Bogomolova, E.M., Y.A. Kurochkin, and A.N. Minaev. "The Study of Moose Behavior on the Kostroma Moose Farm." *Alces* Suppl. 2 (2002): 37–40.

ITN Source. "Reuters moose farm video, http://www.blinkx.com/watch-video/russia-russian-farm-tries-to-domesticate-moose-and-produce-moose-milk-known-for-its-unique-healing-powers/r-rB3_9gloODHawI6jDYYA.

Minaev, A. "Moose as a Domestic Animal: The Kostroma Moose Farm." Accessed May 12, 2011, http://moosefarm.newmail.ru/e000.htm.

Moose Milk Makes for Unusual Cheese." *The Globe and Mail.* Toronto: June 26, 2004.

Yazan, Y., and Y. Knorre. "Domesticating Moose in a Russian National Park." *Oryx* 7 (1964): 301–304.

CHAPTER TWENTY-FIVE

Brownlee, K., E. Leigh Syms, V.F.J. Crichton, and B.J. Smith. "An Ancient Burial Site and an Ancient Moose Antler." *The Moose Call* 15 (2002): 1, 7–8.

Chepstow-Lusty, A. "Agro-pastoralism and social change in the Cuzco heartland of Peru: a brief history using environmental proxies." *Antiquity* 85 (2011) 328, 570–582.

Hearne, S. *A Journey to the Northern Ocean: The Adventures of Samuel Hearne.* Victoria: Touchwood Editions, 2007.

Krzywinski, A., A. Niedbalska, and A. Krzywinska. "Collection and Freezing Semen of the Moose Bull." *Swedish Wildlife Research* Suppl. 1 (1987): 761–765.

Lantz, D.E. "Deer Farming in the United States." *USDA Farmers' Bulletin* 330 (1908).

Lister, A.M. "Evolution of Mammoths and Moose." In *Morphological Change in Quaternary Mammals of North America.* Edited by R.A. Martin and A.D. Barnosky. 178–204. Cambridge: Cambridge University Press, 1993.

Seton, E.S. *Life-histories of Northern Mammals: An Account of the Mammals of Manitoba.* Volume I. Grass-eaters. New York: Charles Scribner's Sons, 1909.

Stott, G. "The Twig Eater." *Equinox* (January–February 1993): 20–29.

Syms, L. "An Ancient Moose: Racking Up New Insights into Very Ancient Heritage." *The Manitoba Museum Annual Report.* Winnipeg: Manitoba Museum, 2002–2003.